IMAGES
of America

HYDE PARK

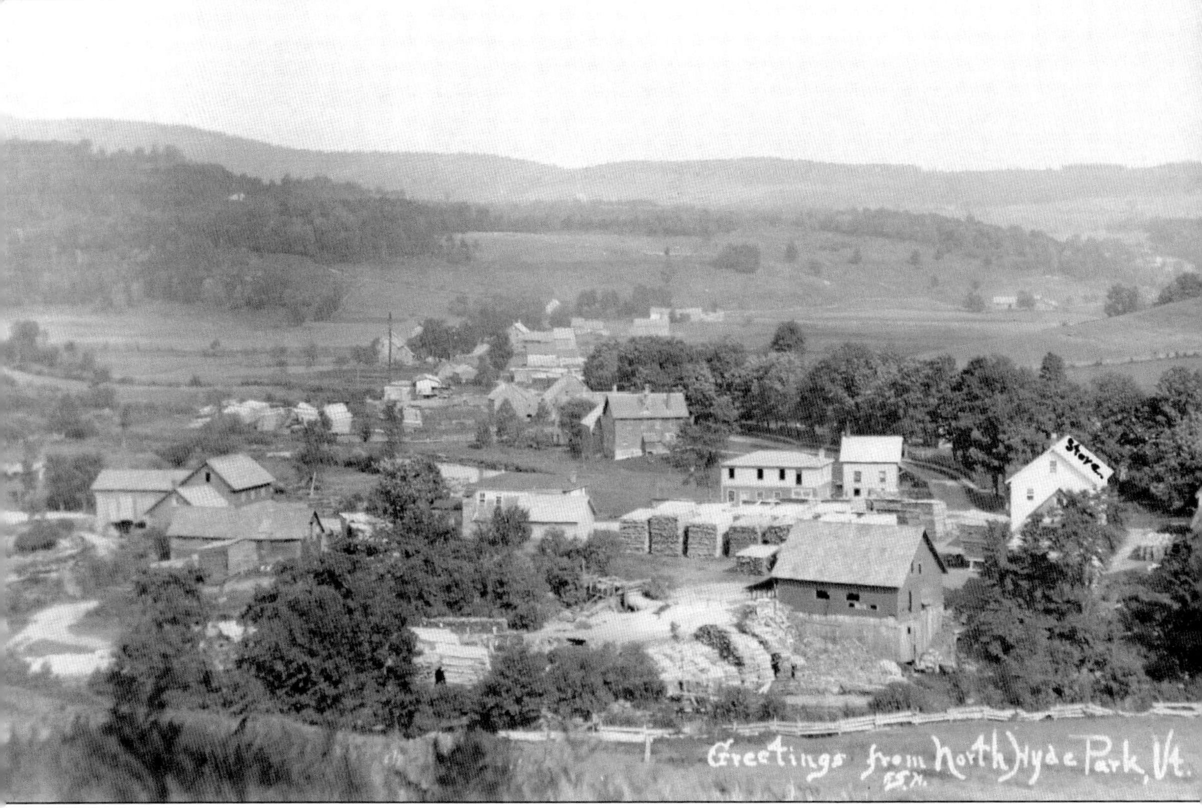

This c. 1920 view of North Hyde Park was taken from the hillside located west of the village. Note the clearings on the distant hillsides, which are today forested. Many clearings, such as these, were needed for the numerous farms located in and around town. (Courtesy of the Graves/McAllister family.)

On the Cover: This image shows two young boys on Maple Street (later renamed Ferry Street), who, by the looks of the gloves on their hands, appear ready to play baseball. Many sports activities of this nature were very popular with youth during this time period. It should be noted that this street also carried the name Water Street when the village was first settled. (Courtesy of the Heath/Savage family.)

IMAGES
of America

HYDE PARK

James and Monica Heath

ARCADIA
PUBLISHING

Copyright © 2014 by James and Monica Heath
ISBN 978-1-4671-2228-3

Published by Arcadia Publishing
Charleston, South Carolina

Printed in the United States of America

Library of Congress Control Number: 2014932468

For all general information, please contact Arcadia Publishing:
Telephone 843-853-2070
Fax 843-853-0044
E-mail sales@arcadiapublishing.com
For customer service and orders:
Toll-Free 1-888-313-2665

Visit us on the Internet at www.arcadiapublishing.com

We would like to dedicate this book to our children, Makesha L. and Jordan J. Heath, and also our granddaughter, Monica Marie Heath, as an inspiration to learning and preserving our local history. We would also like to dedicate it to all the citizens of Hyde Park, both past and present, whose efforts go unsurpassed in making this such a great community.

Contents

Acknowledgments		6
Introduction		7
1.	North Hyde Park (The North Village)	9
2.	Hyde Park Village	53
3.	Rural Hyde Park	95
4.	Odds and Ends	121

ACKNOWLEDGMENTS

We would sincerely like to say "thank you" for the generosity and support we received from community members, friends, and families who supported us and provided images in the authoring of this book. We are also indebted to the Vermont Historical Society and local historians for providing us with historical information. We would like to also acknowledge the following individuals and organizations for their contributions of photographs and images that they allowed us to use in this book: Francis Favreau, Robert and Caroline Jones, Roberta Grimes, Jane and Eleanor (Grimes) Goodrich, Marguerite Stewart, Norma (Thompson) Savage, Velma (Thompson) Rushford, Everton and Marjorie Graves for the McAllister collection, Don and Doug Bullard for the Vernon Bullard collection, Robert Barnes, Donald Johnstone, Linda Jones, Wade Larose, John and Judy Davis, Amy Noyes and the Lanpher Memorial Library for the Page/McFarland collection, Loren and Jean Aither, the late Ruby (Amadon) Day, Arland "Bud" Ploof, Evertt Demeritt, and Madonna Parker.

We would like to also acknowledge the following books, which provided us with a great deal of historical information:

Child, Hamilton. *Gazetteer and Business Directory of Lamoille and Orleans Counties, Vt.* Syracuse, NY: Journal Office, 1883.

Hemenway, Abby Maria. *The Vermont Historical Gazetteer, Vol. 2.* Burlington, VT: A.M. Hemenway, 1871.

Town of Hyde Park and its Bicentennial Committee, The. *Hyde Park—Vermont Shire Town of Lamoille County.* Essex Publishing Company, 1976.

Town of Hyde Park History Book Committee, The. *Hyde Park, Vermont Then and Now.* Hyde Park, VT: Town of Hyde Park Book Committee, 2007.

INTRODUCTION

Hyde Park is a small town in Vermont rich in history and culture. As with so many small towns in Vermont, its original settlement was established by Revolutionary War soldiers from Massachusetts, Connecticut, New Hampshire, and New York who passed through this region en route to Canada and the surrounding forts through the Lake Champlain corridor. The soldiers who knew each other provided a common link among the small towns being granted in this northern region. Hyde Park would see two of these early settlers, John McDaniel and Capt. Jedediah Hyde.

Captain Hyde, for whom the town would be named, was born on August 24, 1738, in Norwich, Connecticut. He was the son of Rev. Jedediah Hyde, a Separatist of the Congregational Church. Captain Hyde was an officer in the Revolutionary War and served in both the Army and the Navy. He also fought at the Battle of Bunker Hill. From January 1, 1777, to January 1, 1780, he was quartermaster sergeant of the 4th Regiment of the Connecticut Line. After obtaining the rank of captain, he was always known as Capt. Jedediah Hyde and was "quite noted for his politeness and easy address," as quoted by Zadock Thompson. In the following years, he married Mary Waterman and had eight children. His firstborn from this marriage was a son, Jedediah Jr., who was born on November 5, 1761, in Norwich, Connecticut. At the age of 14, Jedediah Jr. also joined the Revolutionary War. After the war, he became a schoolteacher and taught in Williamstown, Massachusetts, and Pawlet, Vermont. Both he and his father were surveyors and would survey the lines for the town of Hyde Park and its proprietors.

When Lamoille County was formed in 1838, Hyde Park was appointed the distinction of being the shire town of the county by the Vermont Legislature due to its geographical and political location. When first chartered on August 27, 1781, the town had an area of 23,040 acres and was bounded north by Eden, east by Wolcott, southeast by Morristown, and west by Johnson. This changed somewhat in 1899, when Morrisville and Hyde Park reached a compromise on the annexation of property that was approved by the Vermont Legislature. This would reduce the town's total acreage to 21,210. It also should be noted that the original intent of the proprietors was to have the village sited where Albert M. Whitcomb's farm was located in Centerville.

In years to come, Hyde Park would experience much economic growth and development due to the ingenuity of pioneering families, such as the Page, Fitch, McFarland, Campbell, Bullard, and McAllister families, amongst others. Roads would improve, farms would develop, churches and schools were built, and a number of other businesses—including blacksmiths, cobblers, stores, printers, and mills—would come into town. With his successful calfskin business, Carroll Smalley Page was one of these influential men. He also had a strong political career, serving as governor of Vermont, a Vermont representative and senator, and a US senator.

Our intent is to reflect a small portion of Hyde Park's history and growth through the photographs and images displayed within this book. We wish to visually show that the heartbeat of the community is its people and the roles they play within that community. You will see images of merchants, farmers, teachers, students, loggers, mill workers, homemakers, and so many others who make up the pulse of our community. You will sense, feel, and reflect on the changing times as you view the various photographs and images. You will be able to take a walking tour through both Hyde Park and North Hyde Park Village as you go from page to page.

In closing, you will not be disappointed with the rich history of this unique town. Like so many towns, its history links us all together through the brave men and families who ventured forward to seek out a new life and culture.

One

North Hyde Park (The North Village)

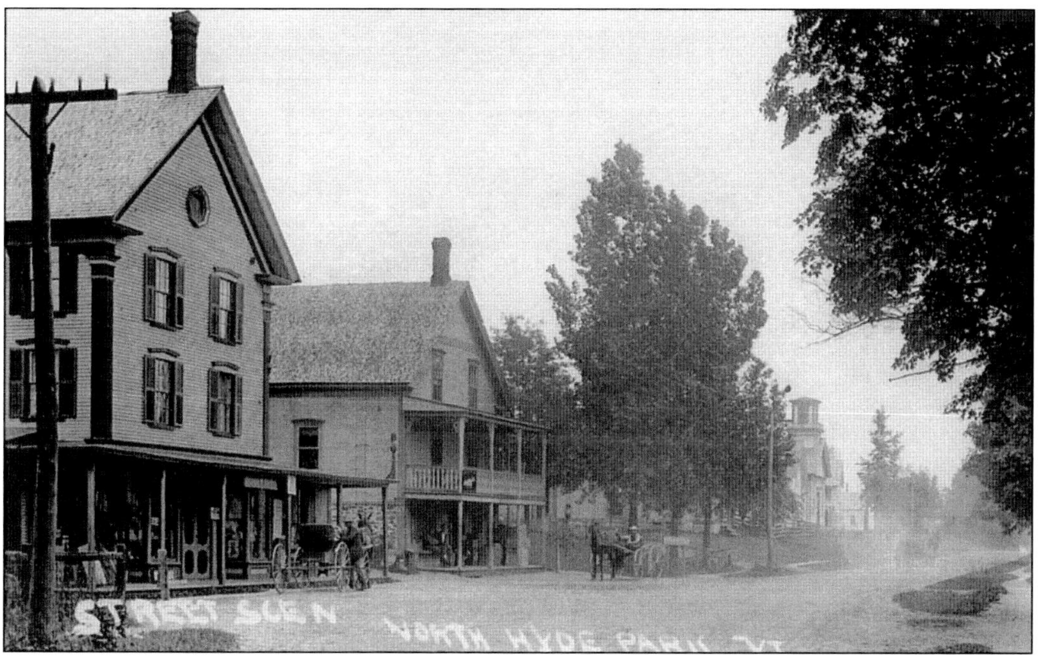

Seen here is a c. 1900 photograph of Main Street in North Hyde Park. The horse and buggy was still the main mode of travel during this time of economic growth in the town. The building to the far left is still standing to this day; however, the one to its immediate right was gutted by fire in 1975 while under the ownership of Don and Ann Atherton. The top portion was rebuilt, and this structure also stands as of today. (Courtesy of the Graves/McAllister family.)

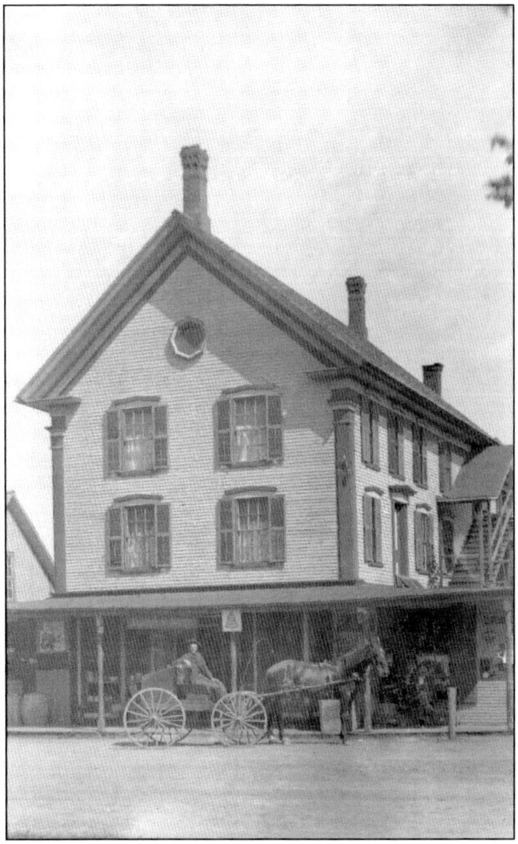

L.E. Harrington's store was better known to folks as Ed Sherlaw's store. In 1918, Sherlaw purchased the business, which he ran until selling it in 1938. This building was later purchased by Ken Deuso and used only as a place of residence. (Courtesy of Linda Jones.)

Ed Wedge was the owner and operator of the Deering Machinery Company around 1920. Located on Main Street, this building later became home to several other businesses, including a general store for the Mace and Atherton families. (Courtesy of Robert and Caroline Jones.)

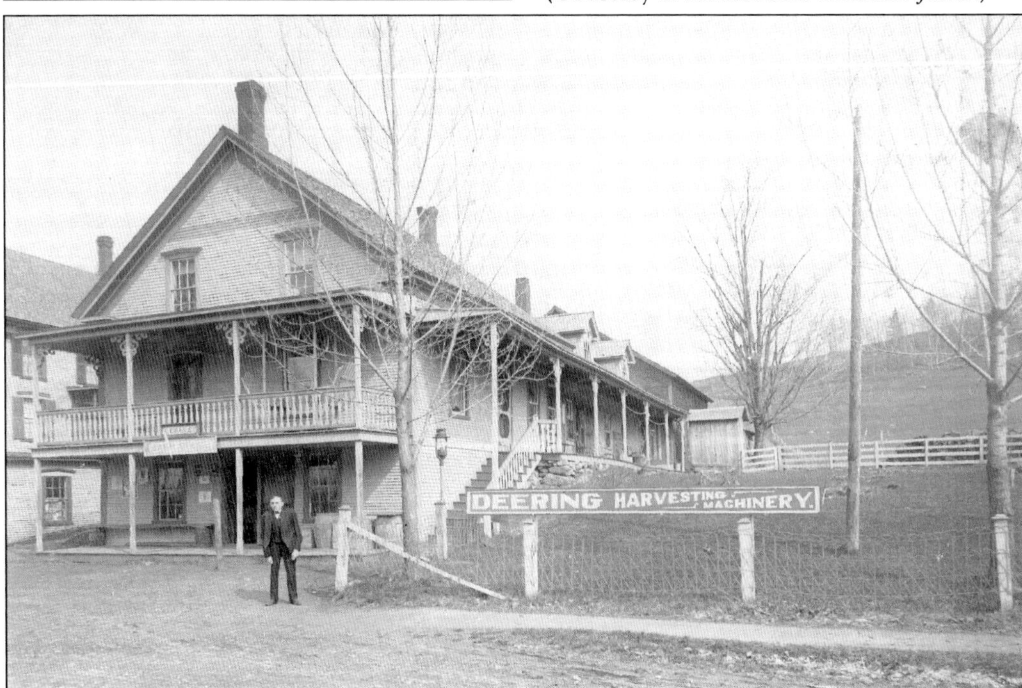

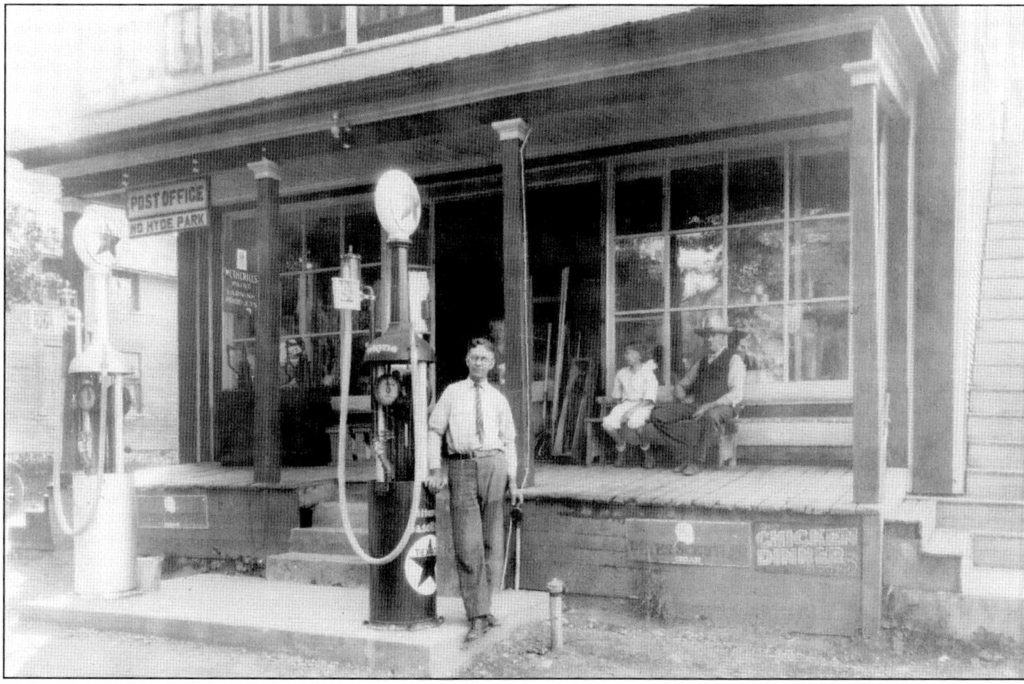

Don McAllister, who came to North Hyde Park from Stowe, is seen here standing by the old gas pumps in front of his store. Frank Hazard purchased the store in 1885, and McAllister bought the store from Hazard in 1922. The store also served as the post office for the village for many years, which was common practice with many general stores around Vermont. (Courtesy of the Graves/McAllister family.)

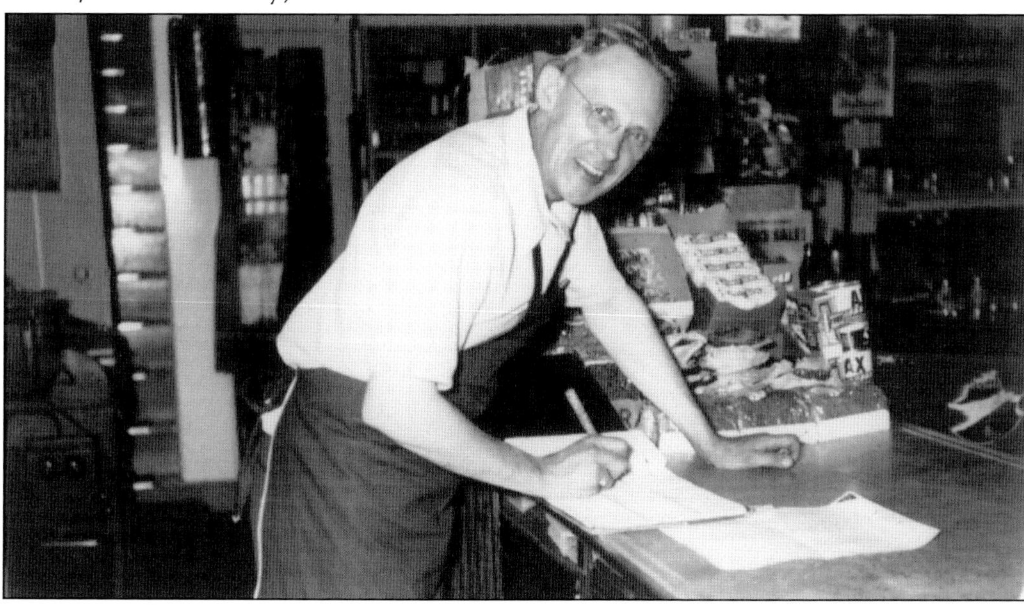

George McAllister smiles while working at the counter of D.S. McAllister & Son General Store in North Hyde Park. McAllister and his wife, Clarissa (Orvis) McAllister, took over the store from his father, Don. The McAllister family owned this business for 47 years until it was sold to Dexter Stewart in September 1969. (Courtesy of the Graves/McAllister family.)

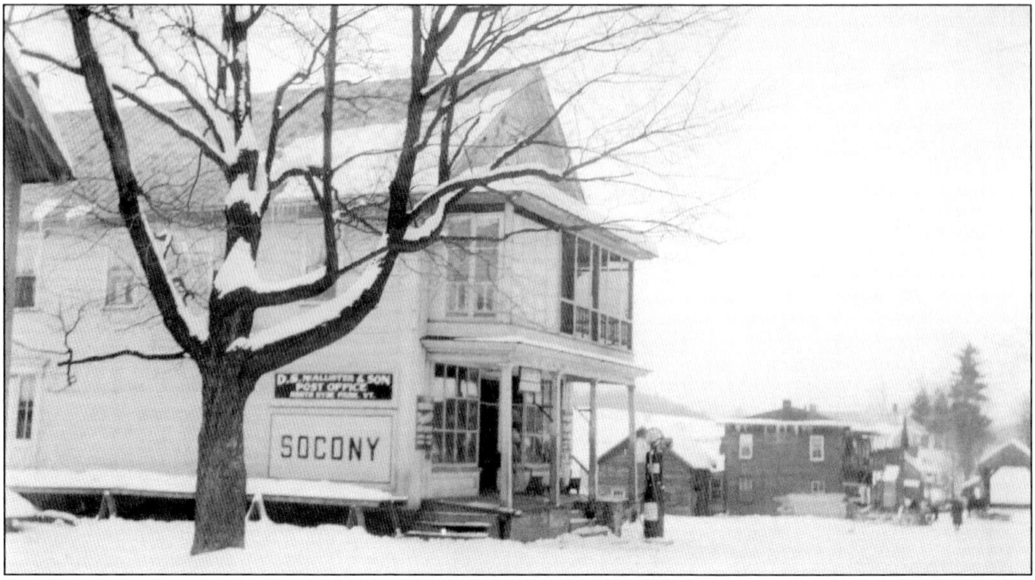

Located next to Bullard Lumber Company on Main Street, D.S. McAllister & Son General Store was also home to the post office and the owners of the store, George and Clarissa McAllister, who lived upstairs. According to the book *Hyde Park—Vermont Shire Town of Lamoille County*, the upstairs was partitioned into apartments by Frank Hazard in 1885. The covered bridge on the far right in this photograph was located on the main road that led north to Eden. (Courtesy of the Graves/McAllister family.)

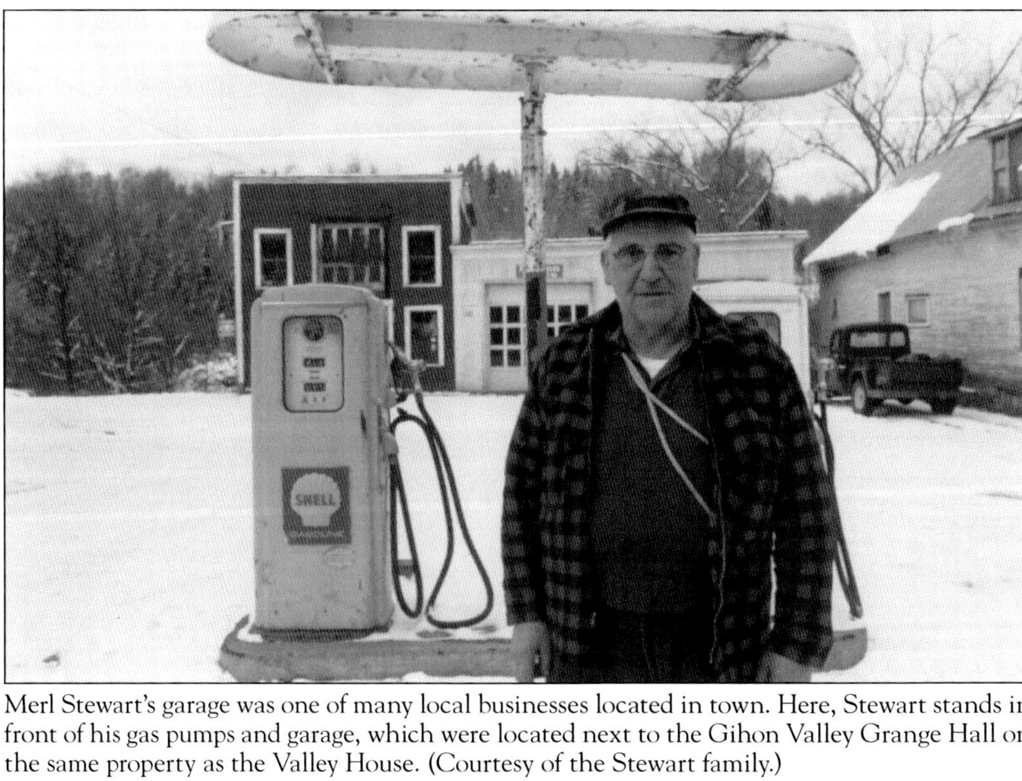

Merl Stewart's garage was one of many local businesses located in town. Here, Stewart stands in front of his gas pumps and garage, which were located next to the Gihon Valley Grange Hall on the same property as the Valley House. (Courtesy of the Stewart family.)

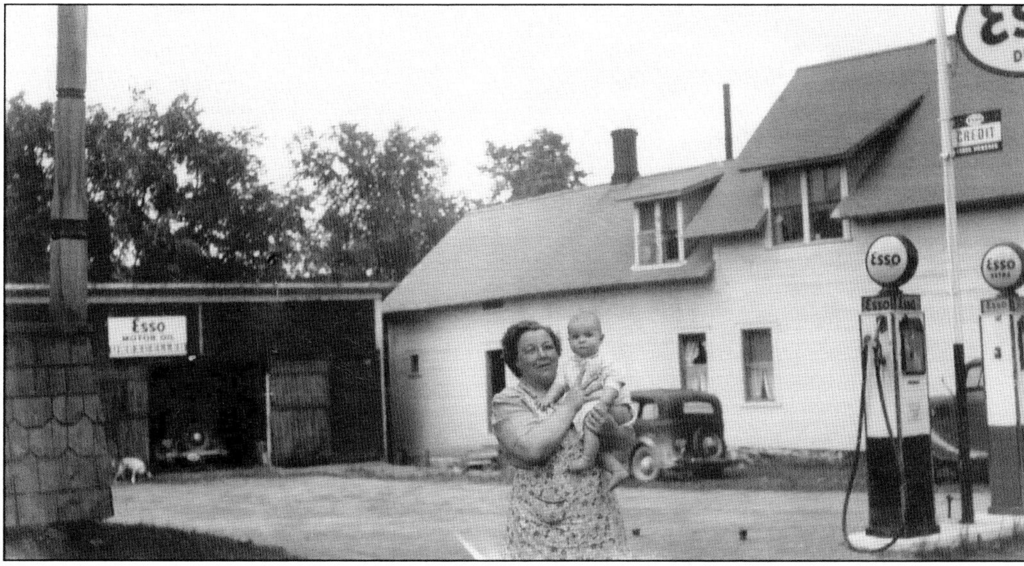

Merl Stewart's wife, Dorothy "Dot" Stewart, stands in front of their home on Main Street in North Hyde Park with son Dexter in her arms. As evidenced by the gas pumps and cars in this image, this photograph depicts the earlier days of Merl's business. (Courtesy of the Stewart family.)

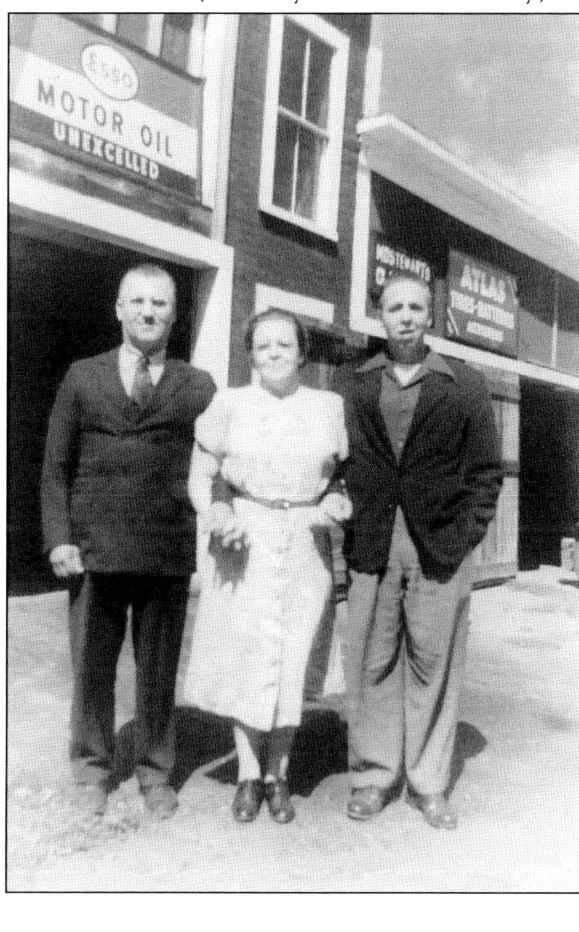

Merl (left), Dorothy, and Dexter Stewart stand in front of Stewart's garage. Notice the signs located along the top of the garage—signs like these were common for advertising and displayed that the business was generally a carrier and sponsor of a product. (Courtesy of the Stewart family.)

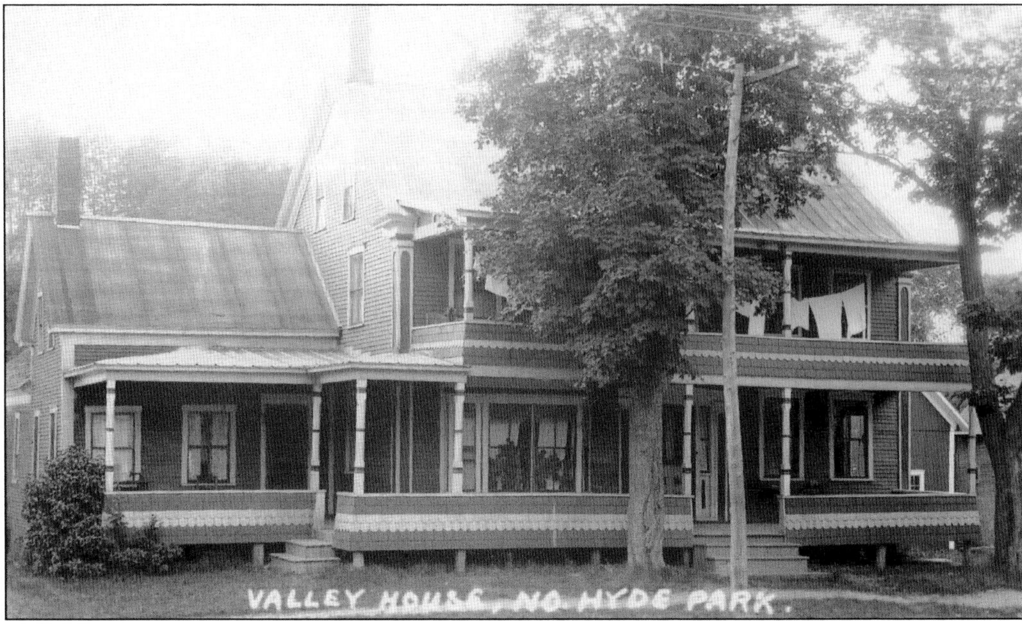

The Valley House was a quaint hotel located on Main Street going through North Hyde Park Village. It was owned and operated by L. Porter Butts for 25 years until he sold it and built a house directly across the road from it. This old hotel was a warm and delightful sight for new and old visitors passing through the area. In later years, it became the home of Merl and Dot Stewart, who also established an automotive business in a garage in back of the property. (Courtesy of the Larose/Manning family.)

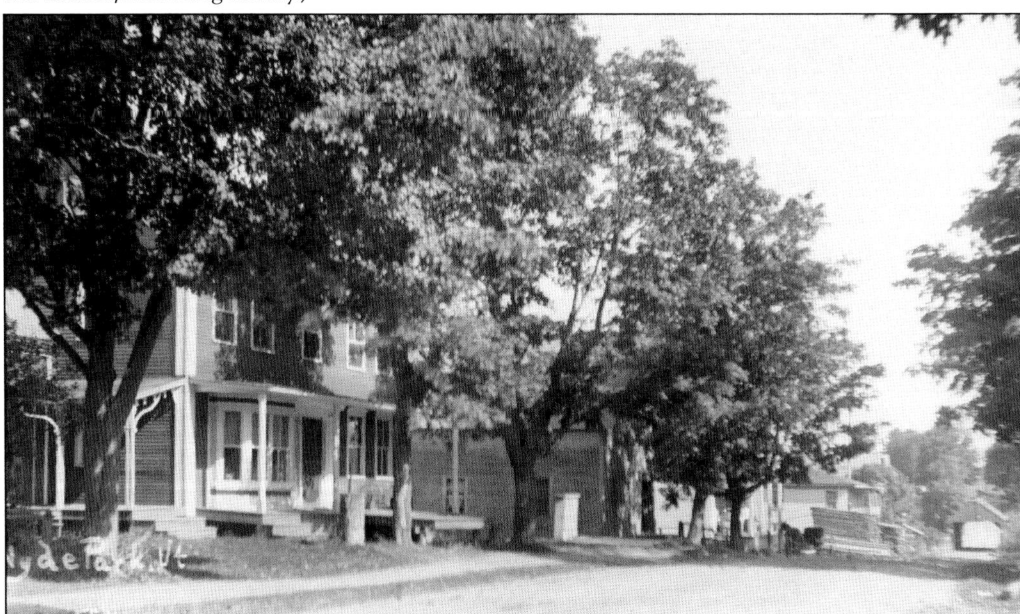

This image of upper Main Street in North Hyde Park was taken prior to the flood of 1927, as evidenced by the covered bridge at the far right of the photograph. A horse and buggy sits in front of D.S. McAllister & Son General Store, which was located next to the Bullard Lumber Mill. Note the lumber piles next to the road. (Courtesy of the Heath/Savage family.)

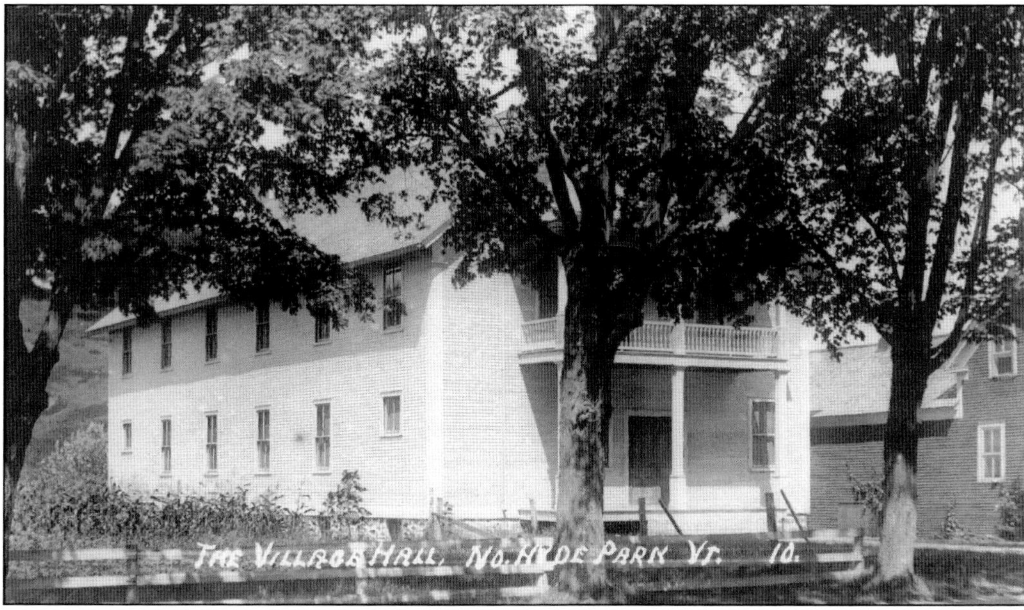

The Valley Hall in North Hyde Park opened in October 1910 and would later be known as the Gihon Valley Grange Hall. Originally, the first floor was used for plays and dances, and the second floor housed the Grange and a small library. The third floor was designated to be the GAR Hall. Because of its size and the wonderful stage on the first floor, the North Hyde Park School held many performances there. It is now home to the Hyde Park Historical Society. (Courtesy of the Heath/Savage family.)

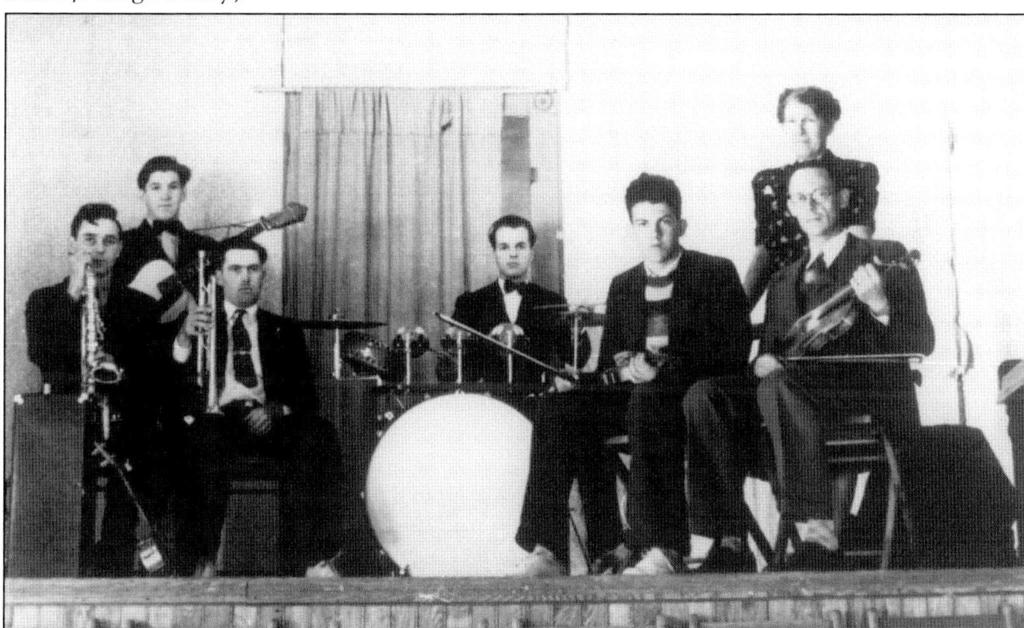

The Gihon Valley Grange Orchestra, pictured in 1940, was a popular provider of entertainment for community events. Pictured, from left to right, are Carroll Page, Proctor Gray, Wesley Hanscom, Merrill Foss, June Kneeland, George McAllister, and Agnes Hodges. (Courtesy of the Graves/McAllister family.)

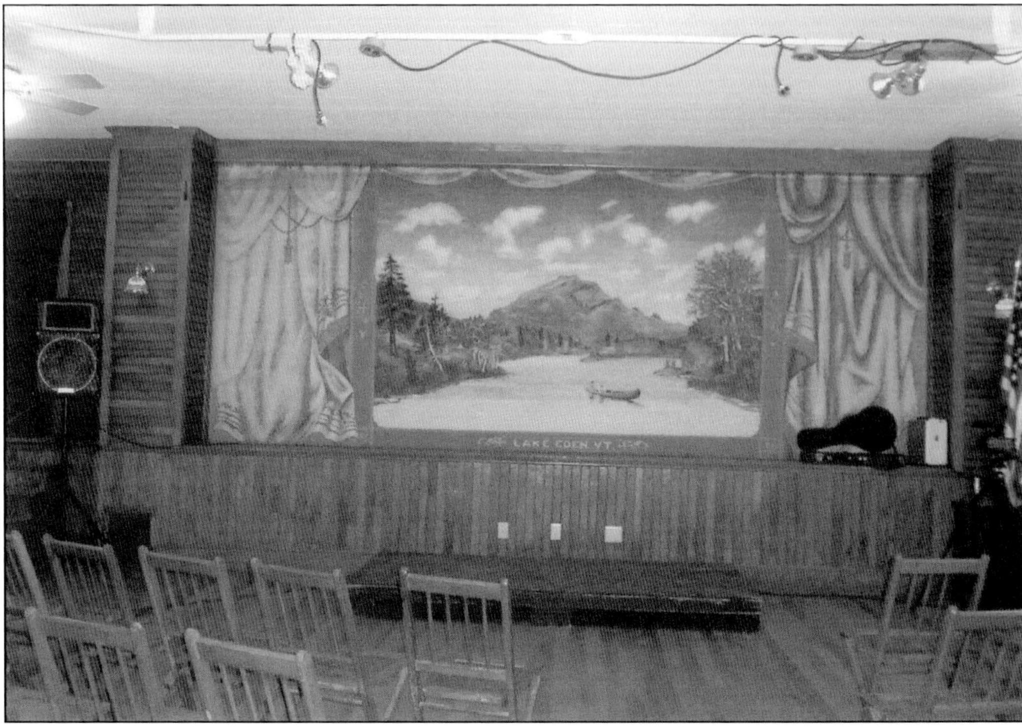

Pictured hanging in Gihon Valley Grange Hall, this curtain depicts a scene of Lake Eden with Mount Norris in the background. It was painted by Charles Andrus in March 1911 and later restored by the historical society. (Courtesy of Robert and Caroline Jones.)

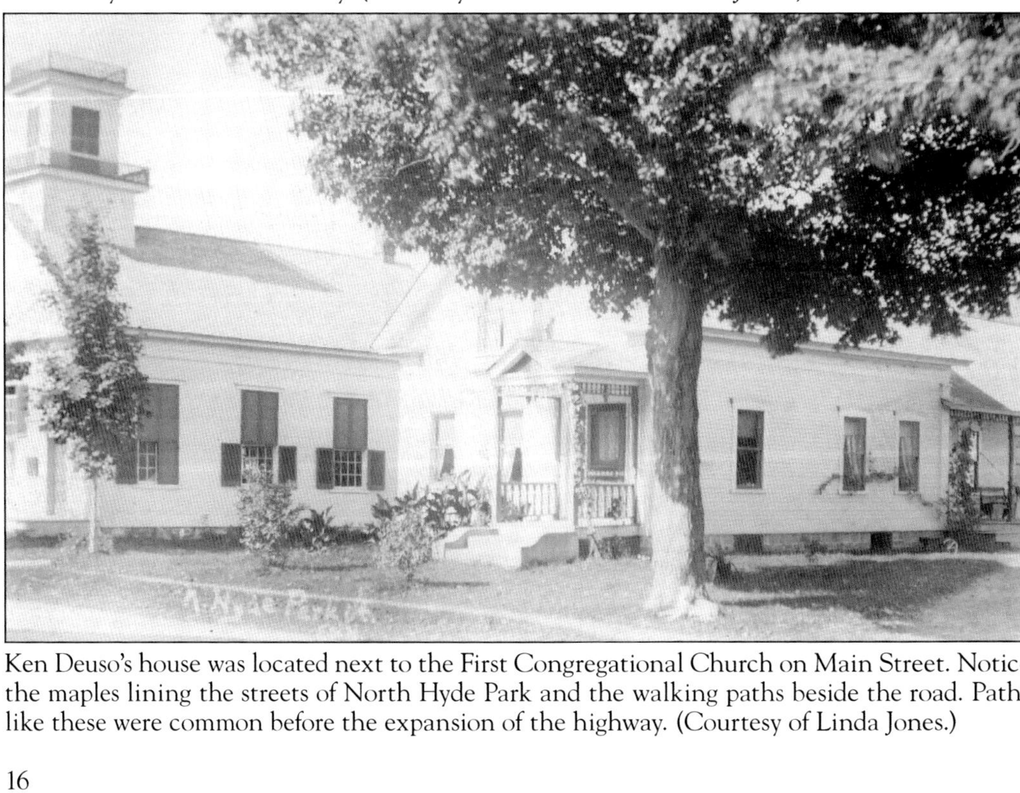

Ken Deuso's house was located next to the First Congregational Church on Main Street. Notice the maples lining the streets of North Hyde Park and the walking paths beside the road. Paths like these were common before the expansion of the highway. (Courtesy of Linda Jones.)

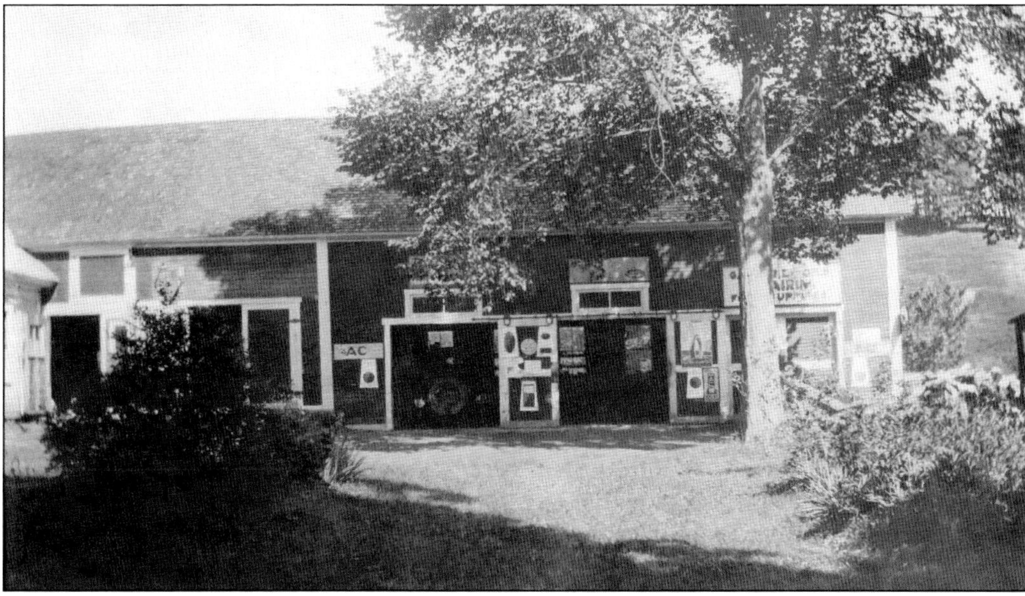

Shown is the trucking business of Delbert Locke. The business is connected to his home. The property was later sold to Ken Deuso. Many small businesses contributed to the small town's local economy. (Courtesy of Vernon Bullard.)

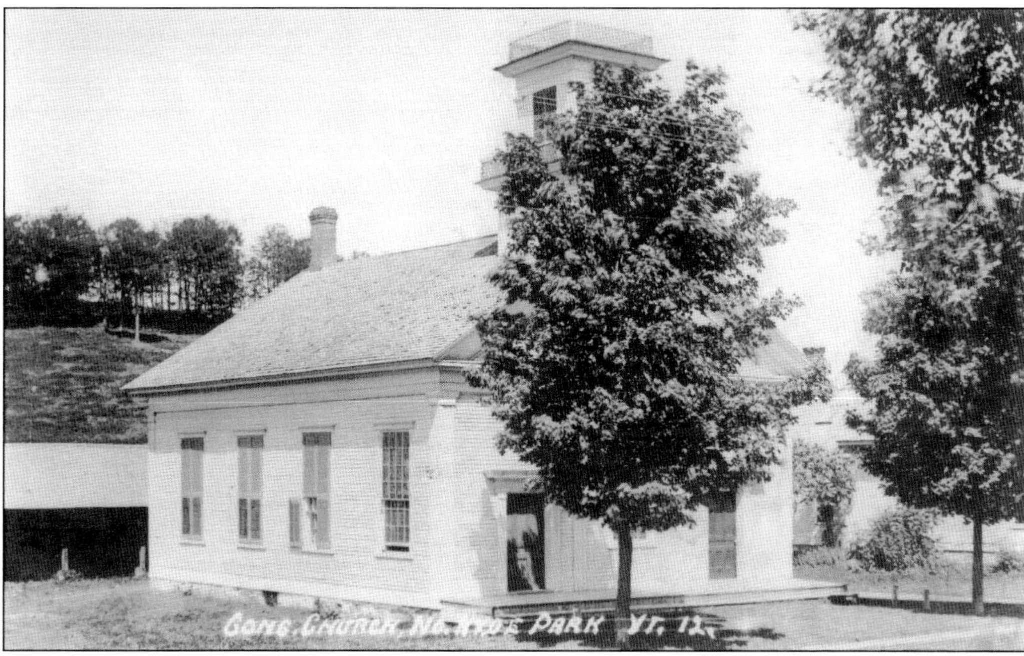

Located on Main Street in North Hyde Park, the First Congregational Church dates back to 1858, when an ecclesiastical committee met in the home of Nathan Walker to vote to move forward with the establishment of the church. Visible in this image are the carriage sheds—a common feature of most churches during this time period—located in back of the church. (Courtesy of the Heath/Savage family.)

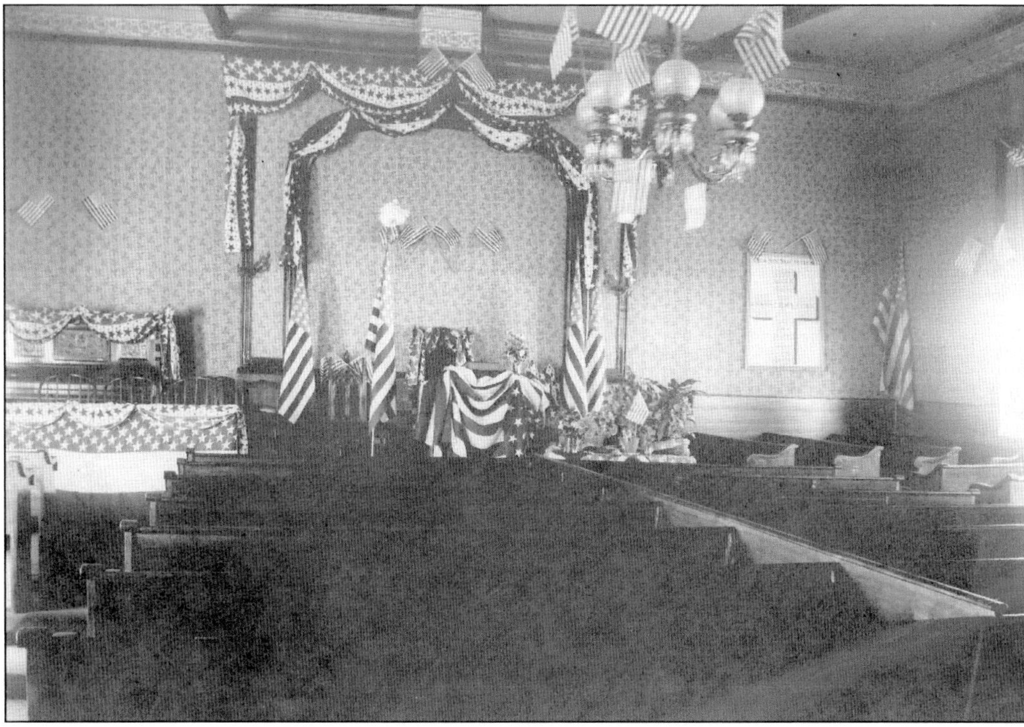

The interior of the First Congregational Church is pictured before it was remodeled due to damage by a fire. The church pews located in the right-hand corner are no longer present, although pews were reestablished in the left-hand corner to accommodate the church choir. The pulpit was donated by the church in Waterville in April 1898. (Courtesy of Robert and Caroline Jones.)

The view in this image looks north on Main Street in North Hyde Park. Notice the footpaths and large maples that line both sides of the dirt road. Scenes like these were common among the small towns of Vermont. (Courtesy of Linda Jones.)

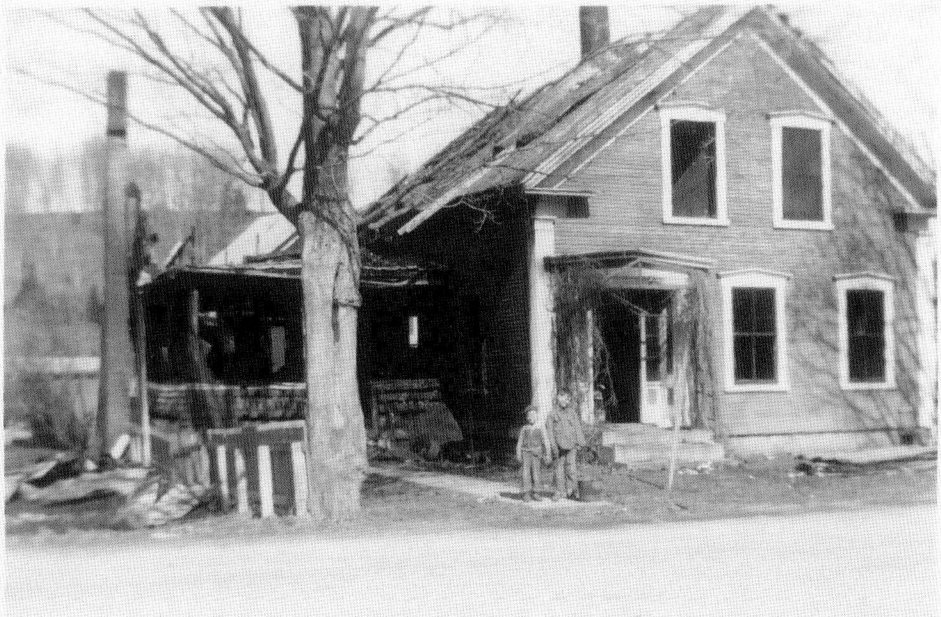

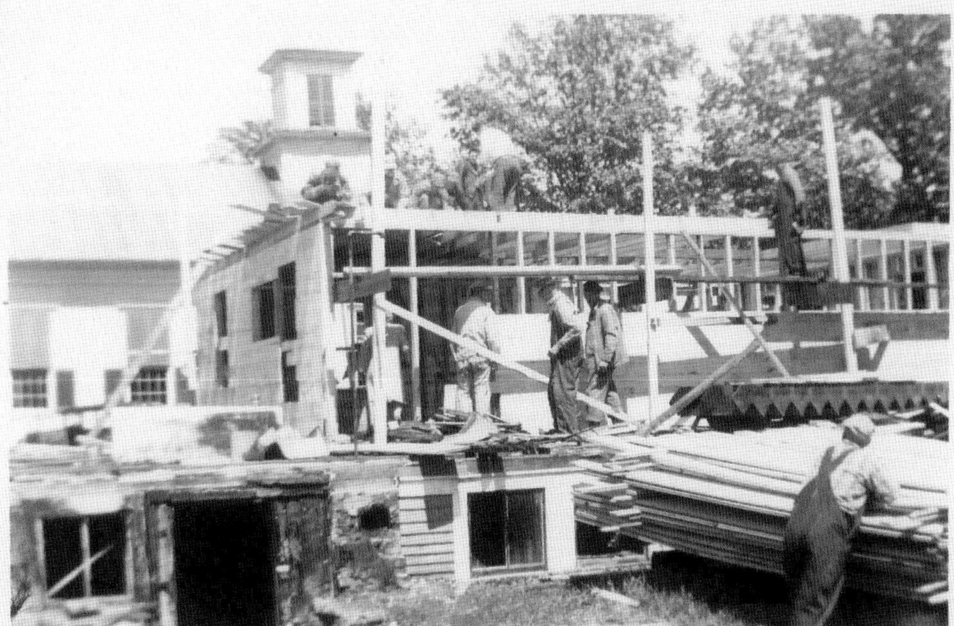

The upper image shows the original Griswold home after it burned down. The construction of the new Griswold home, located next to the First Congregational Church in North Hyde Park, is shown in the lower image. This was the original homesite of the Griswold family and is presently the home of David Griswold. (Courtesy of Vernon Bullard.)

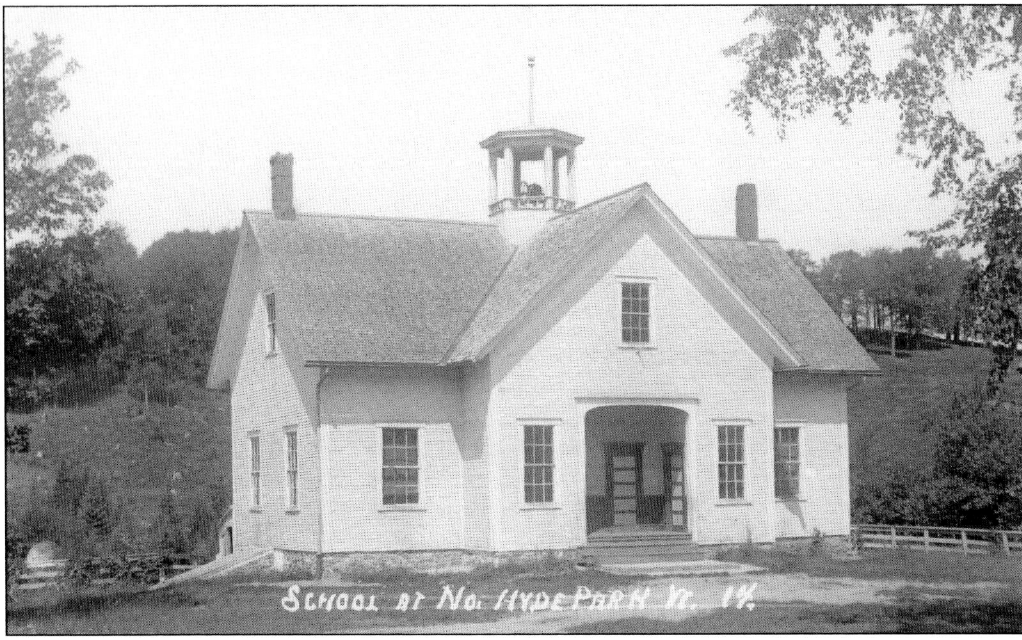

The two-room schoolhouse shown here in North Hyde Park was closed in June 1966. James Heath, one of the authors of this book, was in the last class of five students that attended all six grades in this school. The first room on the right was known as the "Little Room" because it housed grades one through three (there was no kindergarten in those days). Of course, the room on the left was called the "Big Room," as it housed grades four through six. The lunchroom was in the basement. (Courtesy of the Heath/Savage family.)

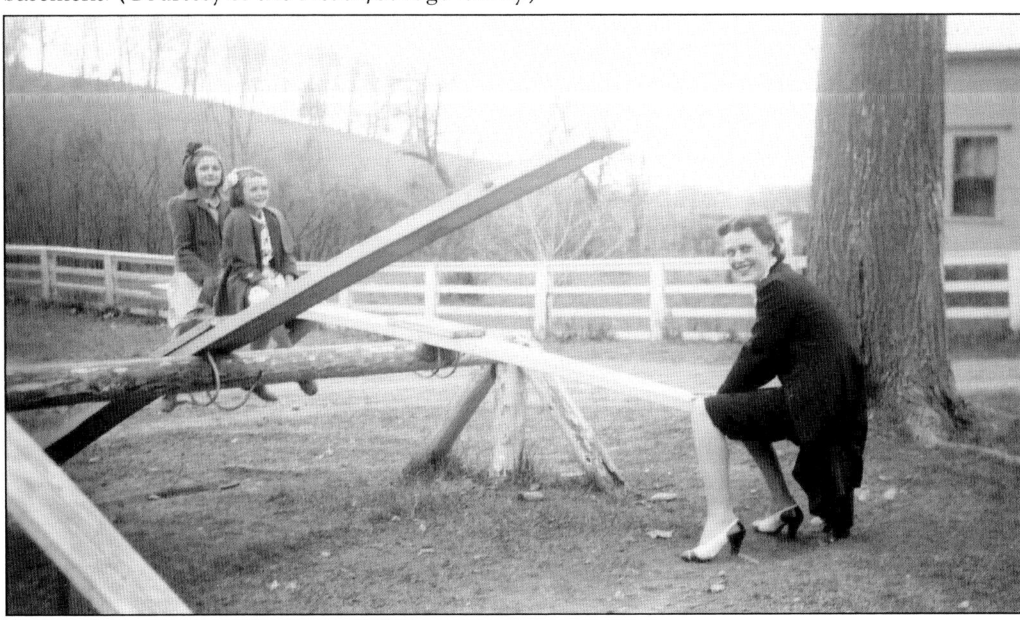

The playground located in front of the North Hyde Park School was complete with a swing set, teeterboard, and slide. Pictured here on the teeterboard in the fenced-in schoolyard are, from left to right, Barb, Marjorie, and Royalynn McAllister. Kickball and baseball were played in the field located in back of the school. (Courtesy of the Graves/McAllister family.)

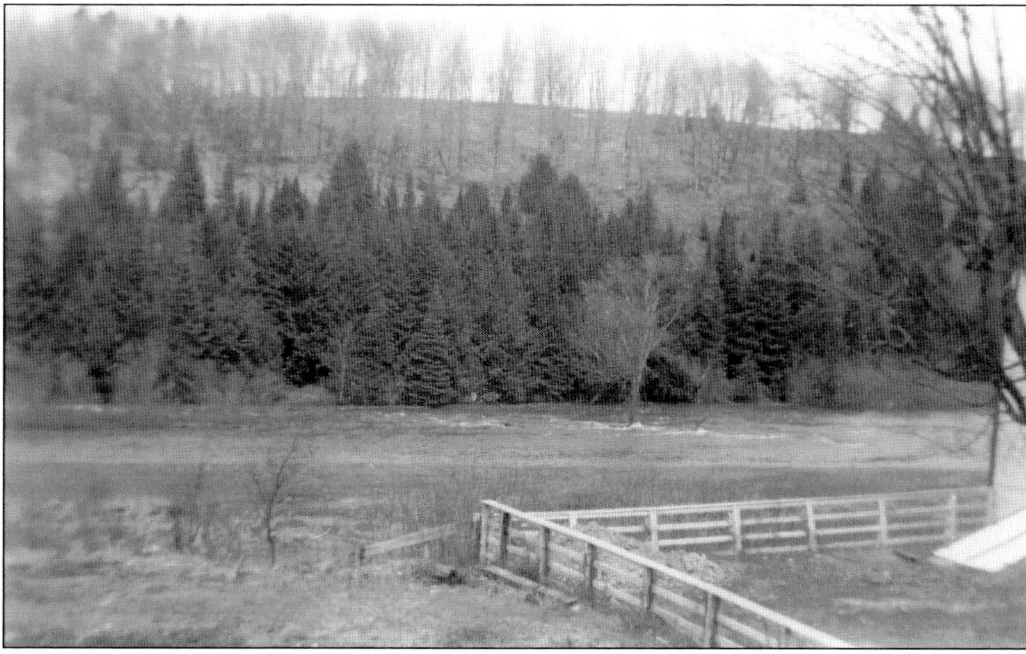

Due to the rapid change in temperatures, springtime flooding is relatively common in Vermont when spring arrives. This photograph was taken in back of the North Hyde Park schoolhouse, where the Gihon River overflowed its banks. (Courtesy of Vernon Bullard.)

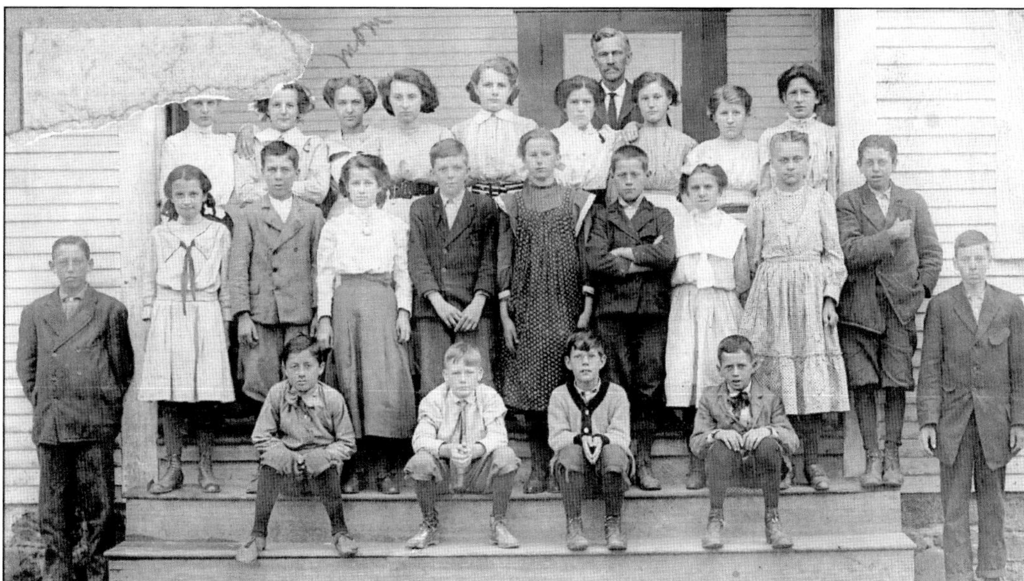

The class photograph at the North Hyde Park School in June 1911 includes, from left to right, are (first row) Leo Grimes (standing), Gerald Kneeland, Gaylord Westover, Randsom Griswold, George McNally, and Neal Sargent (standing); (second row) unidentified, Harold Jones, Glenella Foss, Harold Souther, Helen Amadon, Clarence Wedge, Muriel Bailey, Mildred Beardsly, and Temple Grimes; (third row) Arlie Wescom, Freda Parrin, Grace Heath, Hazel French, Addie Stone, Doris Kneeland, Penniah Foss, Florence Kneeland, and Flossie Jones; (in back) teacher George Allen. (Courtesy of the Heath/Savage family.)

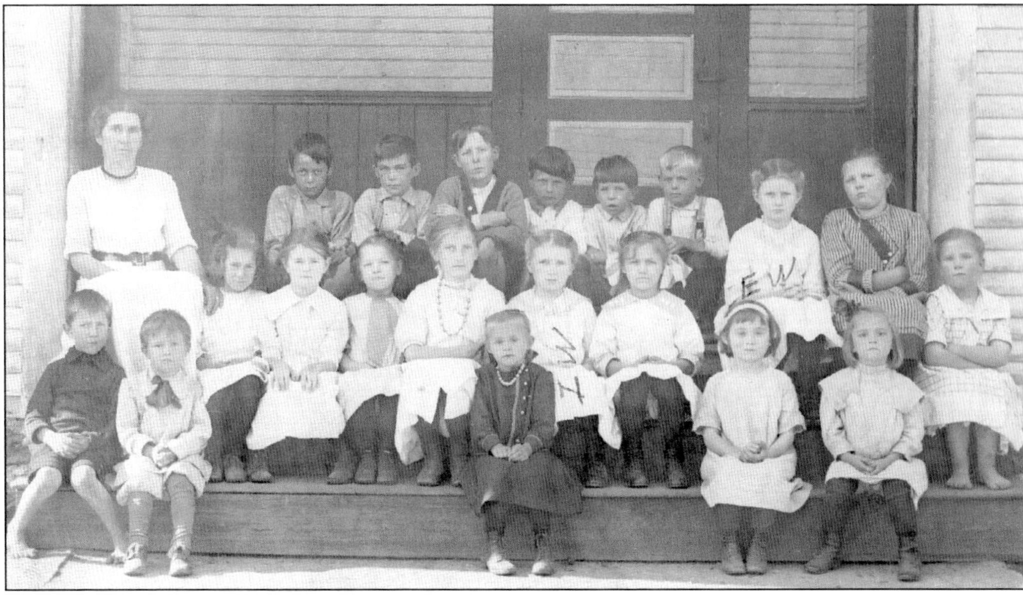

Seen here is a c. 1913 photograph of students on the steps of the North Hyde Park School. The only two students identified in this photograph are "IW" (Iva Whitcomb) and "EW" (Eula Whitcomb), who were the children of Vernon and Florence Whitcomb. They lived on the Whitcomb farm on Ferry Street that was later occupied by Eula and her husband, Ralph Thompson. (Courtesy of Norma [Thompson] Savage.)

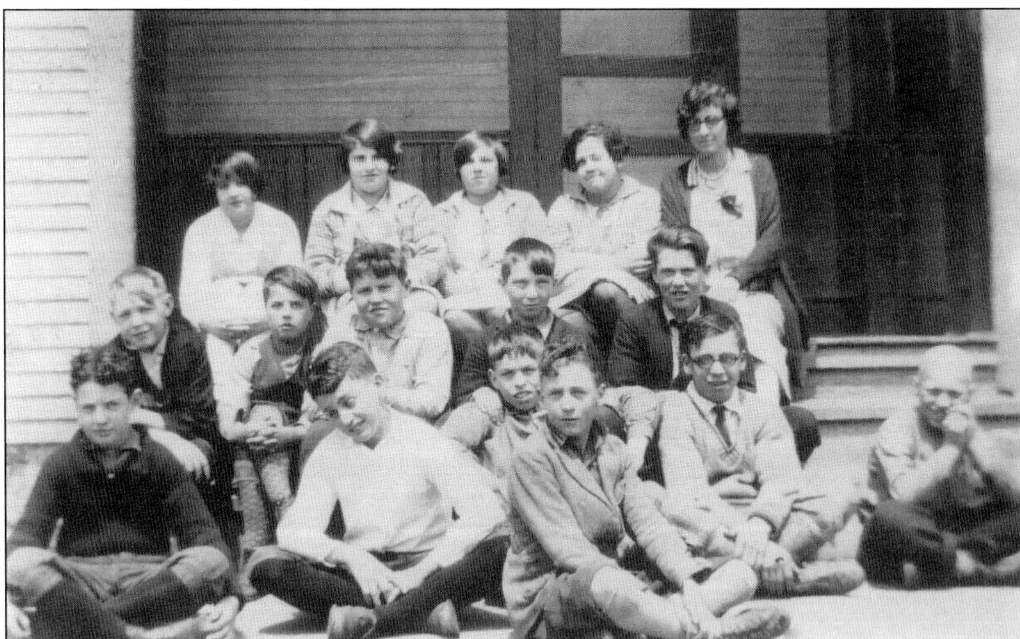

Teacher Helen Bucklin and her class from the "Big Room" are pictured around 1930. From left to right are (first row) Roy Mudgett, Leo Davis, Arnold Larose, Donald Flanders, Henry Morris, and Wilton Larose; (second row) Earl Gray Jr., Merrill Foss, Erald Hanscom, Maurice Heath, and Wesley Hanscom; (third row) Evelyn Foss, Helen Page, Elaine Crocker, Maysel Coan, and Helen Bucklin (teacher). (Courtesy of the Stewart family.)

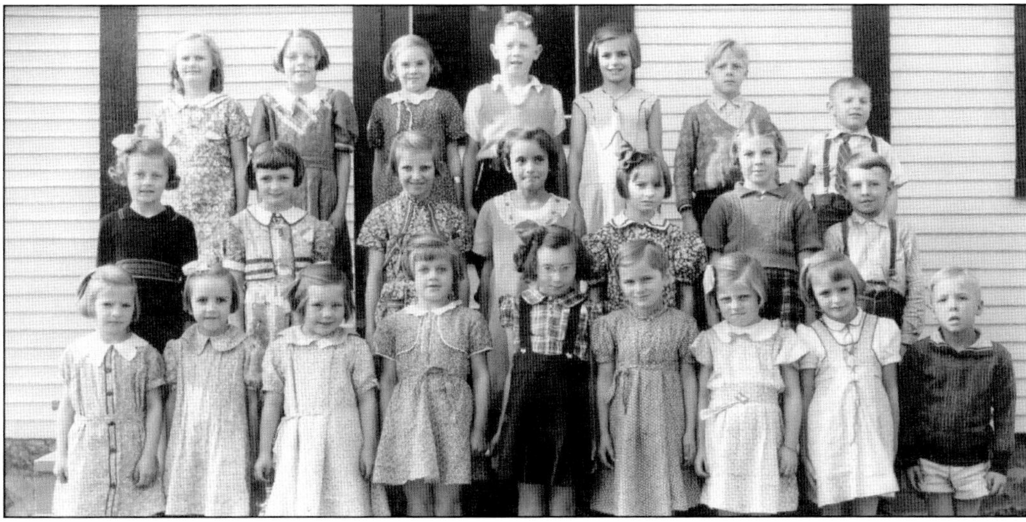

The first-grade class of the North Hyde Park Elementary School is pictured in 1938. From left to right are (first row) Margaret Jewet, unidentified, Stella Bedell, Marion Foss, Eleanor Grimes, Joanne Lanphere, Norma Thompson, Marjorie McAllister, and Dexter Stewart; (second row) Janice Wedge, Barb McAllister, Kathleen Jones, Rachel Tallman, Jaunita Larose, Alison Cleary, and Howard Sprague; (third row) Mary Mudgett, Dolly Dudley, unidentified, Cliff Manosh, Bertha Jacobs, unidentified, and Larry Sanborn. (Courtesy of the Stewart family.)

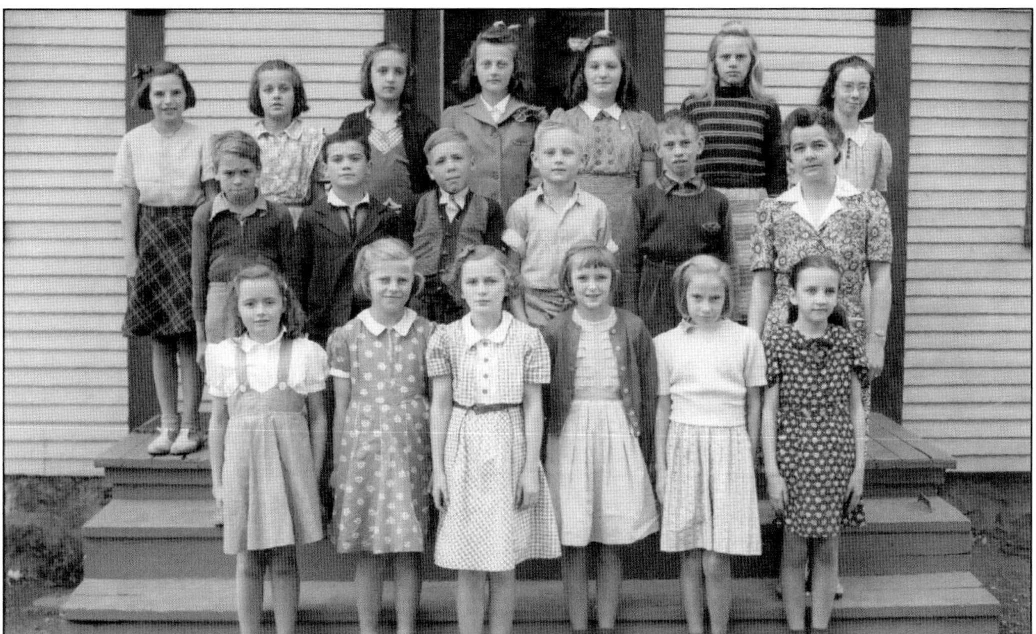

Pictured with their teacher in October 1942 is the fifth-grade class of the North Hyde Park Elementary School. From left to right are (first row) Betty Jones, Norma Thompson, Joanne Lanphere, Marjorie McAllister, Cora Jones, and Eleanor Jones; (second row) Lawrence Manning, Francis Manning, Dexter Stewart, Elroy Langdell, Lee Jones, and Emily Gillen (teacher); (third row) Pauline Hill, Marion Foss, Rachel Tallman, Janice Wedge, Juanita Larose, Beatrix Jones, and Eleanor Grimes. (Courtesy the of Stewart family.)

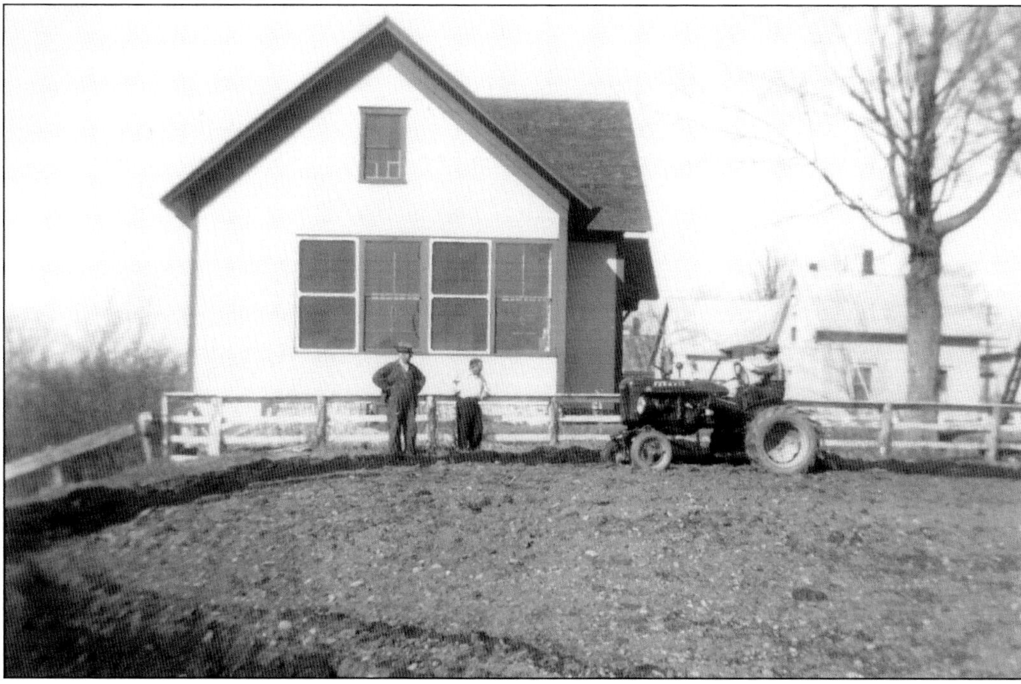

Haven Bullard (left) and company are hard at work plowing a small piece of his land with a Farmall tractor. This property was located between Bullard's home and the North Hyde Park School, which can be seen in the background. (Courtesy of Vernon Bullard.)

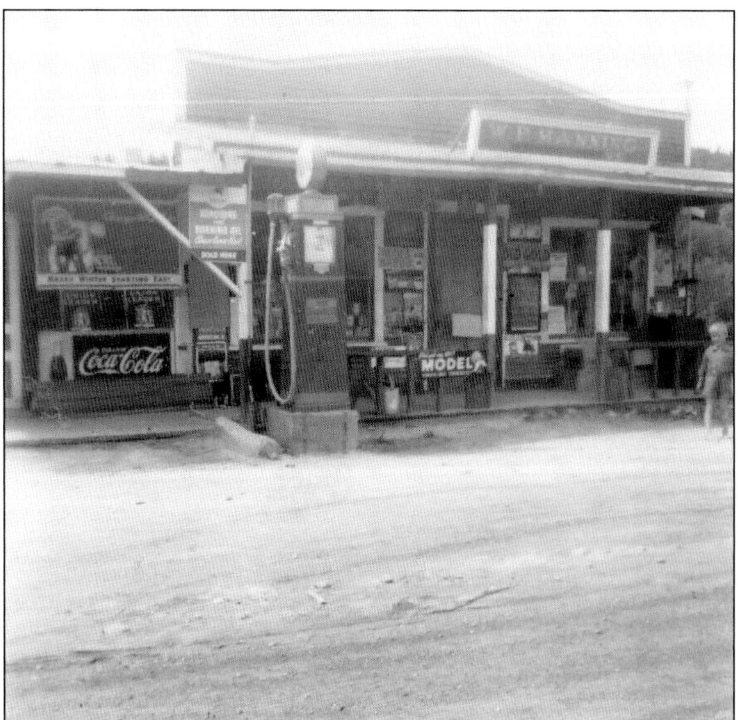

Willard F. Manning's store was located on lower Main Street in North Hyde Park, in the vicinity where the residence of the Gamble family once stood. This small general store carried a variety of dry goods to meet the needs of the community. (Courtesy of the Larose/Manning family.)

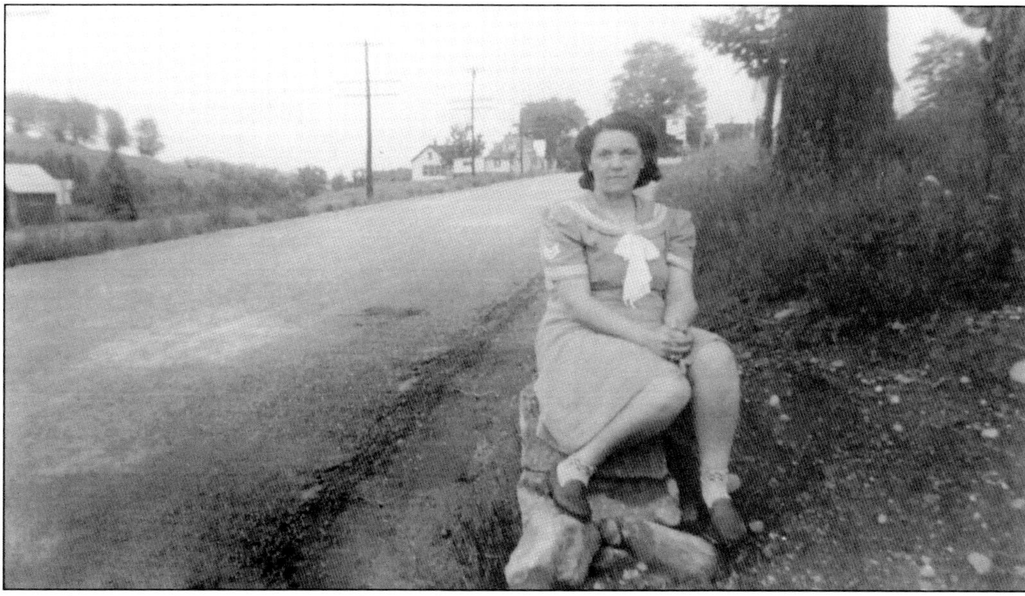

Fern (Manning) Larose sits in front of her home, which was located on Main Street across from Willard Manning's store (later owned by Abner Mason). Notice Francis peeking out from behind the tree. The schoolhouse (in the distance) and Harley and Kate Souther's slaughterhouse (over the bank, to the far left) are also visible in this photograph. (Courtesy of the Larose/Manning family.)

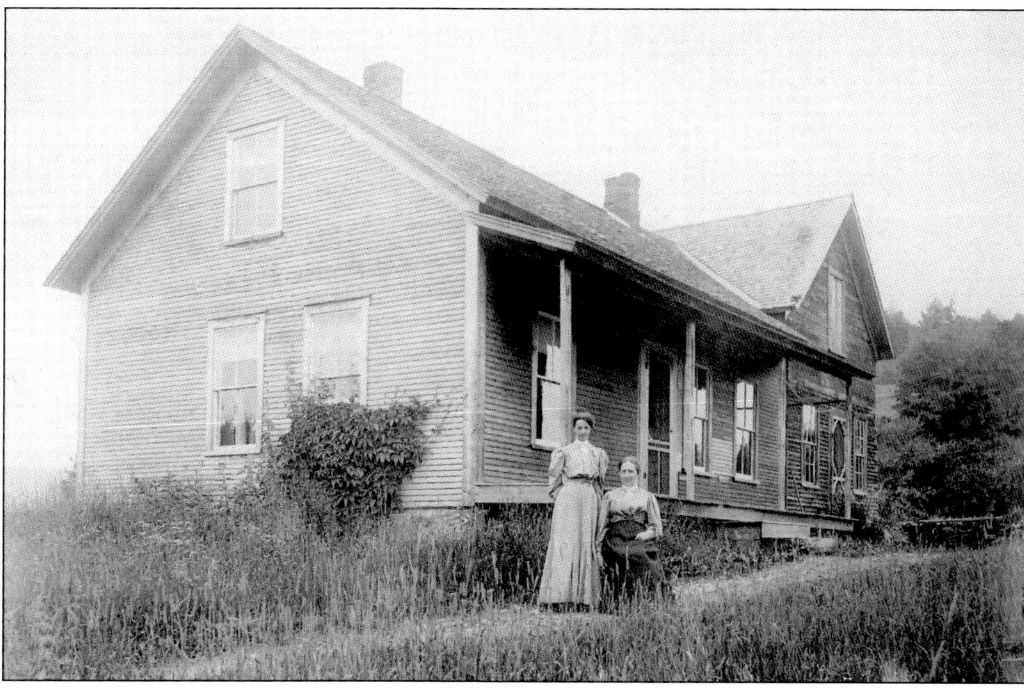

The first framed house in North Hyde Park was built by Daniel Bullard, one of the first settlers of the village. Vivian Bullard, Don McAllister's wife, was the granddaughter of Daniel Bullard. Dr. L.L. Eastman later lived in this house with his wife, Kate. Floyd and Ella Merrill were the last to reside in this home. (Courtesy of the Graves/McAllister family.)

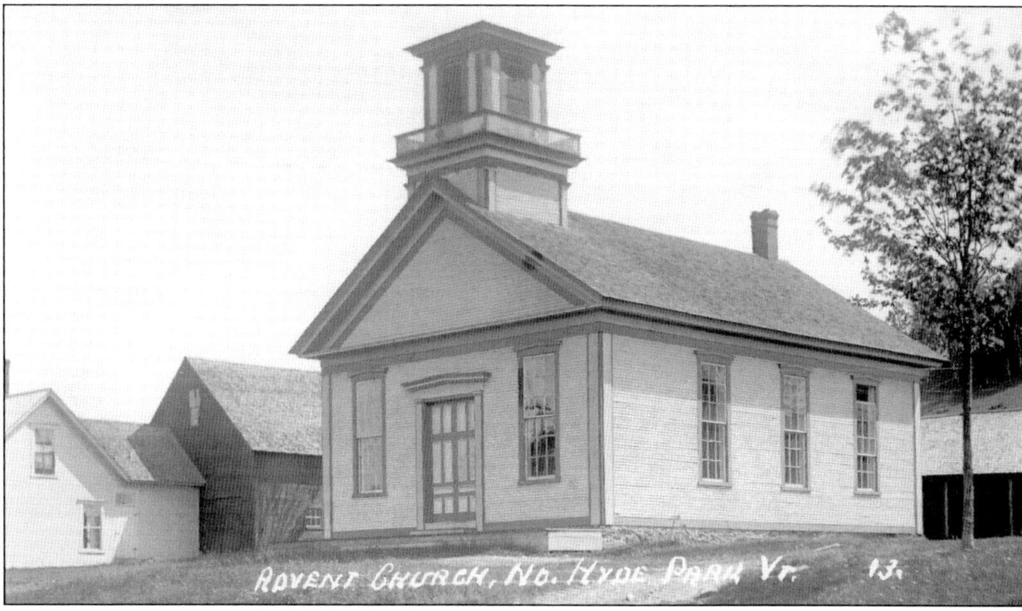

The Advent Christian Church, built in 1867, was located next to Don McAllister's farm on Main Street in North Hyde Park. Rev. Ira Gray of Waterbury was responsible for building the church and also the house, where his great-great-grandson David Griswold now lives. Vernon A. Ober was the Advent preacher for many years in the mid-1900s. (Courtesy of Roberta Grimes.)

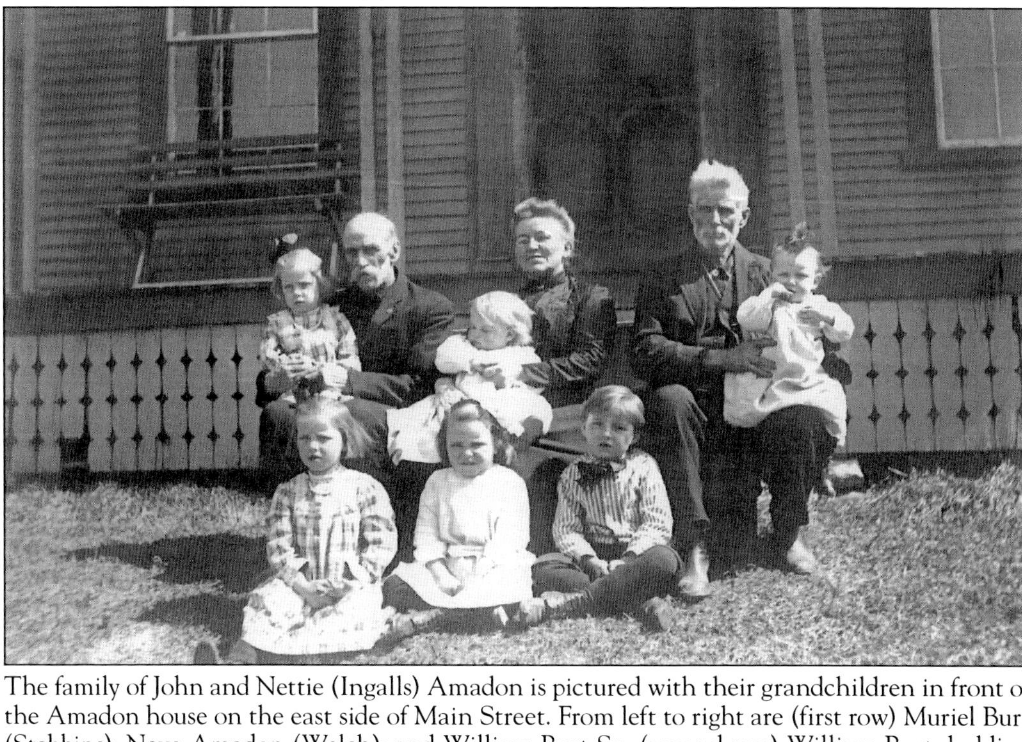

The family of John and Nettie (Ingalls) Amadon is pictured with their grandchildren in front of the Amadon house on the east side of Main Street. From left to right are (first row) Muriel Burt (Stebbins); Neva Amadon (Welch); and William Burt Sr.; (second row) William Burt, holding Opal Burt (Lafountain); Nettie Amadon, holding granddaughter Ruby Amadon (Day); and John Amadon, holding granddaughter Dora Knowles (Sargeant). (Courtesy of Ruby [Amadon] Day.)

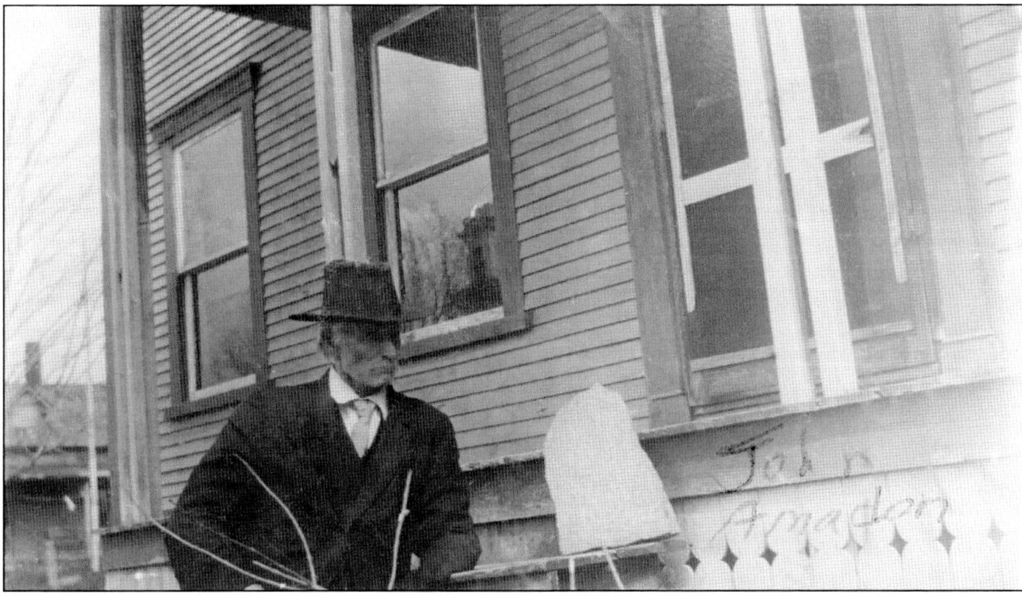

John Henry Amadon stands in front of his home in North Hyde Park. Amadon was a veteran of the Civil War, and his granddaughter Ruby (Amadon) Day, who passed away at the age of 102 in March 2013, told her cousin Monica Heath, the author of this book, stories of attending Civil War reunions (GAR encampments) by train with her grandfather. (Courtesy of the Larose/Manning family.)

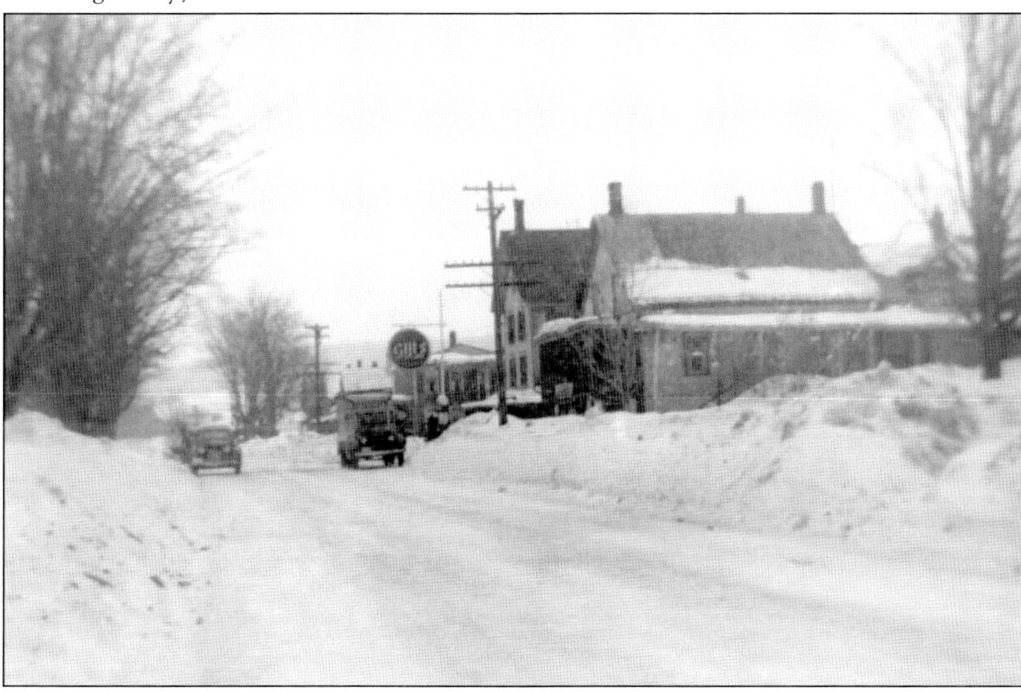

This c. 1930 wintery view looks north up Main Street in North Hyde Park. On the right are the gas pumps, marked by the Gulf sign, located at Mace's General Store. Winter scenes like this one were common in towns around Vermont, with the winter season seeming to last forever at times. (Courtesy of Robert and Caroline Jones.)

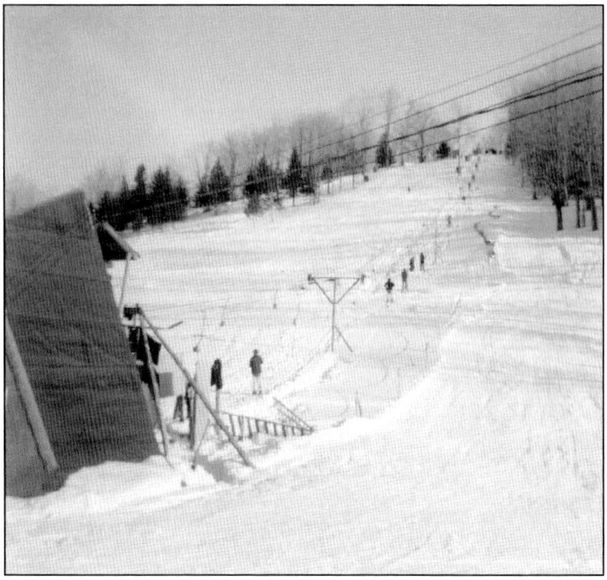

The North Hyde Park Ski Tow was located on the east side of the village. Built by Everton and Marjorie (McAllister) Graves, this ski area was located on the property owned by Marjorie's parents, George and Clarissa McAllister. An all-day lift ticket used to cost $5. (Courtesy of the Graves/McAllister family.)

This area of downhill skiing was designated for beginners. Notice the rope tow, which was used to get the skiers to the top of the hill. At the very bottom of the ski area was a small building where skiers could warm up and pick up a cup of hot chocolate. (Courtesy of the Graves/McAllister family.)

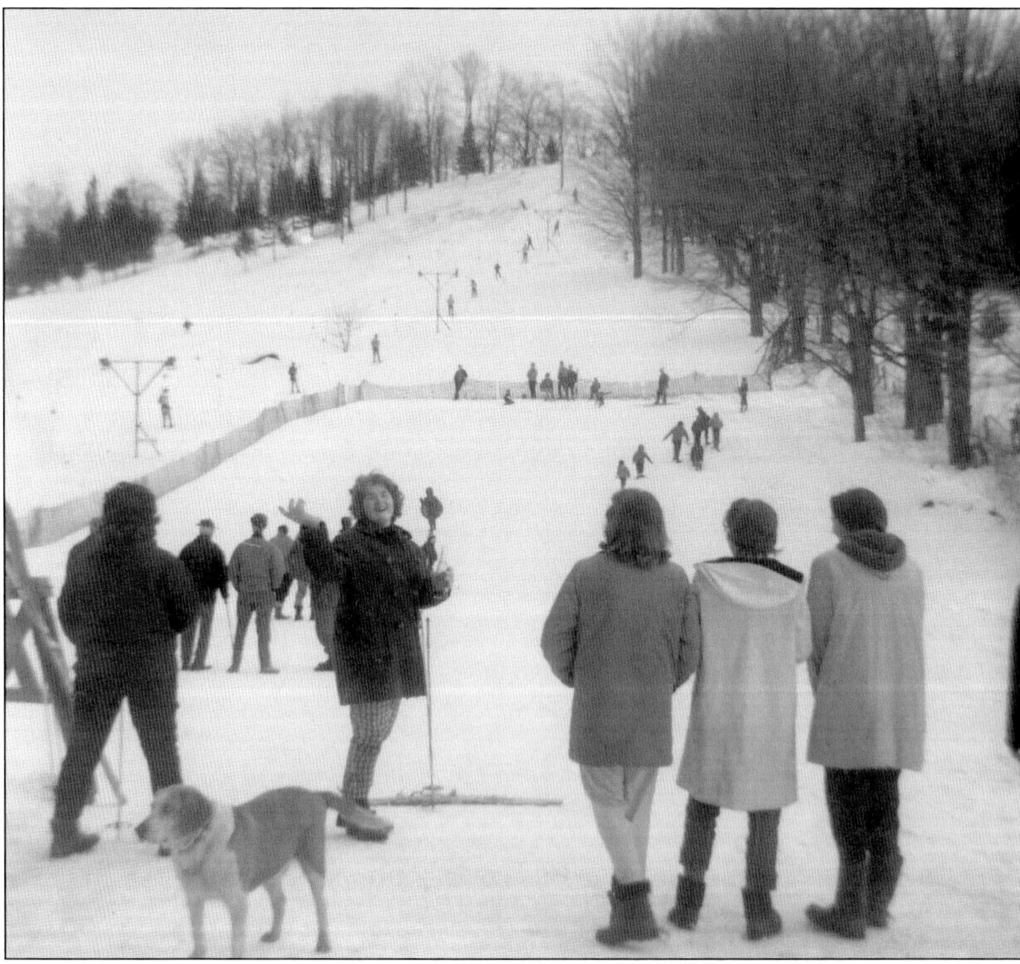

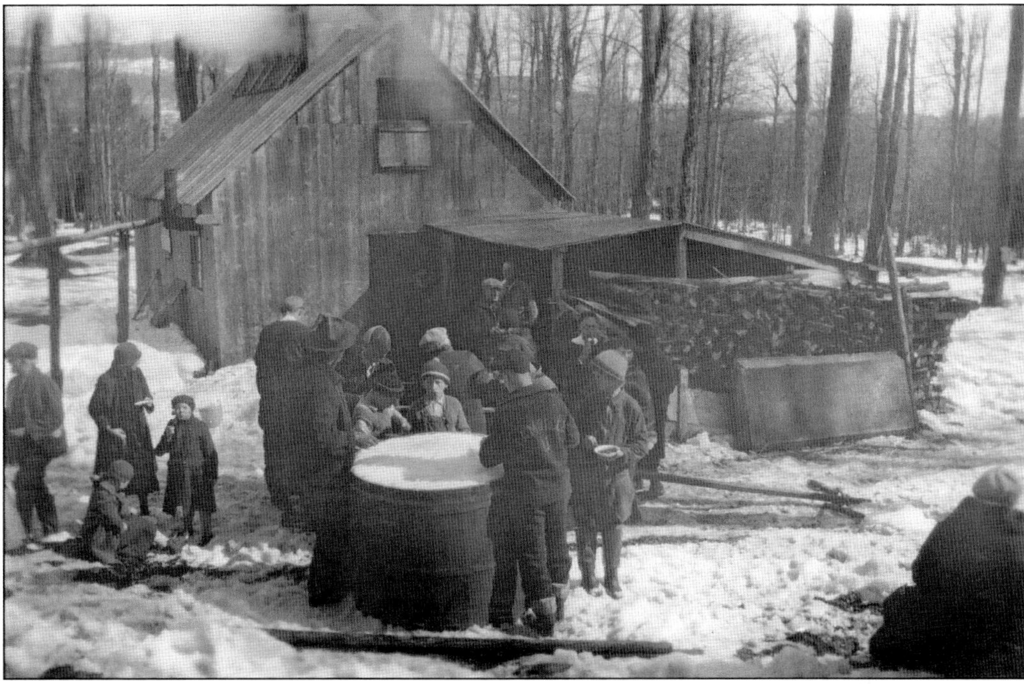

Attendees enjoy a "Sugar-on-Snow" party at George McAllister's sugarhouse in North Hyde Park. Events of this nature were wonderful social outings where community members, families, and friends got together to enjoy the season and the beginning of spring. (Courtesy of the Graves/McAllister family.)

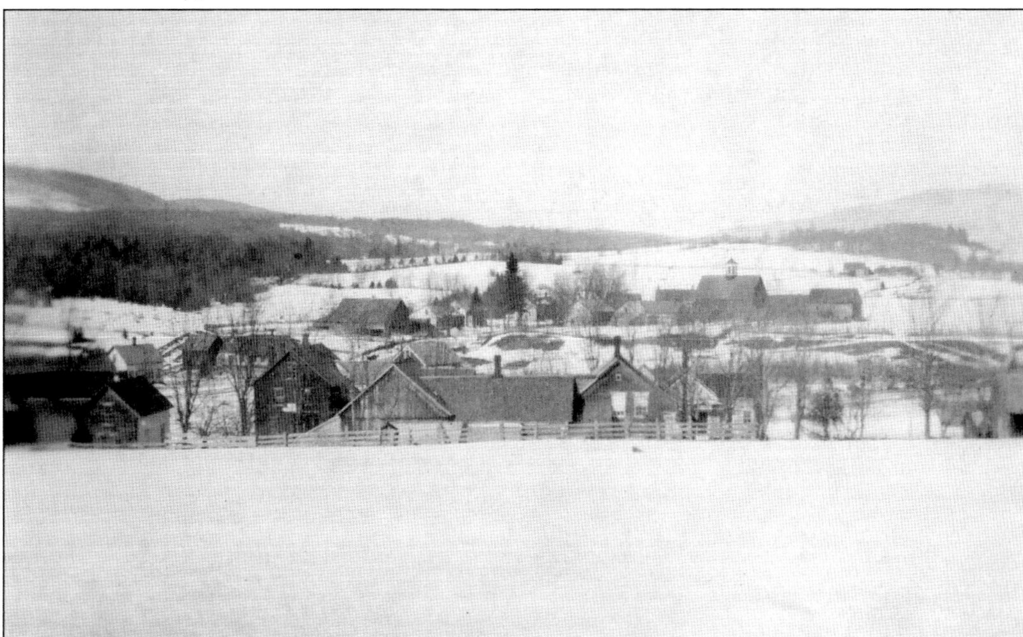

This photograph with a view looking north towards the town of Eden was taken on the south side of Ferry Street. This image reflects the old buildings and barns that once stood outside of town along Route 100. (Courtesy of the Graves/McAllister family.)

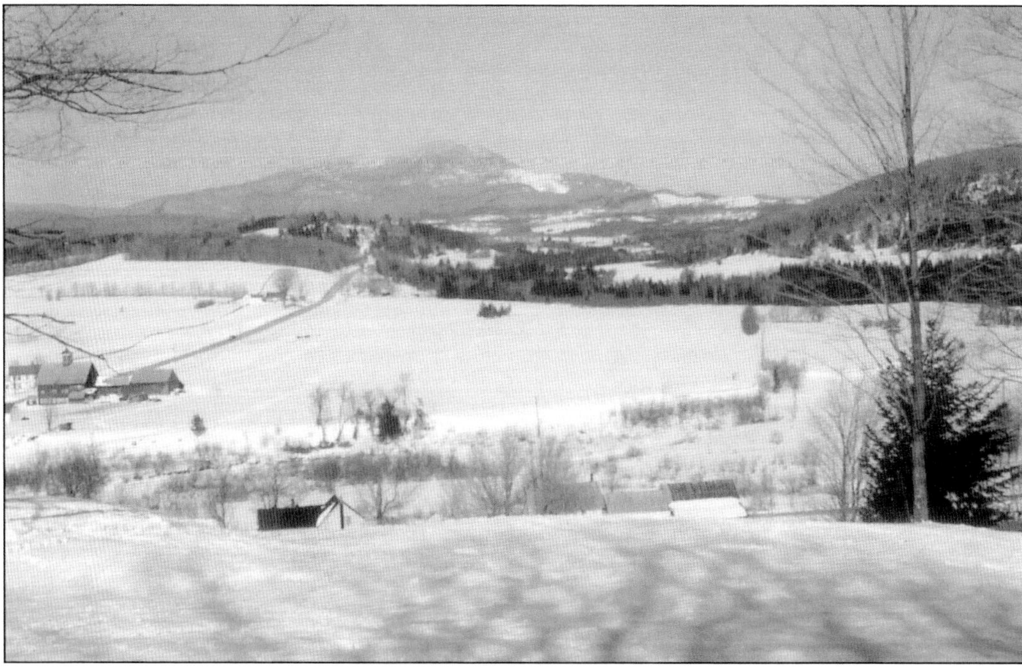

This photograph looking north towards the town of Eden and Belvidere Mountain was also taken on the south side of Ferry Street. If one looks closely at Belvidere Mountain, the waste pile from the first asbestos mine from the early days of mining is visible. To the left are a house and barn owned by Marvin Lock, with the fields of the farm located at the center of this photograph. (Courtesy of the Graves/McAllister family.)

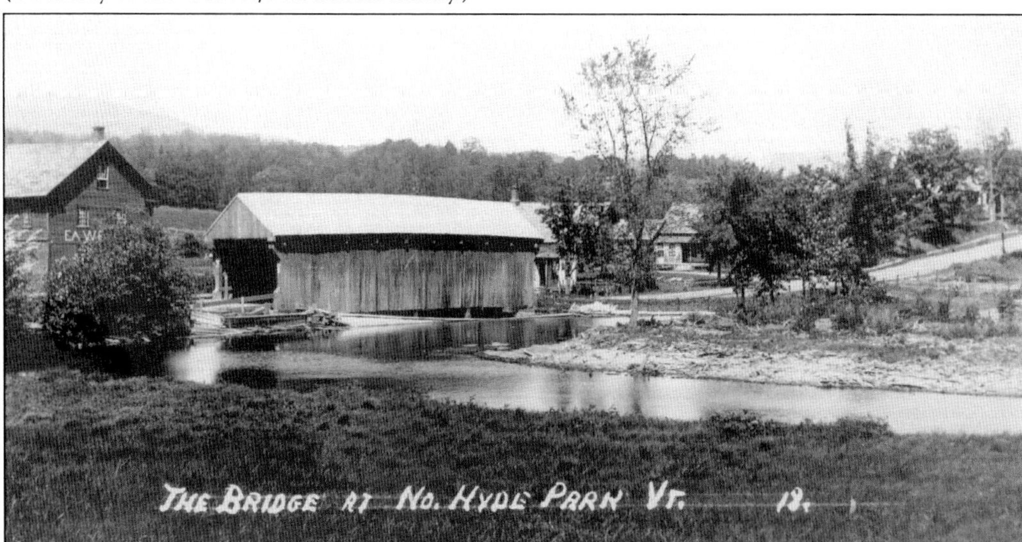

In this view looking across the Gihon River from Ferry Street, one sees the covered bridge leading north towards Eden. It was swept away in the flood of 1927. Next to the bridge on the left is the E.A. Wedge Grist and Starch factory, which had horse sheds in back where people would park their horses and buggies when they went to church. The March 29, 1905, *News & Citizen* reports, "E.A. Wedge has commenced cutting his large stock of logs. John Amadon has charge of the slab department; another trust." (Courtesy of the Heath/Savage family.)

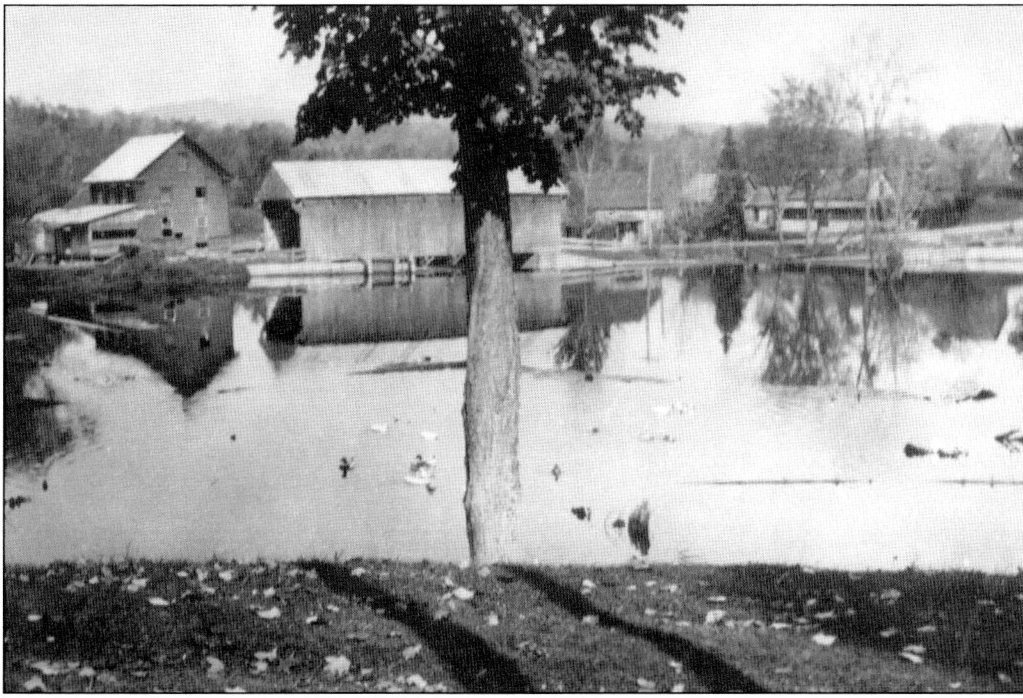

A dam was built to create a pond to provide a water supply to power the E.A. Welch Grist and Starch Factory, located at the left in this image. The millpond also supported many recreational activities, such as fishing and swimming in the summer and ice-skating and hockey, with a warm fire on the bank, during the winter. (Courtesy of the Heath/Savage family.)

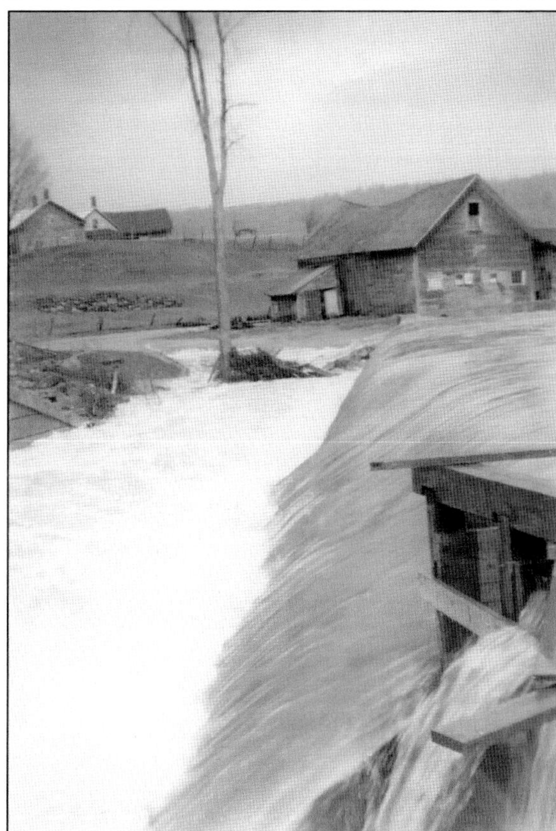

Bullard's milldam was built on the east side of the covered bridge. In this photograph, Frank Sargeant's barn (in the background) is being flooded from the spring runoff. The headwaters of the Gihon River begin from the outlet on the south side of Lake Eden. (Courtesy of Vernon Bullard.)

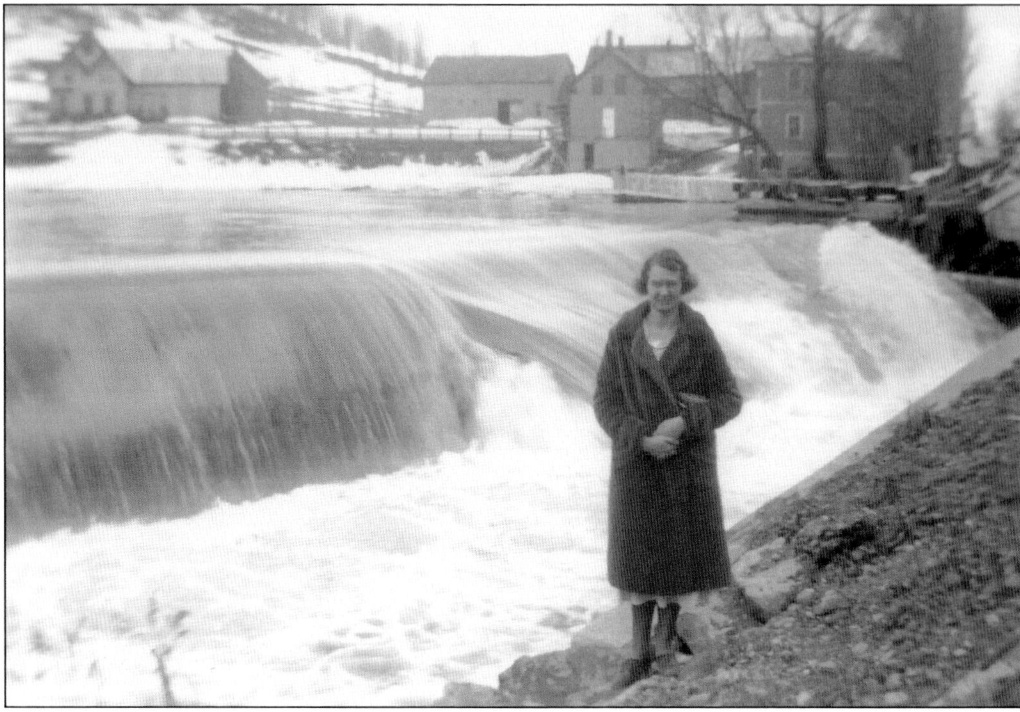

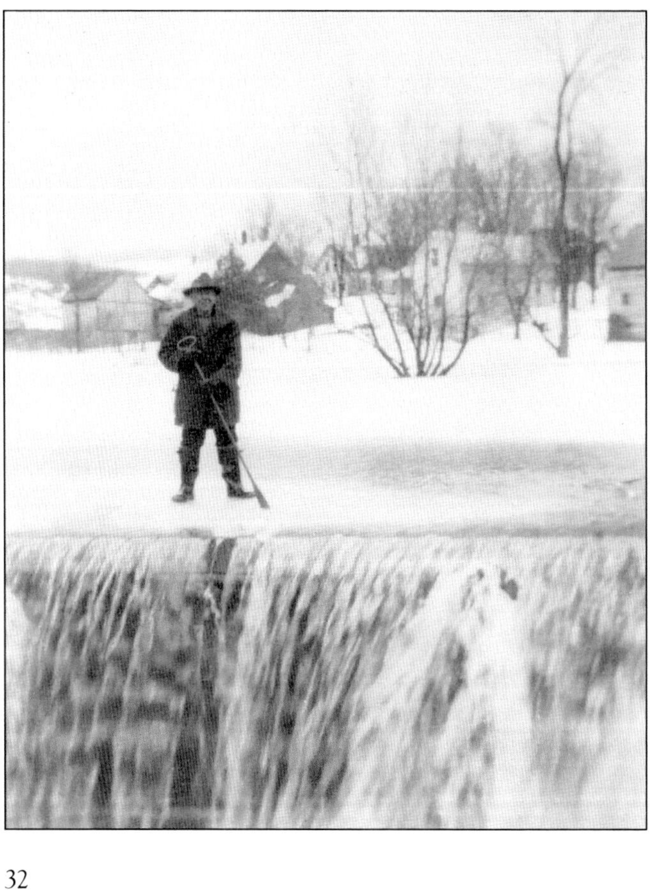

Early spring arrives in this photograph of Mary Griswold, who is standing next to the dam and bridge on the north end of town, with Ferry Street in the background. The Maple Croft house is to the left in this photograph, and Mary Griswold's home is visible just above her head. (Courtesy of Vernon Bullard.)

Haven Bullard stands on the ice near the edge of the milldam. The ice pick in his hands was most likely made in a blacksmith shop and was used for chiseling blocks of ice after they had been sawn for storage in the icehouse. (Courtesy of Vernon Bullard.)

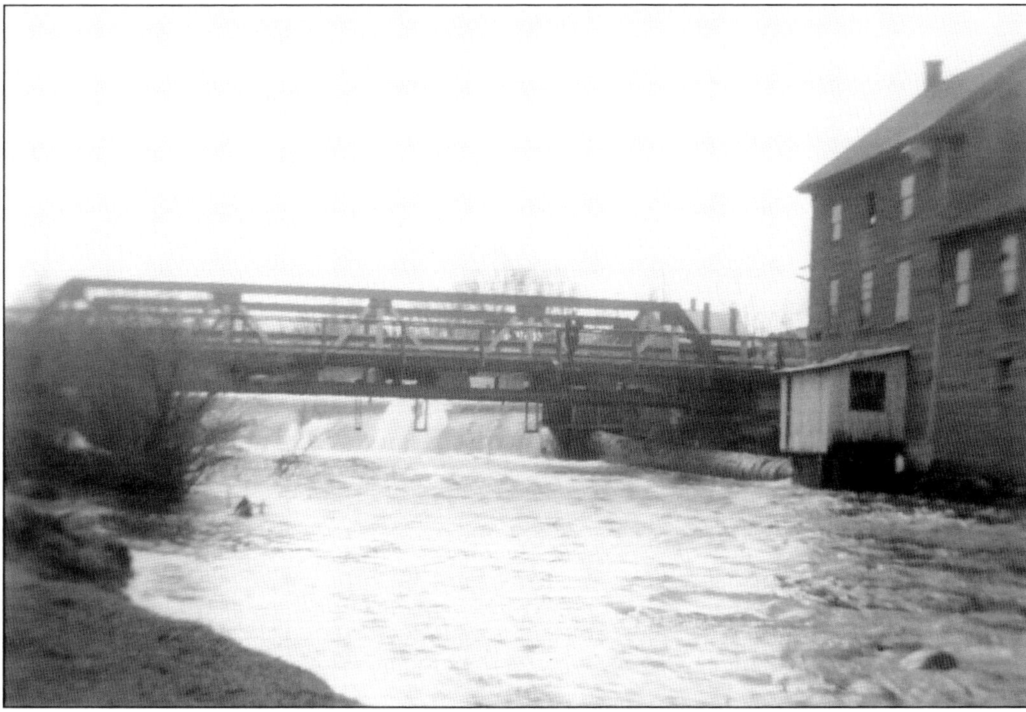

Seen here is the new steel bridge, which was built after the flood of 1927. Many a trout has been caught at the foot of the falls coming over this dam. Notice the old E.A. Wedge Grist and Starch Factory to the right in this image. (Courtesy of Vernon Bullard.)

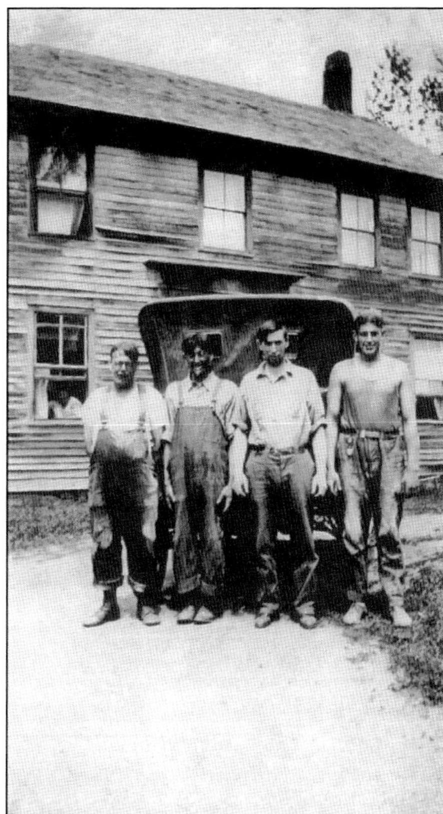

The Grimes brothers are pictured in front of their home, which was later known as the Paul Mudgett house, in North Hyde Park. In 1878, the post office, store, tavern, and dance hall were all located in this building. This was the second framed building erected in North Hyde Park. From left to right are Chester, Temple, Fenno, and Roger Grimes. (Courtesy of Roberta Grimes.)

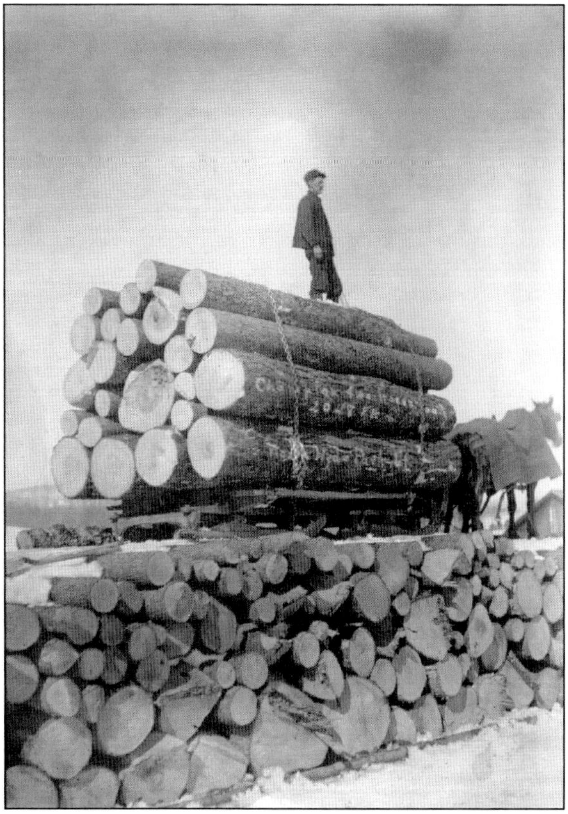

Marshall Sulham stands atop a log load in the yard of Bullard's mill around 1927. Written on the logs in this photograph are the words "Champion Two Horse Load" with "2048 Ft." The Vermont rule was used for scaling logs and is still used today. (Courtesy of the Heath/Savage family.)

This photograph was taken in the log yard of Bullard's mill in North Hyde Park. The building to the right is Cash Griswold's blacksmith shop, originally a tin shop owned by Edwin A. Gallup. Standing on the log are, from left to right, Don McAllister, Charles Parker, Wid Sargent, Arthur Hooper, unidentified, Arthur Foss, unidentified, and Bill Patch. (Courtesy of the Heath/Savage family.)

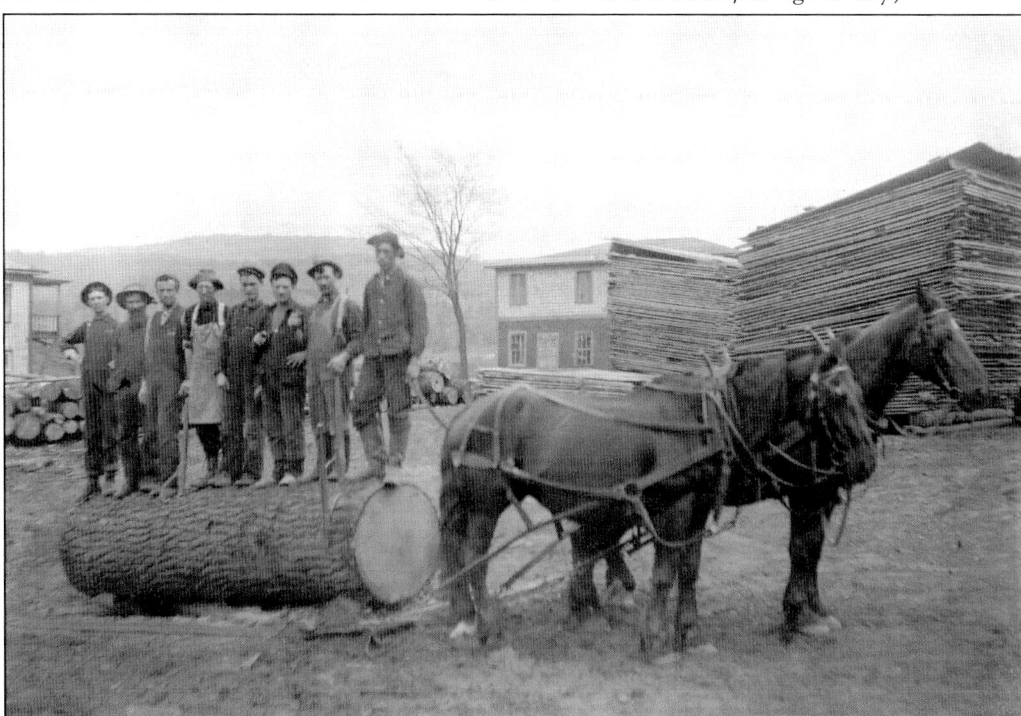

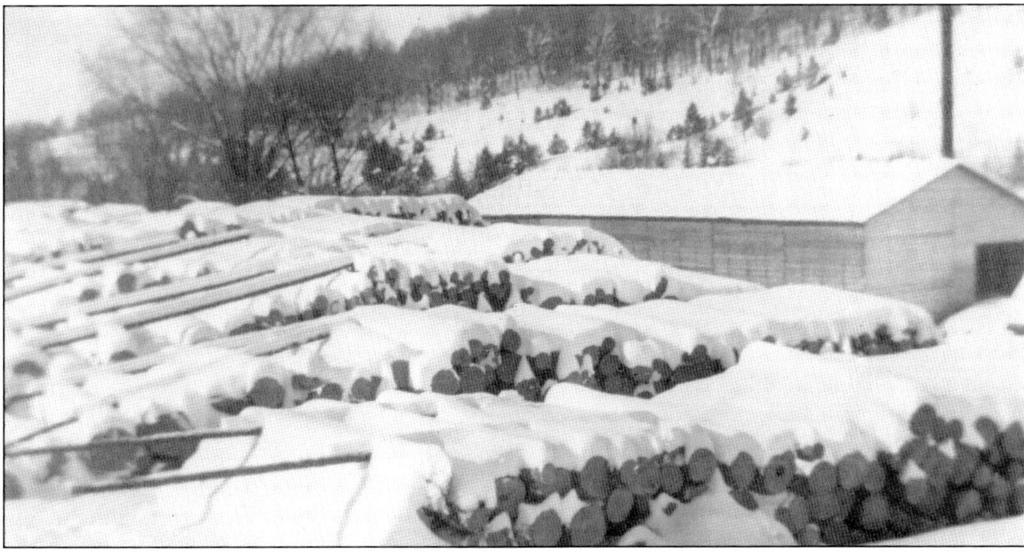

The log yard at Bullard Lumber Company is pictured during the winter months. Lumber mills purchased the majority of their log inventory during winter in order to have them as clean as possible. It was told that on one Friday, 100 loads of logs on draw sleds were waiting to be unloaded in the millyard. These draw sleds were located on all the roads leading into town. (Courtesy of Vernon Bullard and Merrill Heath.)

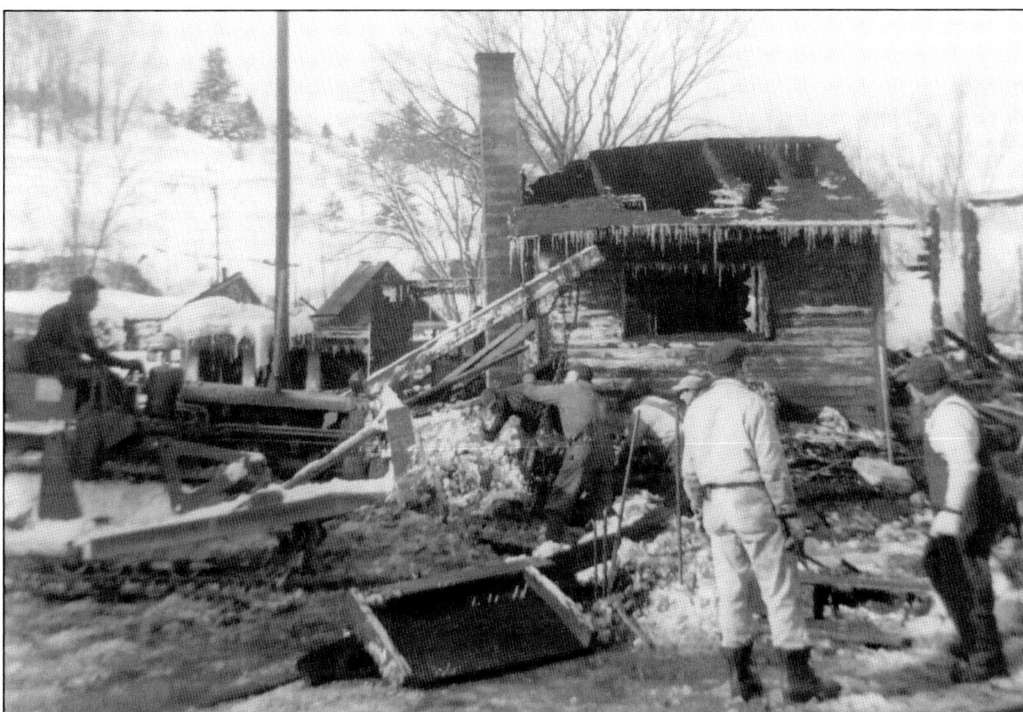

Cleanup begins in this image of the aftermath and ruins from the fire that destroyed several buildings of the Bullard Lumber Company on February 9, 1955. The man in the far-right front wearing bib overalls and a wool hat is Walter Aither, who lived on Ferry Street and worked in the golf-tee factory located at the mill. (Courtesy of Loren and Jean Aither.)

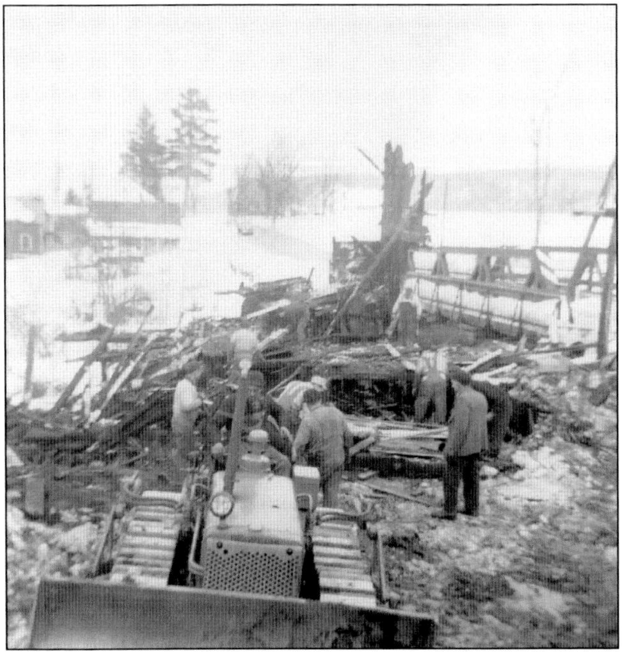

Pictured are the ruins of the old gristmill that was purchased from Harriet Wedge, the widow of E.A. Wedge, by Vernon and Anniebel Bullard on July 22, 1921. The gristmill was located next to the river and bridge on the village's north end. This building was a symbol for many years, reflecting the beginning and growth of North Hyde Park. The man to the right looking on is Wilmer Heath (wearing a jacket and hat), who lived in town on Ferry Street. (Courtesy of Loren and Jean Aither.)

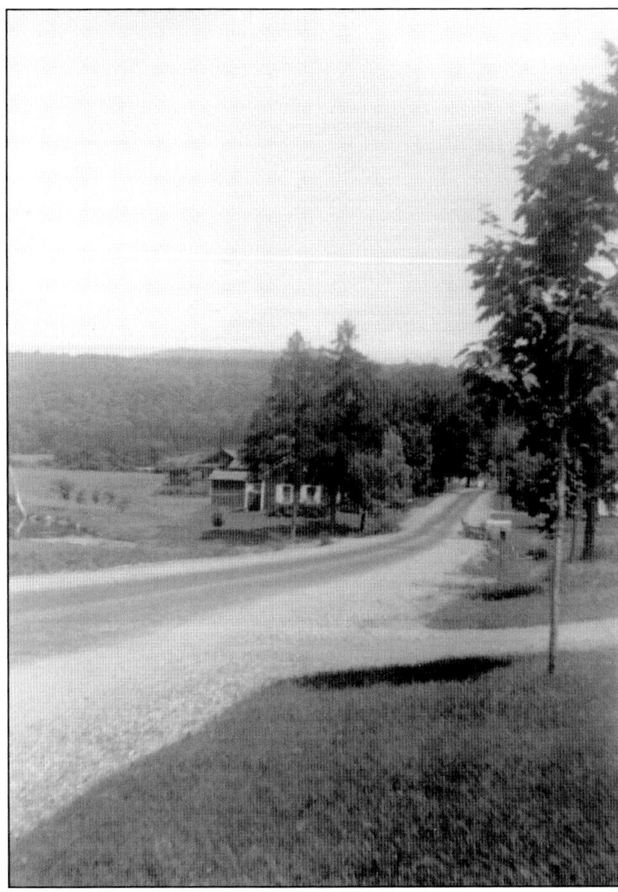

The view in this image looks east on Ferry Street in front of Henry and Helen Smith's home. Down the road on the left is Ralph and Margret (Peg) Mudgett's home, and across from them is the home of Roger and Ila Grimes. The road in this photograph is being prepared for paving. (Courtesy of Roberta Grimes.)

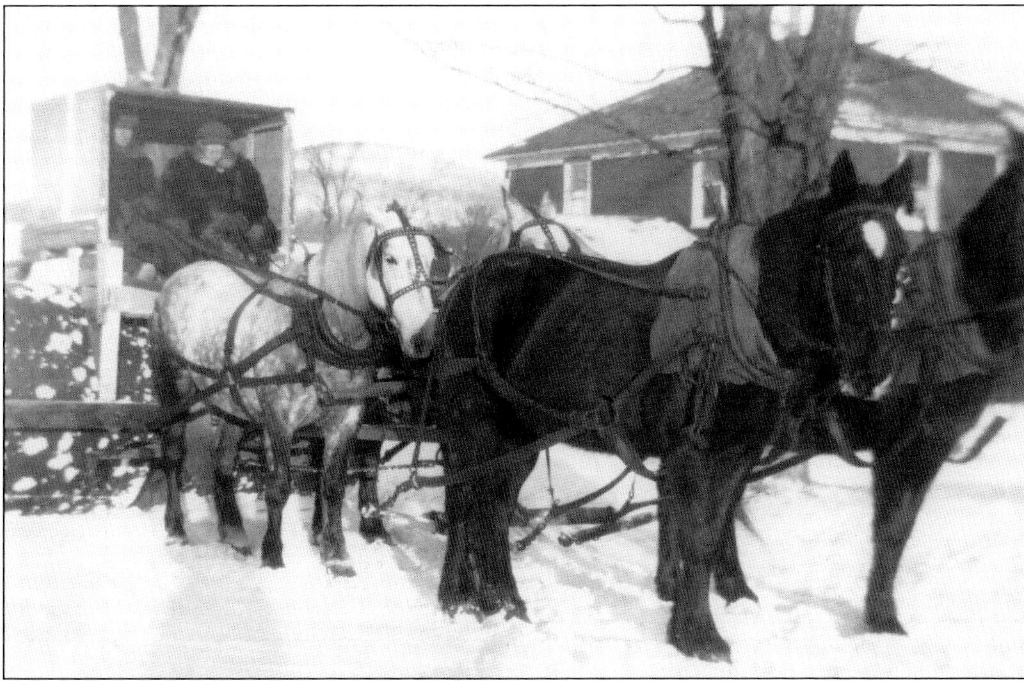

Robert Flanders and road commissioner Harley Hanscom roll the snow on Ferry Street in North Hyde Park in the winter of 1927–1928. Before the days of plowing the roads, snow rollers were used to pack snow in the roads for ease of traveling. Wilmer Heath's home is in the background. (Courtesy of Robert and Caroline Jones.)

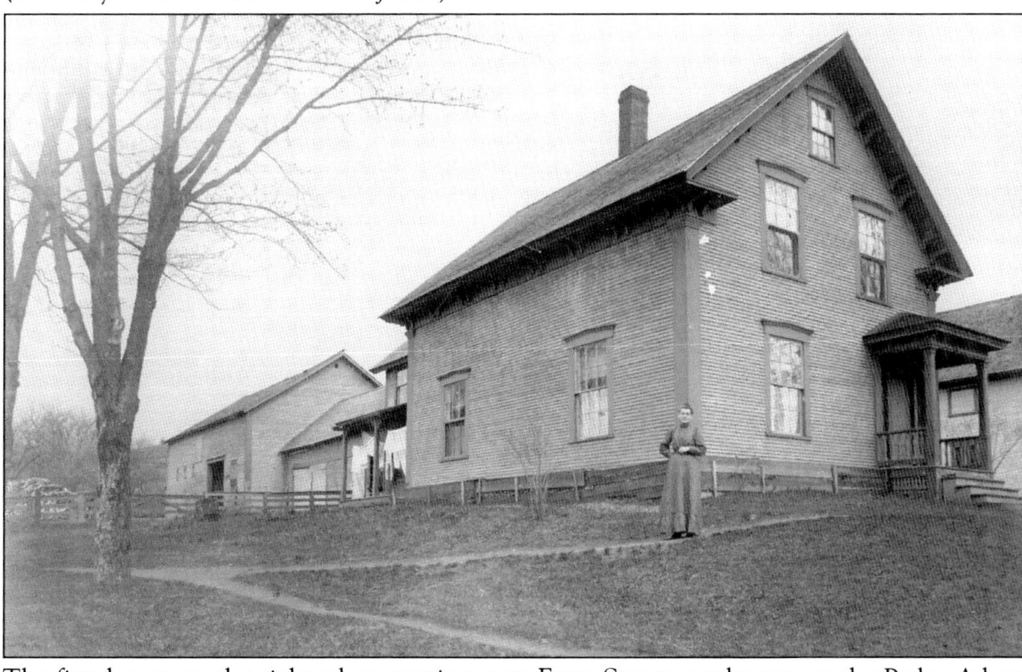

The first house on the right when turning onto Ferry Street was known as the Perley Adams house, and it was later owned by Mike Dewey. The barn in this image is gone; however, the house is still standing. (Courtesy of the Stewart family.)

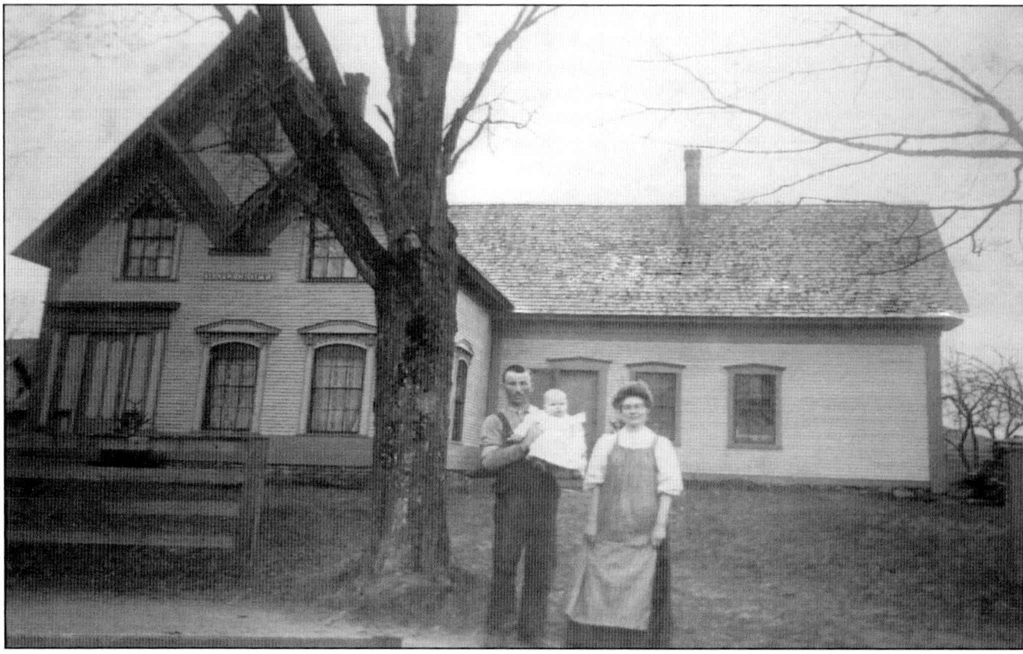

Located on Ferry Street, Maplecroft was referred to as the "Candy Cane" house by the children of Hyde Park because of the trim hanging from the eaves. Jack and Ethel (Thompson) Amadon are pictured with their daughter Geneva, nicknamed "Neva." (Courtesy of Ruby [Amadon] Day.)

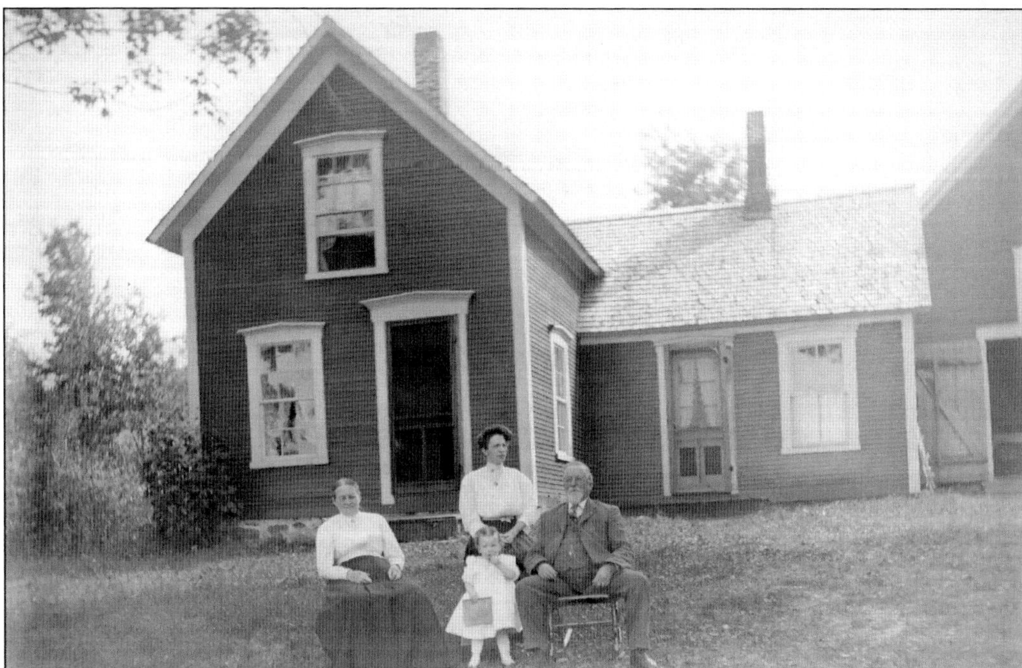

This house was located on Ferry Street at what is now known as the Fenno and Doris Grimes homesite. The structure burned down and was replaced by the Grimes residence. In the photograph are (sitting) Mr. and Mrs. Selby; (standing) H.D. and Alice Warner. After the Selbys' home burned, they lived in the parsonage across from the post office. (Courtesy of Roberta Grimes.)

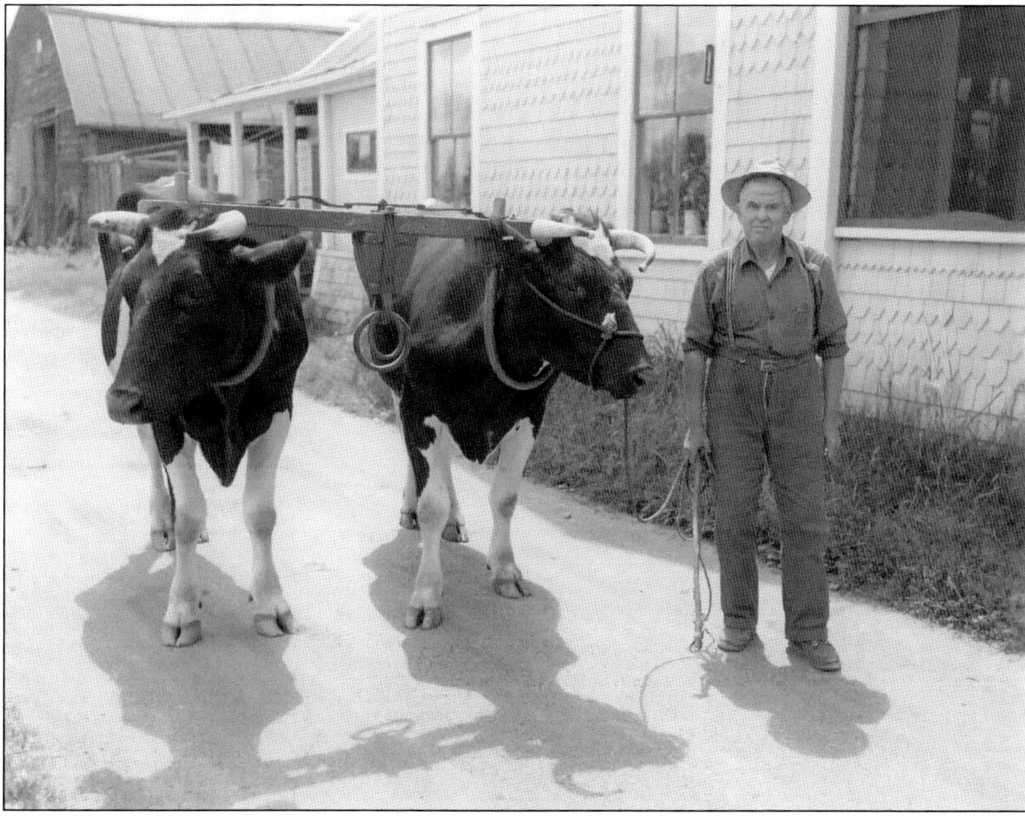

Harley Hanscom stands with his team of oxen next to his home. In a 1959 football game played between the New York Giants and the Cleveland Browns at Yankee Stadium, Harley and his team of oxen appeared on the field at halftime and went through their paces while accompanied by the Burlington High School band. (Courtesy of Robert and Caroline Jones.)

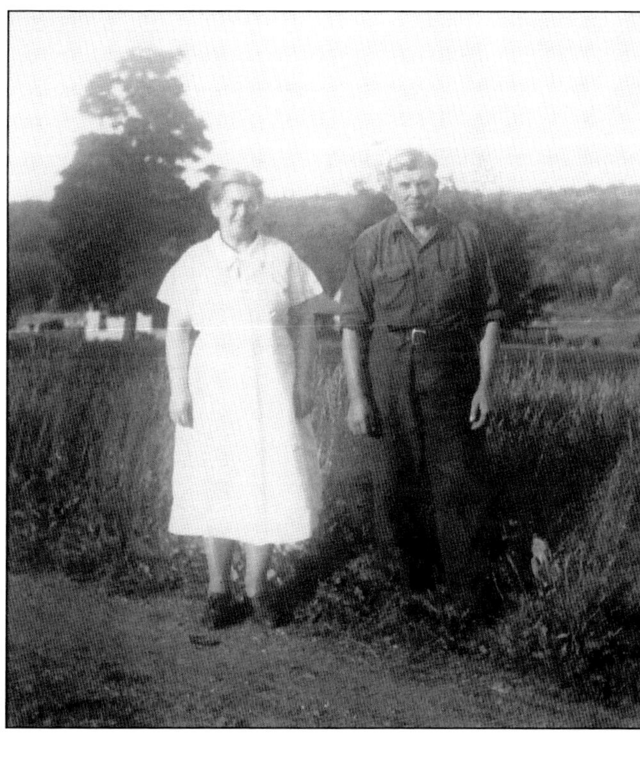

Harley and Ethel Hanscom pose next to their home on Ferry Street. Harley, a lifelong farmer, lived next door to his son Earold. (Courtesy of Robert and Caroline Jones.)

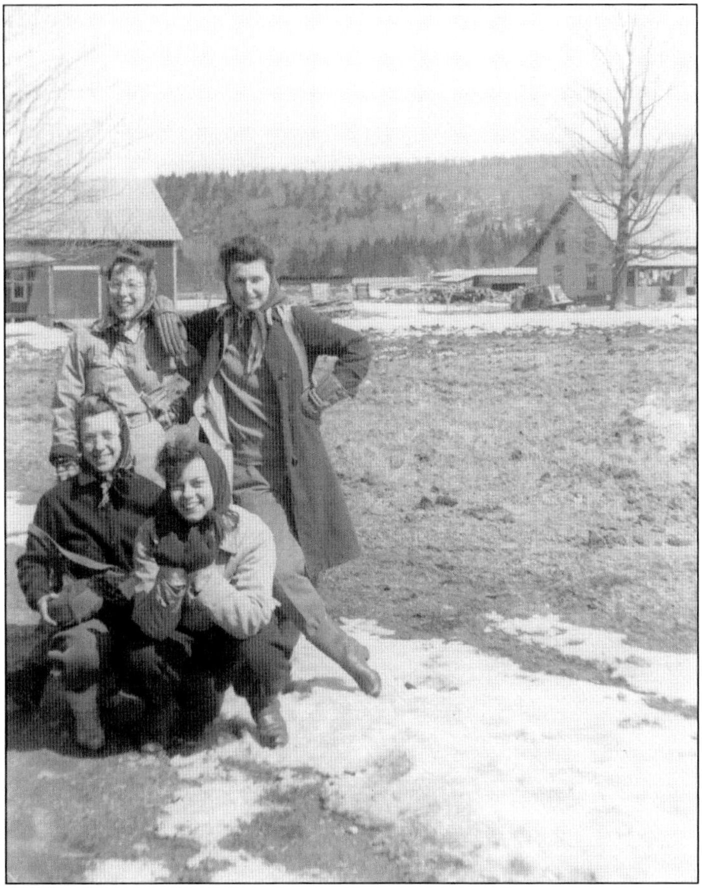

Pictured beside Ethel Hanscom's house on Ferry Street in North Hyde Park, a group of ladies prepares to take a hike up to Thompson Falls. Notice John Dudley's home and mill in the background. (Courtesy of Roberta Grimes.)

Ralph Thompson sits on a rafter of the henhouse that he is building on his farm in North Hyde Park. Ralph and his brother Guy built this together around 1925. (Courtesy of the Heath/Savage family.)

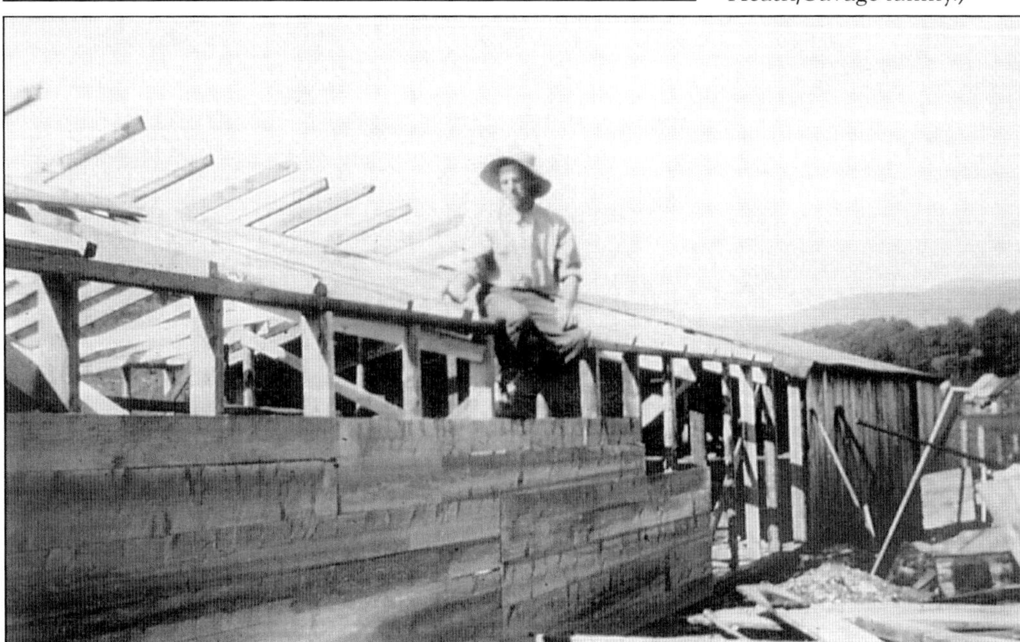

This is a c. 1960 aerial view of Heath Lumber Company, located on Ferry Street in North Hyde Park. The land, which was part of the Vernon Whitcomb farm, was purchased from Florence (Ingalls) Whitcomb. In 1946, Wilmer Heath and his son Merrill founded the mill, which is now named M.B. Heath & Sons Lumber. This mill is the last lumber mill still in operation from the many that existed throughout the town of Hyde Park. (Courtesy of the Heath/Savage family.)

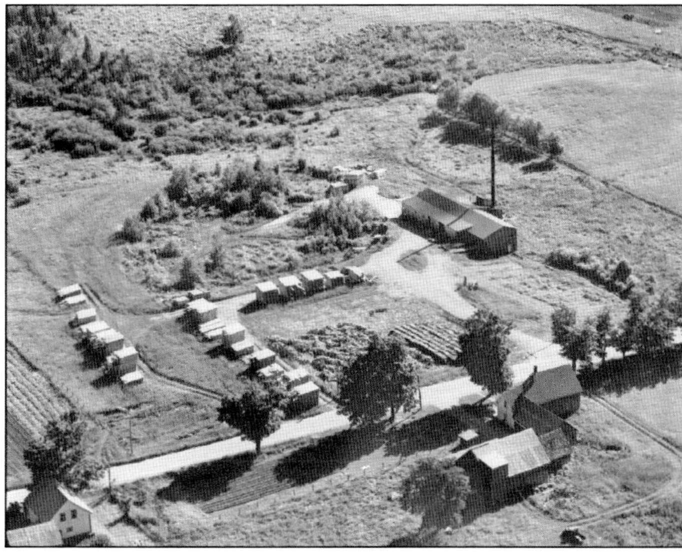

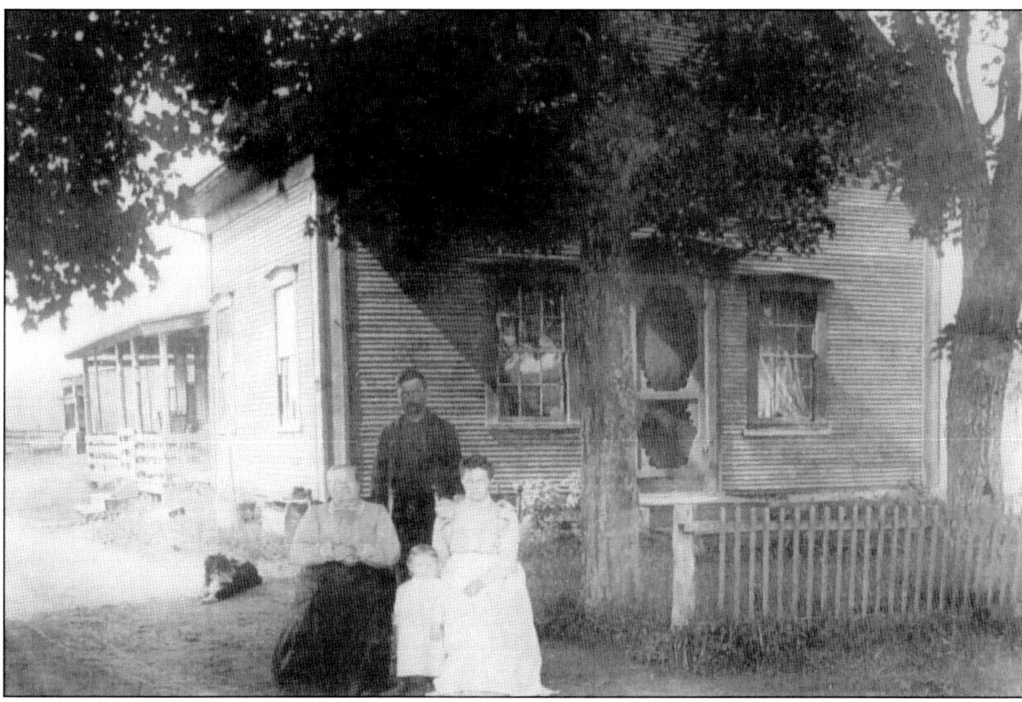

The home of Vernon Whitcomb and his wife, Florence (Ingalls), was located next to Heath Lumber Company on Ferry Street. Pictured, from left to right, are (first row) Amy (Gallup) Ingalls (Florence's mother), Eula Whitcomb, and Florence Whitcomb; (second row) Vernon. Later, Florence gave this house to her daughter Eula (Whitcomb) Thompson and son-in-law Ralph Thompson. (Courtesy of Velma [Thompson] Rushford.)

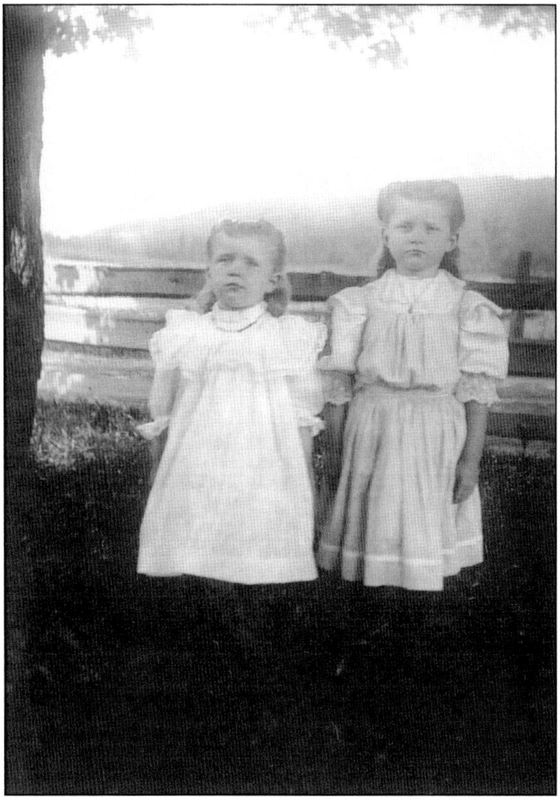

Sisters Iva and Eula Whitcomb are dressed in their Sunday best for services at Advent Church on Main Street in North Hyde Park. (Courtesy of Heath/Savage family.)

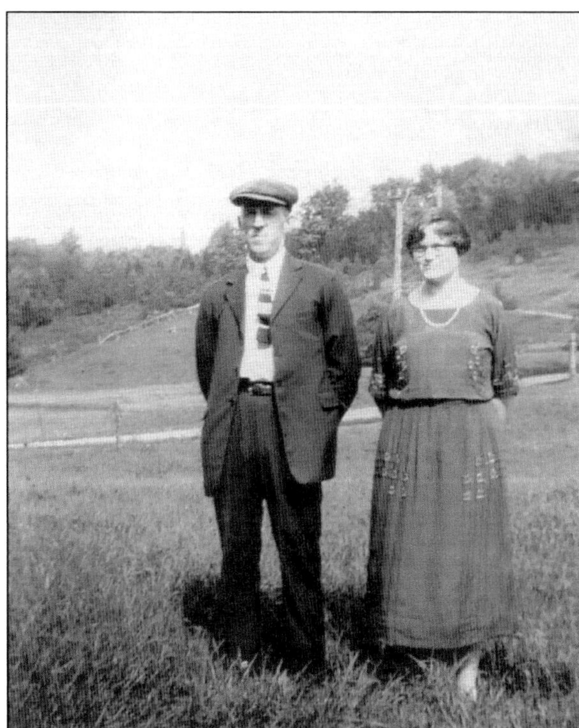

Ralph and Eula (Whitcomb) Thompson are pictured next to their home in North Hyde Park. Ralph, the son of John Thompson, was a soldier in World War I. (Courtesy of the Heath/Savage family.)

The Larose family enjoys a picnic with relatives in front of Hobart Manning's home, located on the upper end of Ferry Street in North Hyde Park. Shown here are Gary Larose (standing); his father, Adrian (seated against the maple tree); and relatives Daniel and Katie (sitting on the grass). The woman on the right is unidentified. (Courtesy of the Larose/ Manning family.)

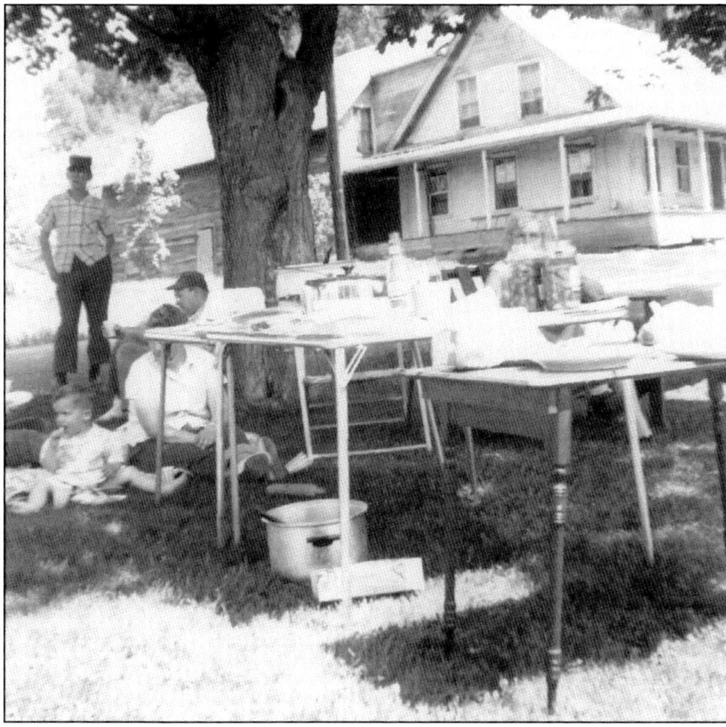

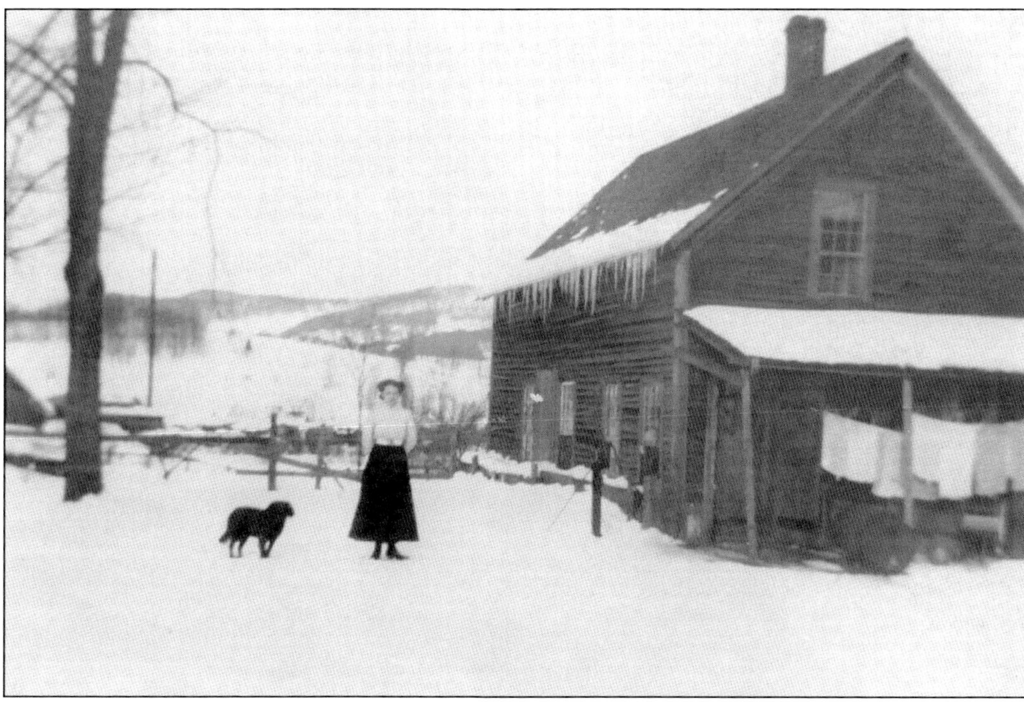

Pictured is the home of Albert and Lenora (Whitcomb) Heath, which was later owned by their grandson Merrill Heath. Albert and Lenora's daughter Grace Heath stands next to the home with her dog. In the background is the Parker & Stearns mill, located next to the Gihon River. (Courtesy of the Heath/Savage family.)

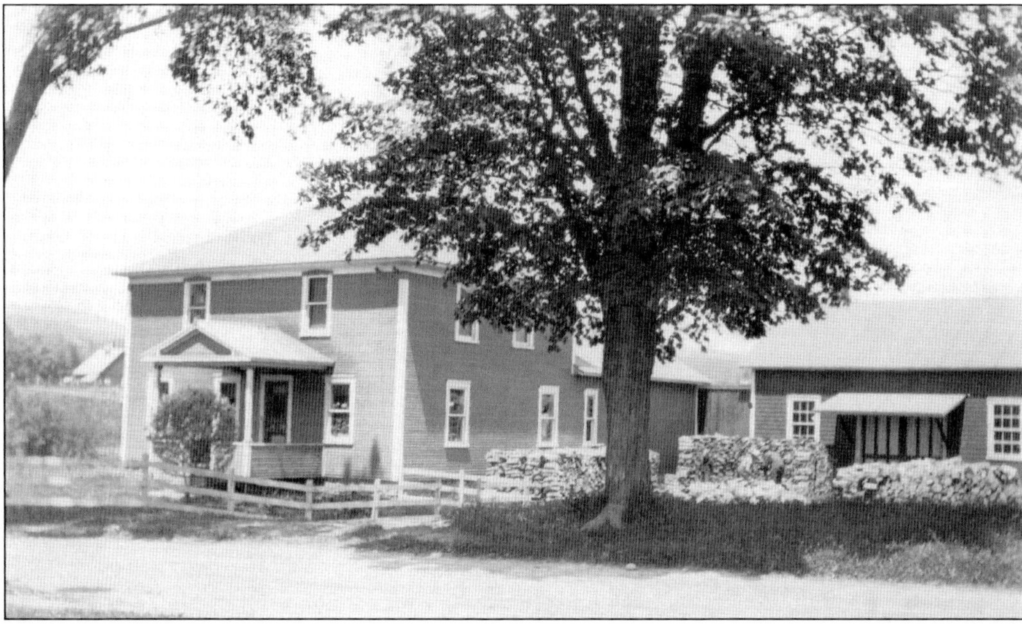

The home of Wilmer and Florence (Bedell) Heath is located next to the residence of their son Merrill Heath on Ferry Street in North Hyde Park. A close look reveals Wilmer and two unidentified people working on the woodpile that was needed each year to heat the house. This home was built in 1915 by Wilmer and his father, Albert Heath. (Courtesy of the Heath/Savage family.)

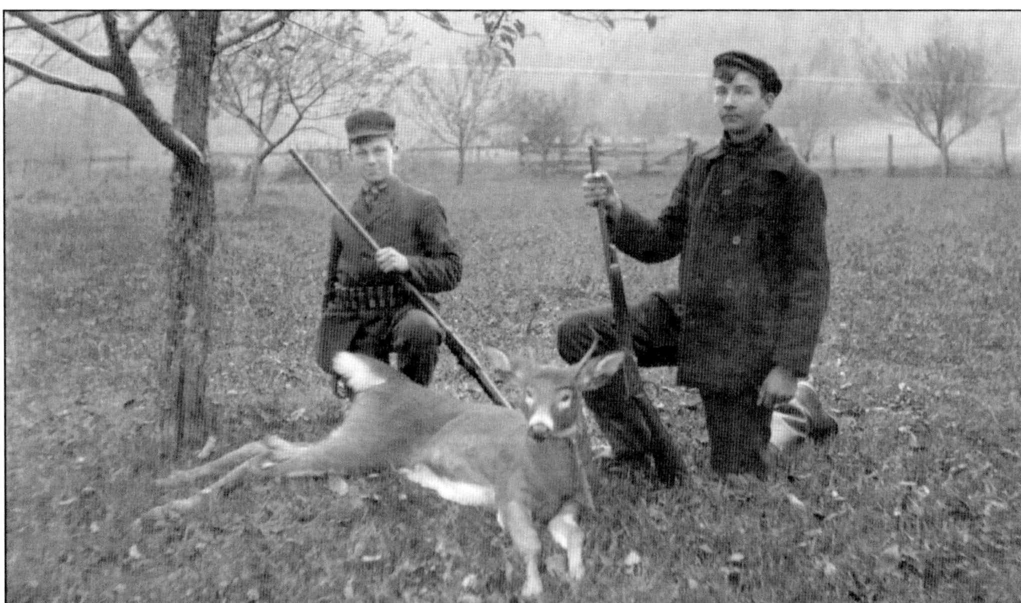

Proud young hunters Nathan Allen (left) and Wilmer Heath pose with a buck in North Hyde Park at the turn of the 20th century. (Courtesy of the Heath/Savage family.)

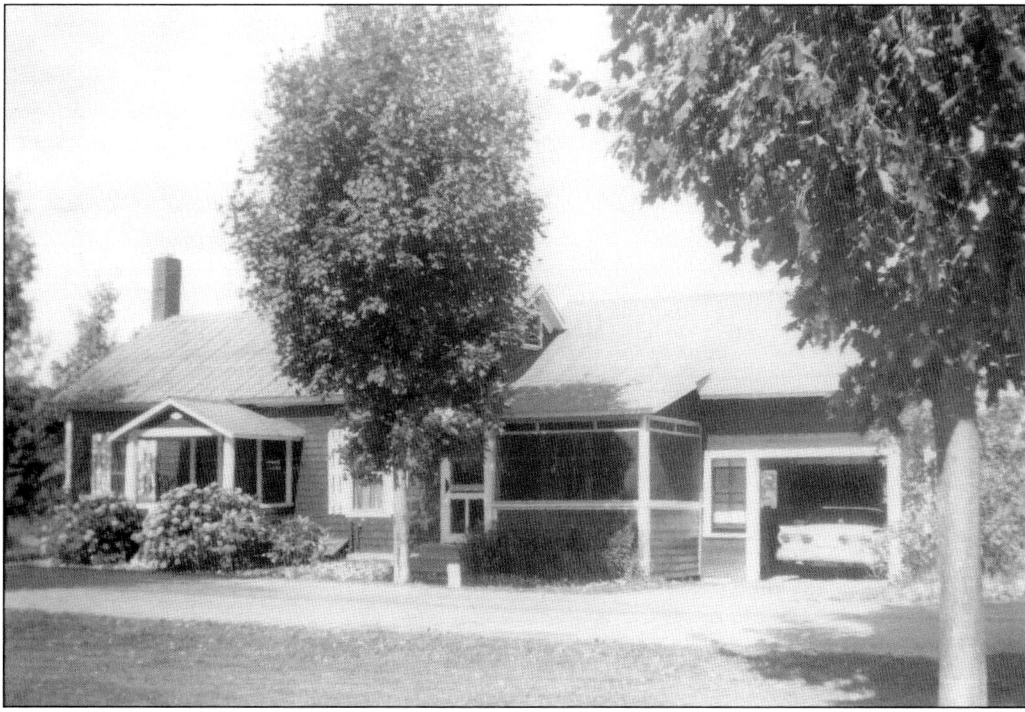

Ralph and Margaret (Peg) Mudgett lived on Ferry Street in North Hyde Park. Peg, an elementary school teacher, taught in the towns of North Hyde Park and Eden for many years. (Courtesy of Roberta Grimes.)

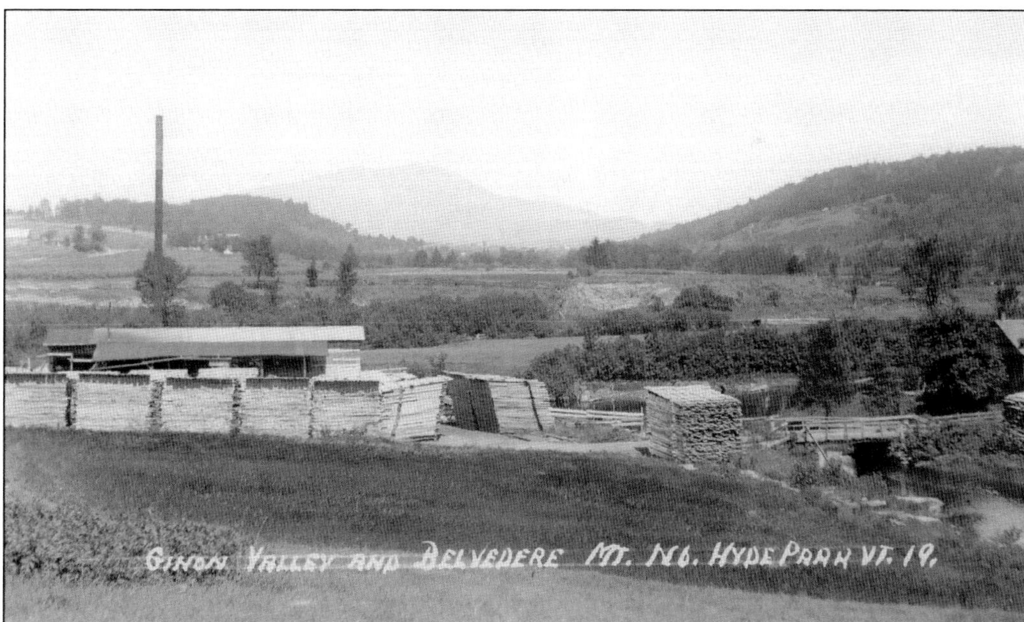

This image of the Parker & Stearns lumber mill on Ferry Street was taken in 1900. The mill was later moved to Eden around 1923–1924. Notice how the lumber stacks are placed next to the road, which was gravel at the time. (Courtesy of Linda Jones.)

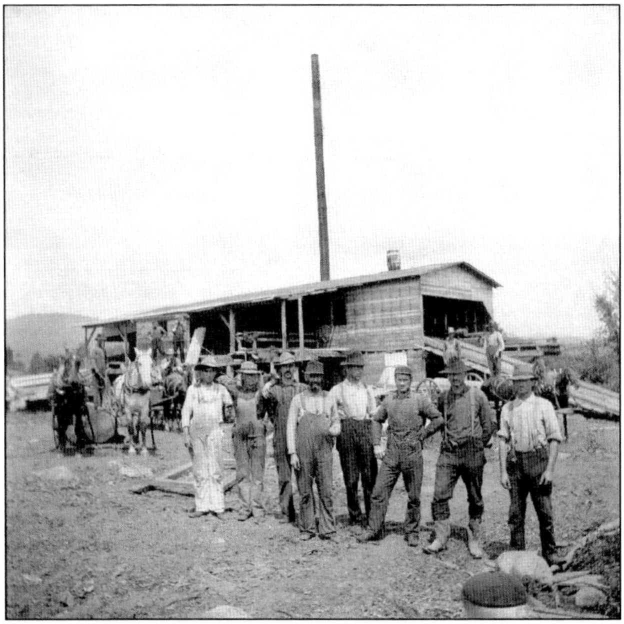

Seen here is the yard crew of Parker & Stearns lumber mill, which was built next to the Gihon River because a water source was needed to power the steam engine. The man on the far right is Albert Heath. (Courtesy of the Heath/Savage family.)

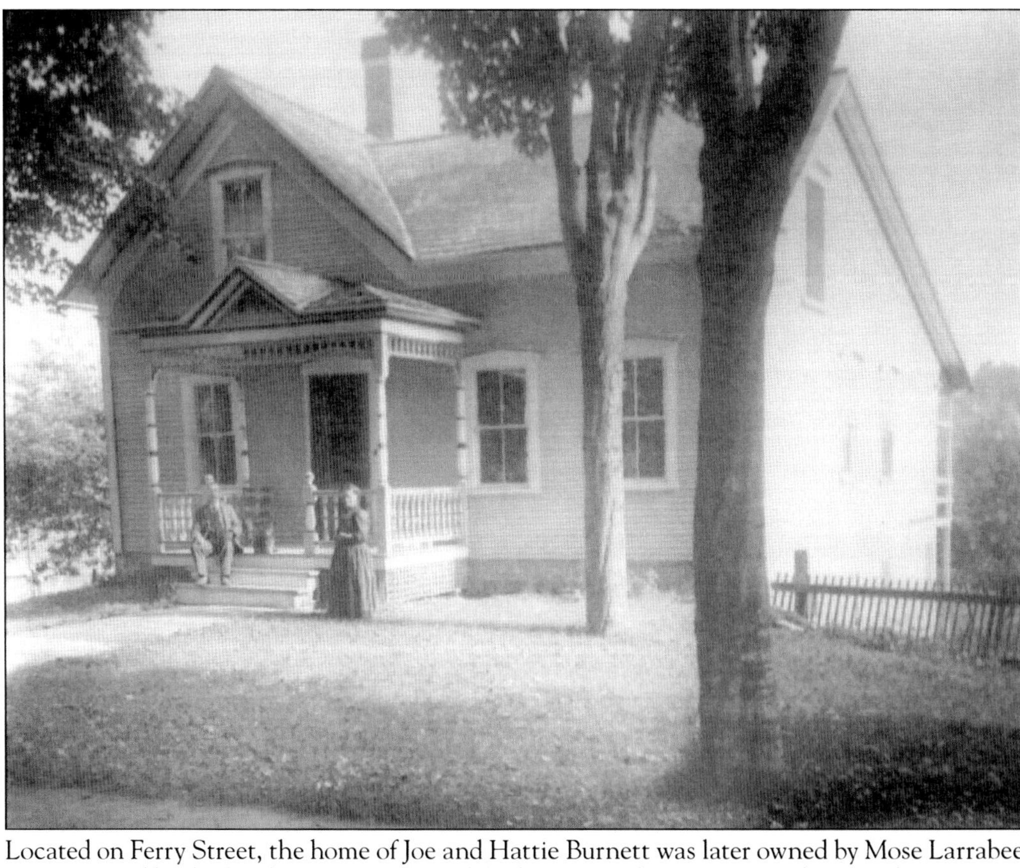

Located on Ferry Street, the home of Joe and Hattie Burnett was later owned by Mose Larrabee, who operated his barbershop business out of the house. Author James Heath remembers going as a young boy to get his hair cut by Larrabee for 25¢. (Courtesy of Velma [Thompson] Rushford.)

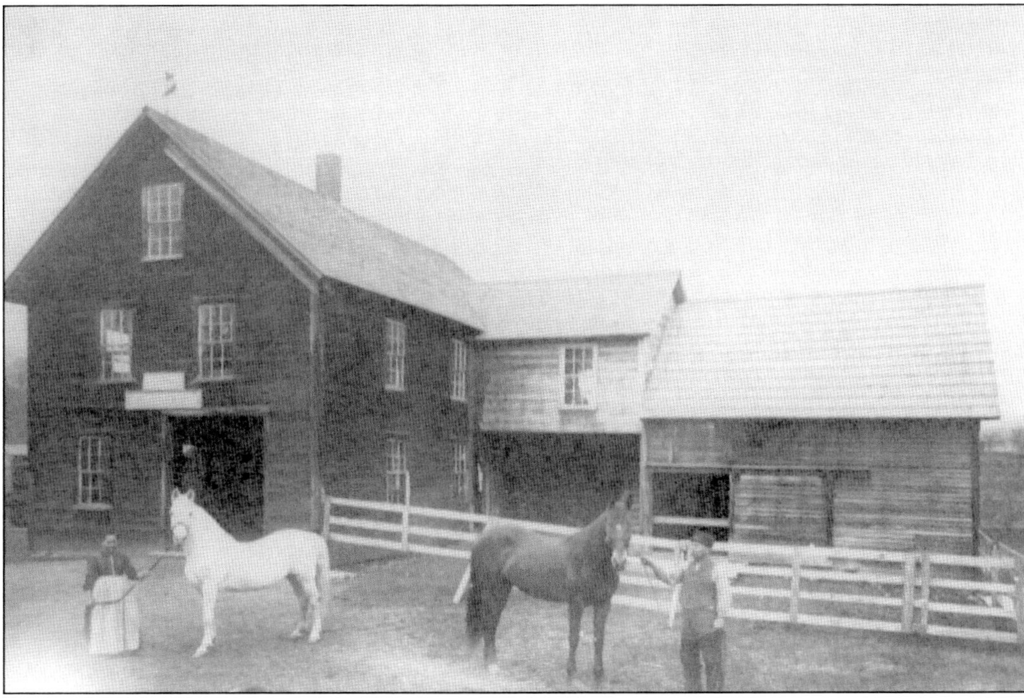

Joe Burnett's blacksmith and furrier shop, pictured around 1899, was one of many small businesses in Hyde Park. During this time period, this trade was practiced by many men because of the high demand for items like horseshoes, draw sleds, peaveys, and cant hooks. (Courtesy of Velma [Thompson] Rushford.)

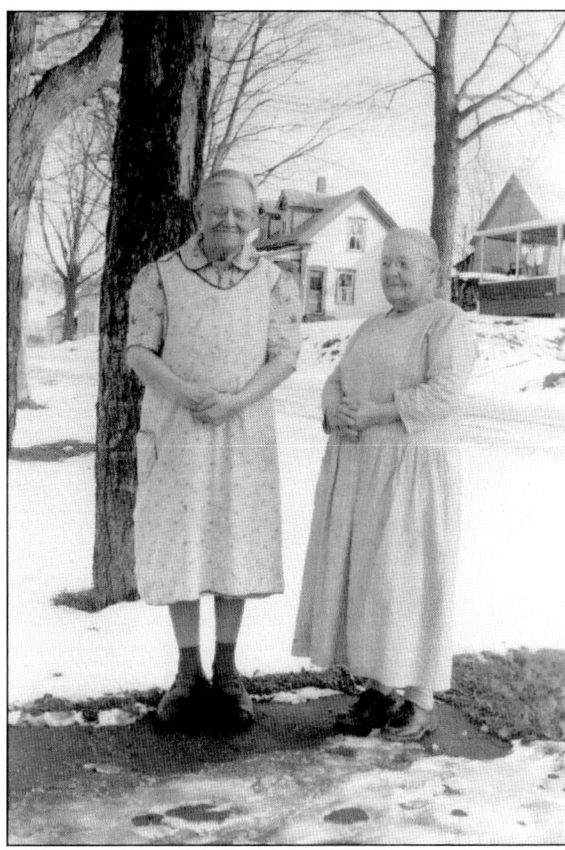

Hattie Bidwell (left) and Mamie Cady stand in front of the home of Joe and Hattie Burnett. According to Eleanor Grimes Goodrich, Cady, a niece of Joe Burnett, went to work for the Burnett's after their daughter Hattie died. (Courtesy of Jane and Eleanor [Grimes] Goodrich.)

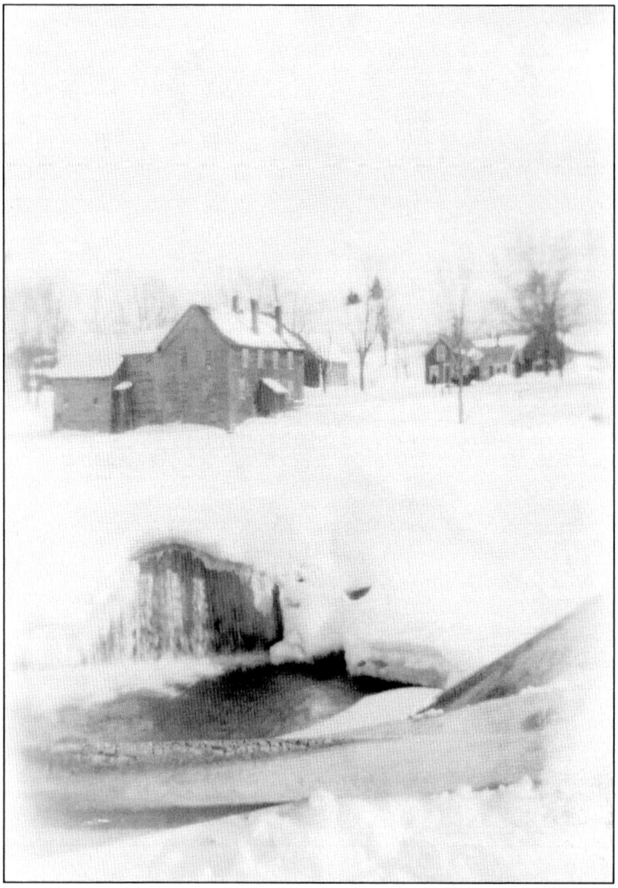

Ice covers the dam in North Hyde Park. The old blacksmith shop (left) and Fenno Grimes's house (right) are also pictured. (Courtesy of Robert and Caroline Jones.)

Seen in this image is a Fourth of July parade on Main Street in North Hyde Park in 1908. Parades were big events for promoting patriotism and community pride. Note how the costumes of the children reflect a past that built their town, state, and country. (Courtesy of the Heath/Savage family.)

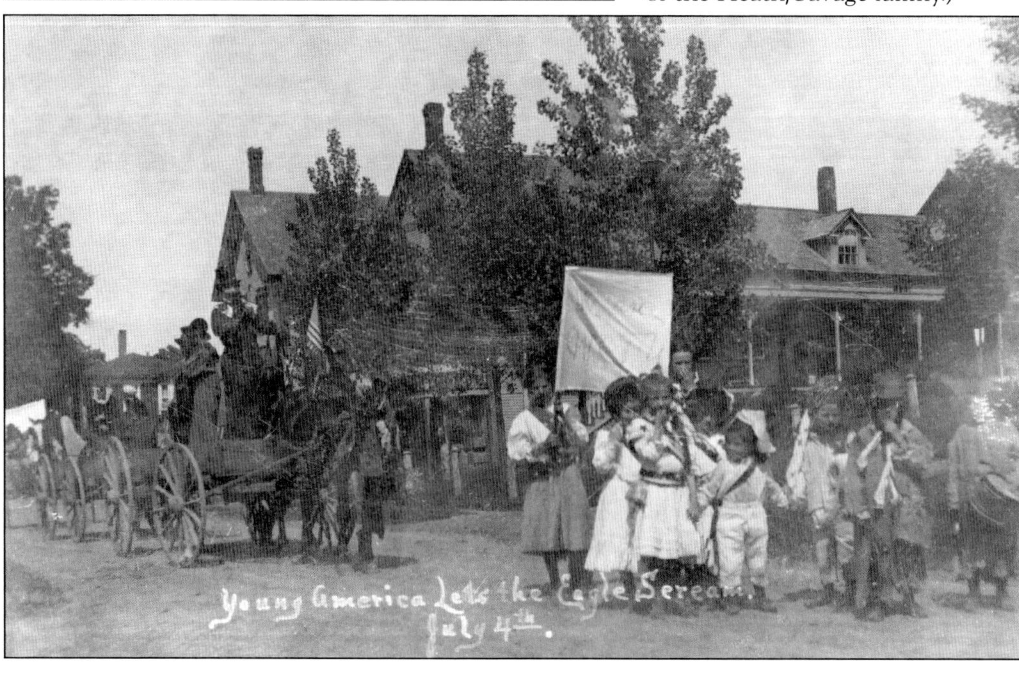

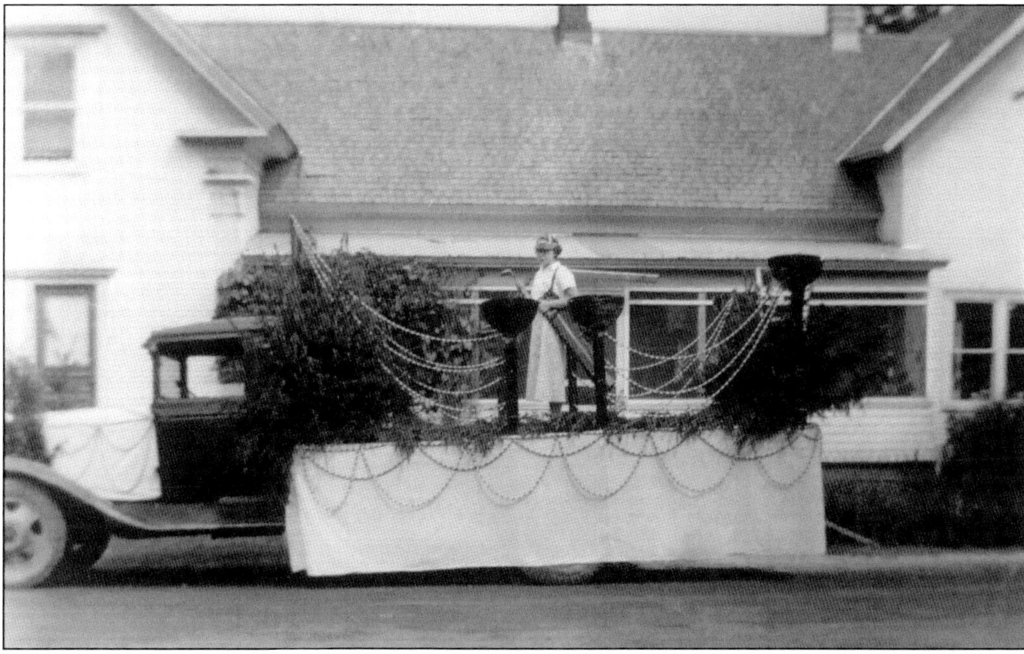

Ruth Bullard stands on a float in front of her home on Main Street in North Hyde Park sometime in the late 1930s. As shown in this photograph, Ruth was an active member of the North Hyde community and engaged in many activities, including the Fourth of July parade. (Courtesy of Vernon Bullard.)

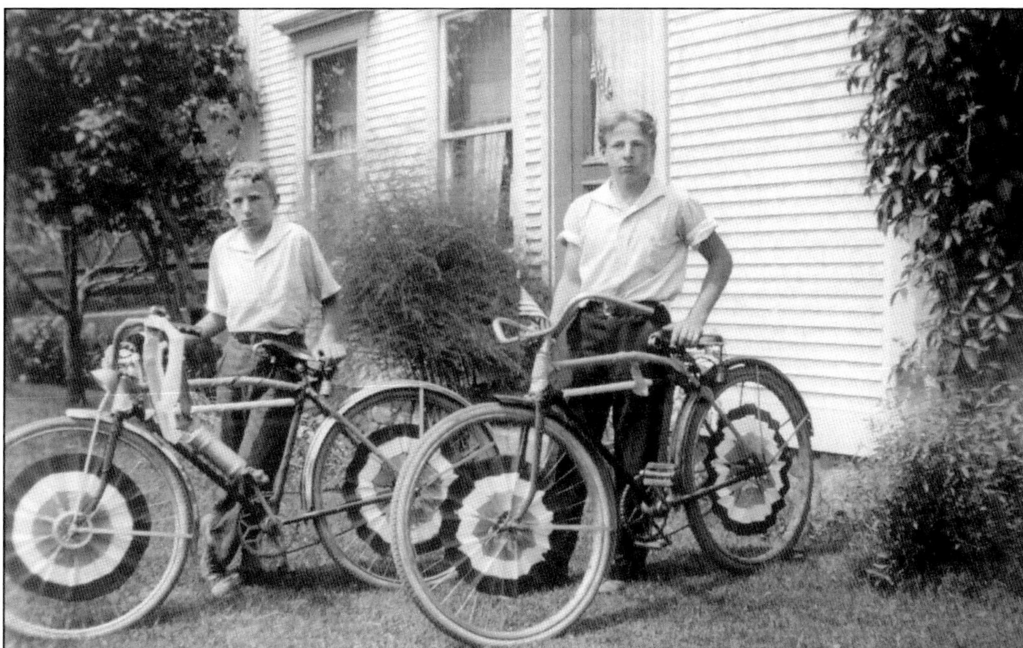

Haven "Bud" Bullard (left) and Vernon "Buster" Bullard, pictured in front of their home, have their bikes ready for the parade on Main Street in North Hyde Park around 1935. (Courtesy of Vernon Bullard.)

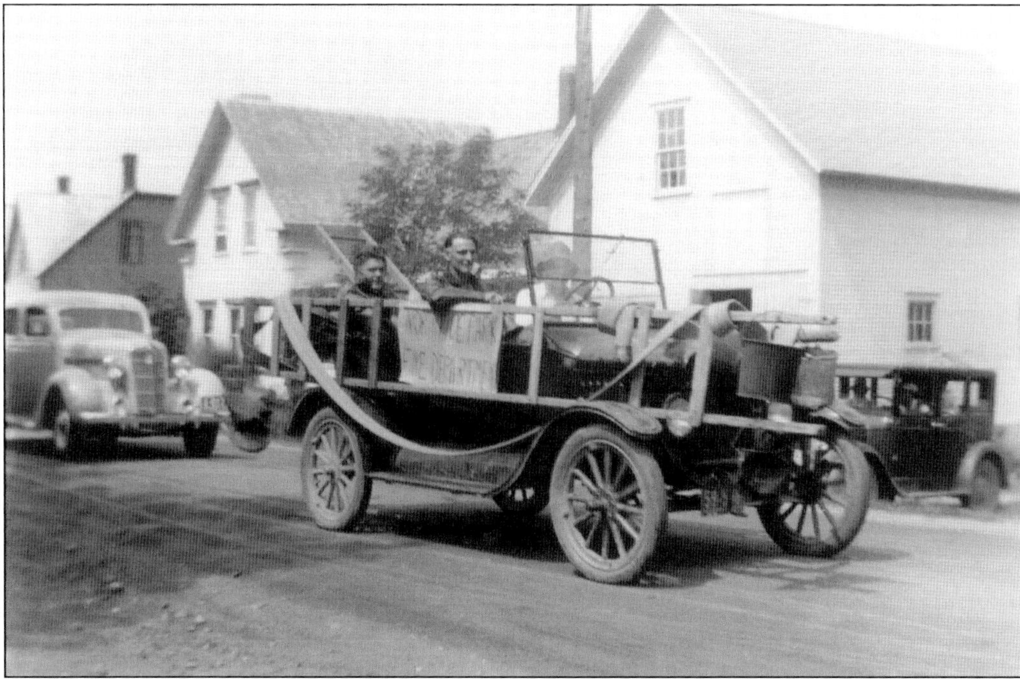

This parade photograph shows the North Hyde Park Fire Department ready to go with ladder, hose, and buckets. Like the many fire departments today in Lamoille County, the North Hyde Park Fire Department was comprised of volunteers. (Courtesy of Vernon Bullard.)

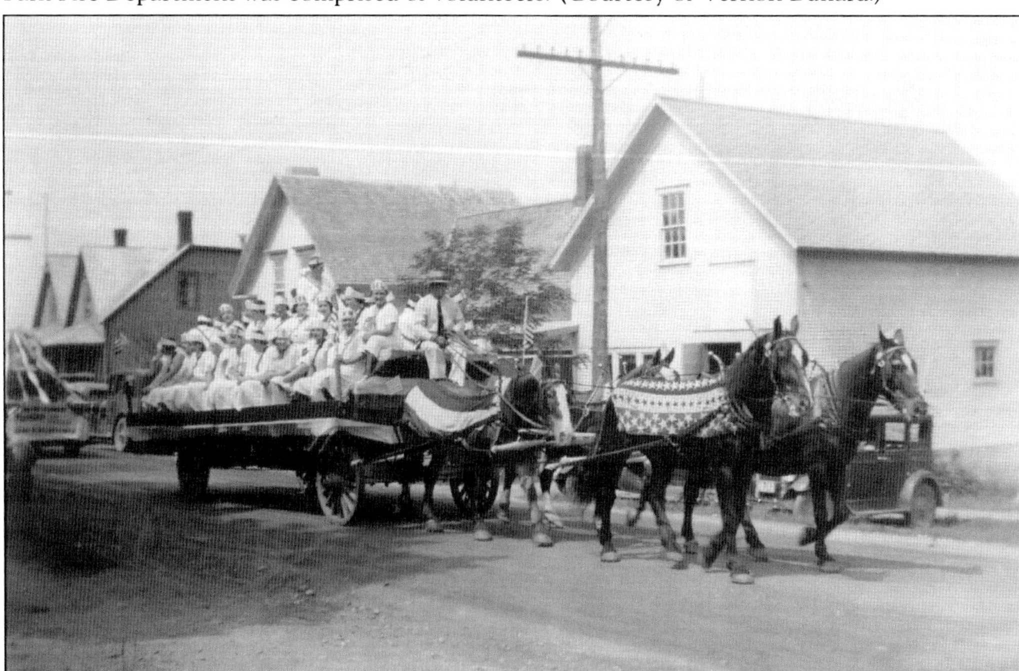

An unknown ladies' group rides in a wagon in the North Hyde Park parade. Social groups of this nature were common in building a strong and united community. The Bullard home is directly behind the wagon, and the Sargent home is to the far left. (Courtesy of Vernon Bullard.)

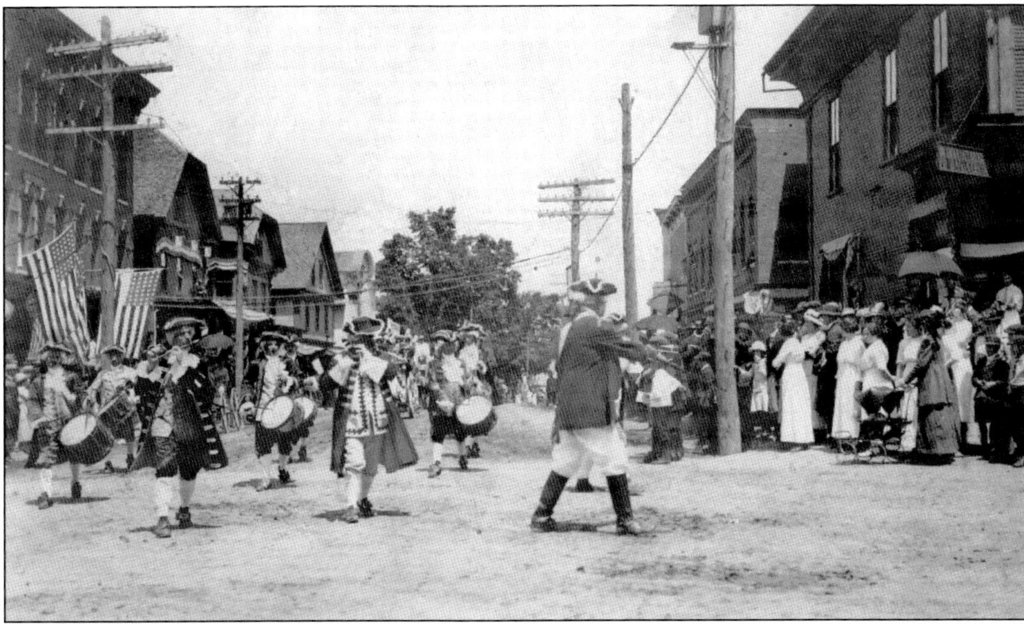

This is a rare photograph of the North Hyde Park Drum Corps marching in the Morrisville Fourth of July parade. Robert Barnes's grandfather, who was also named Robert Barnes, fought in the Civil War and was part of the North Hyde Park Drum Corps until his sudden death in 1902. As is evident from this photograph, this parade was well attended. (Courtesy of Francis Favreau.)

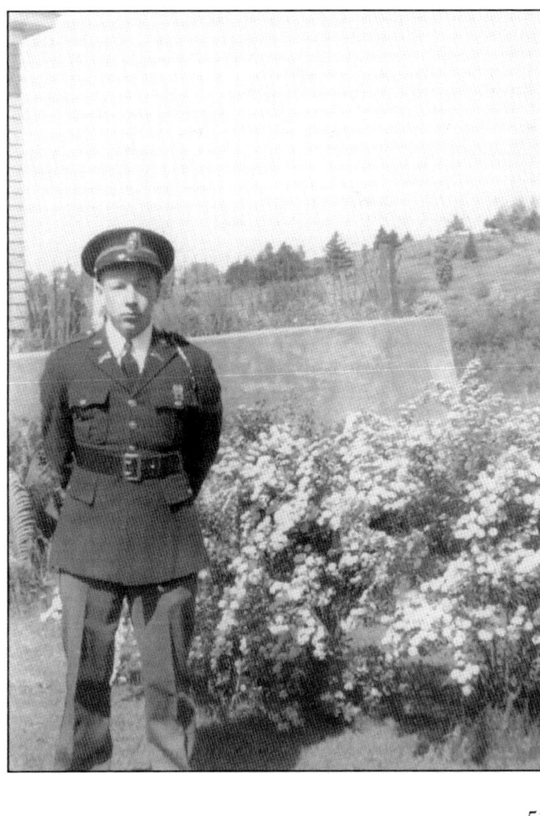

Young Army veteran Vernon "Buster" Bullard stands next to his home in his uniform. Buster graduated from Norwich University and proudly served his country in the African theater, where he met General Patton. (Courtesy of Vernon Bullard.)

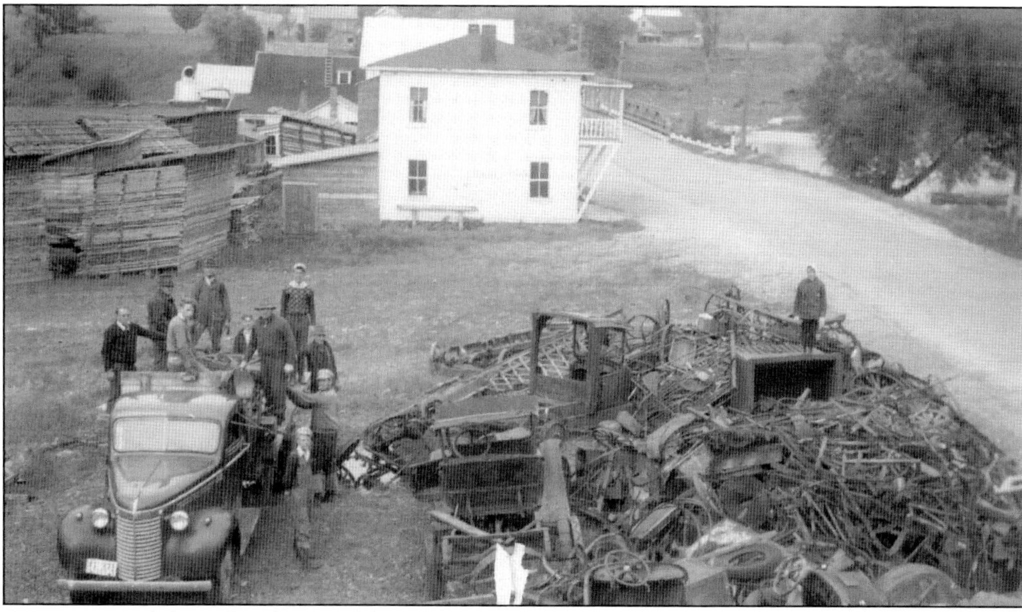

A scrap-metal drive for the World War II war effort was held in North Hyde Park. When the United States entered the war, much-needed support efforts of this nature became common in many communities throughout the country. (Courtesy of the Graves/McAllister family.)

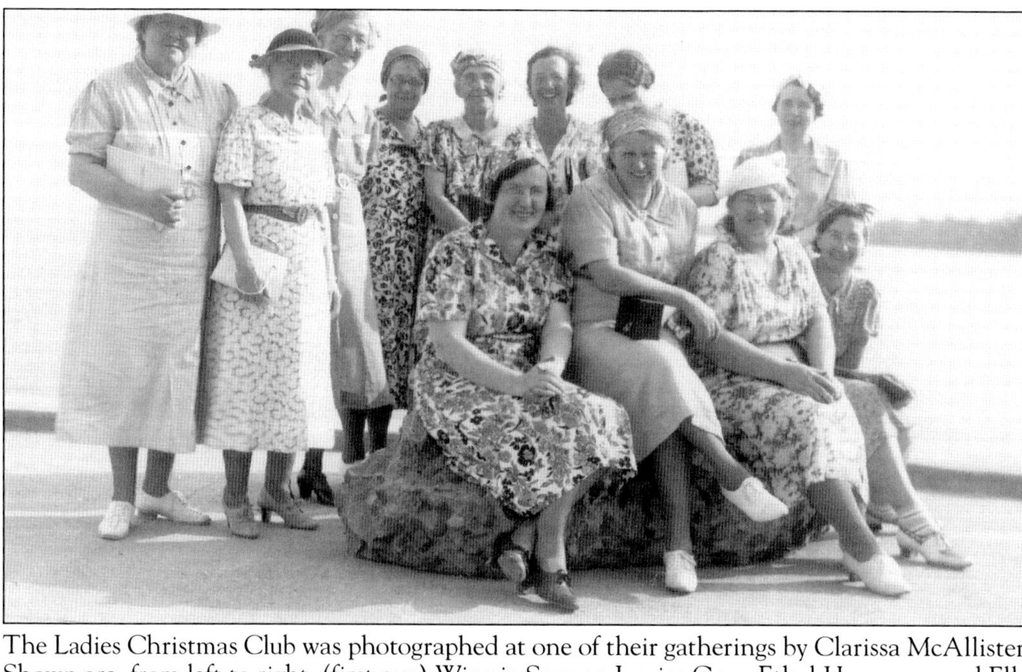

The Ladies Christmas Club was photographed at one of their gatherings by Clarissa McAllister. Shown are, from left to right, (first row) Winnie Sawyer, Louise Gray, Ethel Hanscom, and Ella Merrill; (second row) Mina Gillen, an unidentified visitor, Stella Stearns, Vivian McAllister, Mable Griswold, Madge (Jones) Thompson, Daisy Foss, and Marion Gillen. (Courtesy of the Graves/McAllister family.)

Two

Hyde Park Village

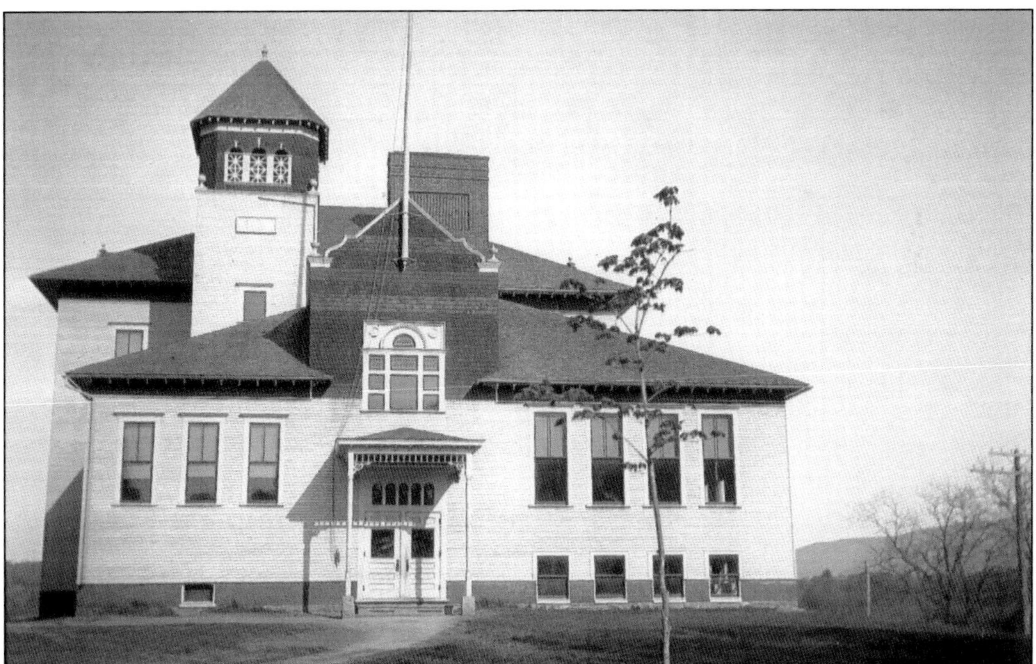

Lamoille Central Academy (LCA) was constructed in the late 1800s on what was known as the Aaron Keeler homesite. LCA was organized in 1857. The school was previously located on the second floor of the town hall. (Courtesy of Francis Favreau.)

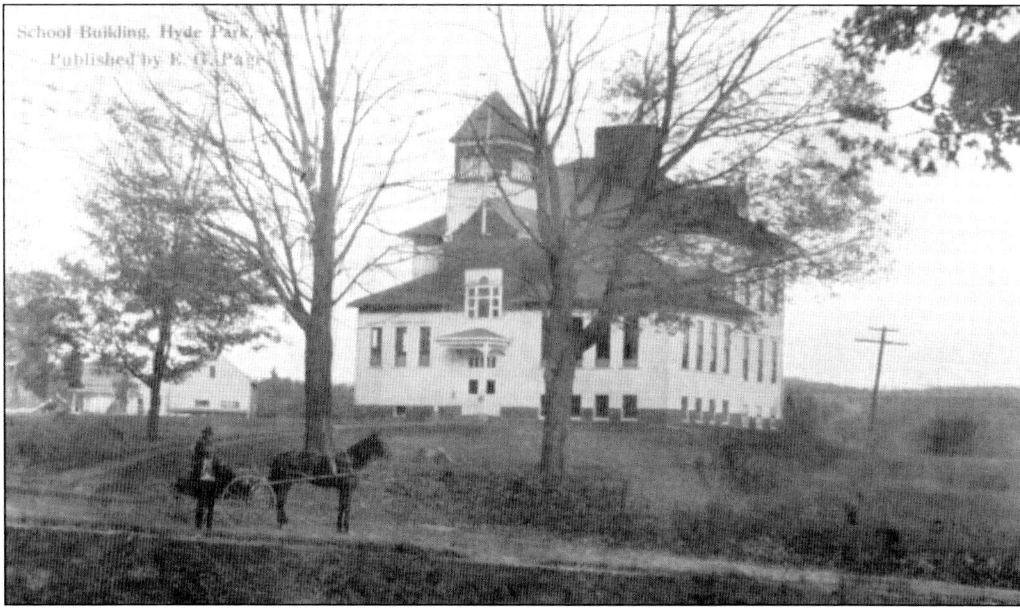

This image of Lamoille Central Academy with a horse and buggy out front gives a clear view of the property as it was when Aaron Keeler lived there. Keeler's home, one of the older houses in town, was mostly demolished, except for a few parts of the structure, which were moved across the street. (Courtesy of the Page/McFarland family.)

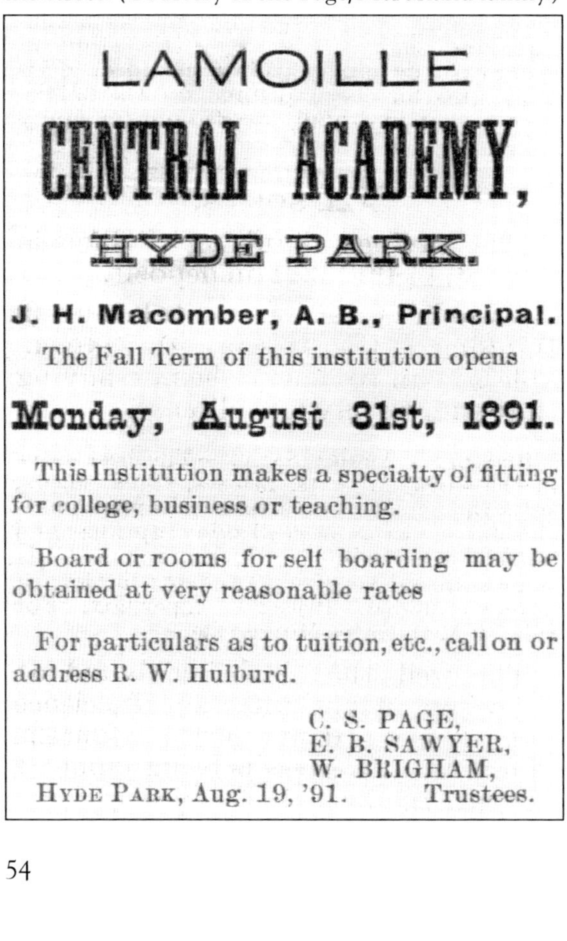

LAMOILLE
CENTRAL ACADEMY,
HYDE PARK.

J. H. Macomber, A. B., Principal.

The Fall Term of this institution opens

Monday, August 31st, 1891.

This Institution makes a specialty of fitting for college, business or teaching.

Board or rooms for self boarding may be obtained at very reasonable rates

For particulars as to tuition, etc., call on or address R. W. Hulburd.

C. S. PAGE,
E. B. SAWYER,
W. BRIGHAM,
HYDE PARK, Aug. 19, '91. Trustees.

Shown here is an ad displaying the announcement of Lamoille Central Academy's fall term. At its inception in 1857, LCA would publish a schedule showing the tuition fees of the various courses offered for enrollment. For example, English was $3.50, French $2, and music was the most expensive, at $9 to learn the piano. It should be noted that the very first school in Hyde Park was in Judge Sawyer's barn in 1800. (Courtesy of Francis Favreau.)

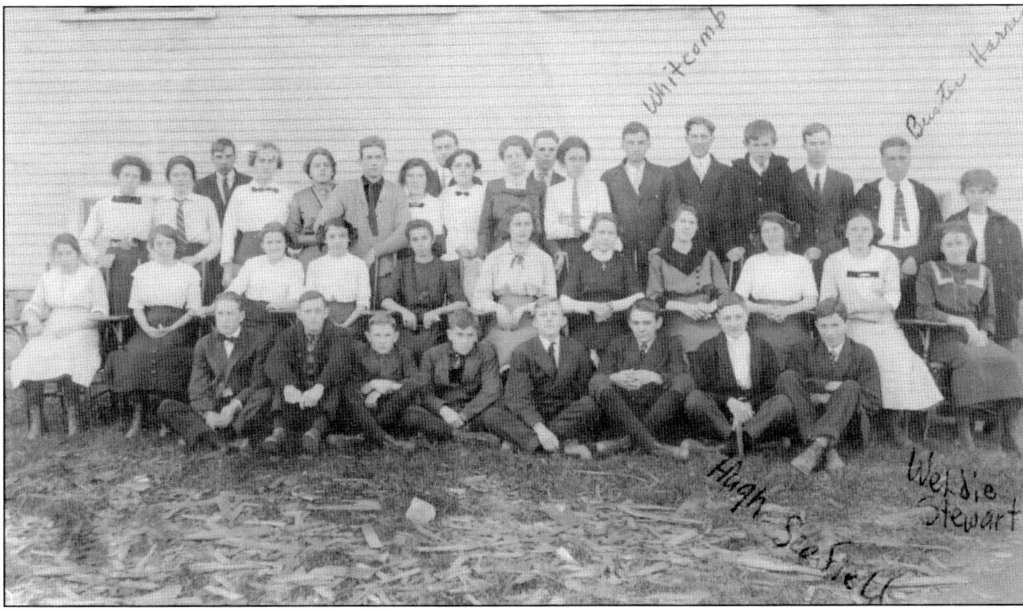

This class photograph of students at LCA was one of many taken throughout the years of the school's history. Note that some of the names of the students are written on the photograph. (Courtesy of the Larose/Manning family.)

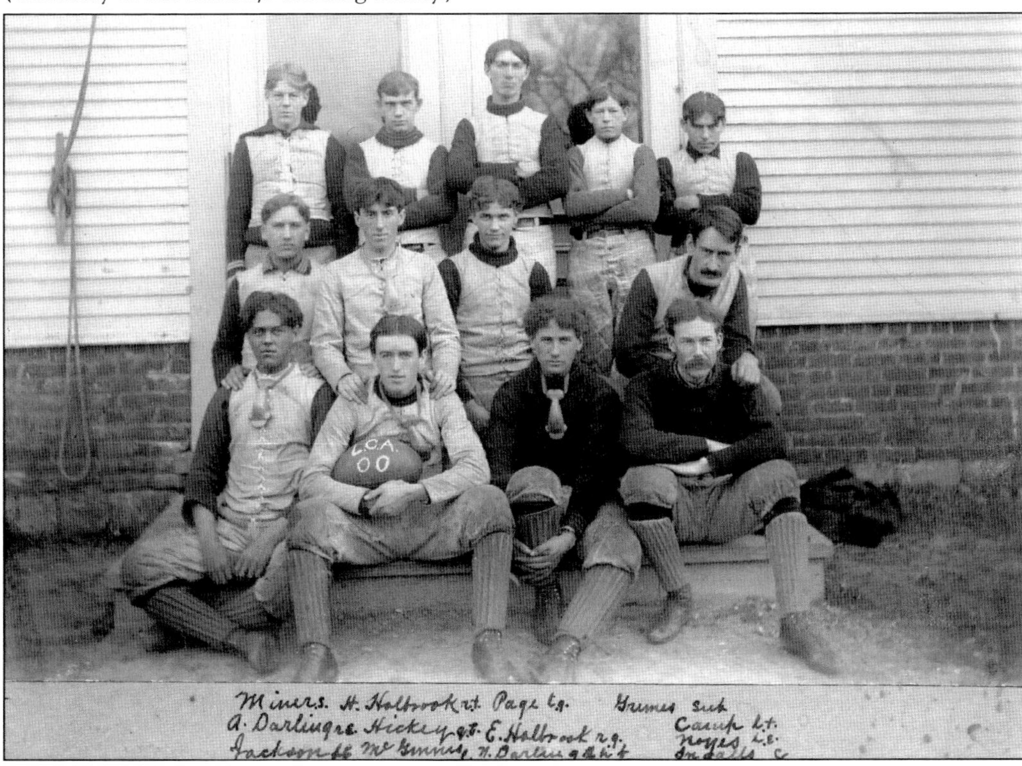

This photograph of the LCA football team was taken in 1900. The names of some of the players and the positions they played are listed on the photograph; however, the sequence of who is who is unknown. (Courtesy of Francis Favreau.)

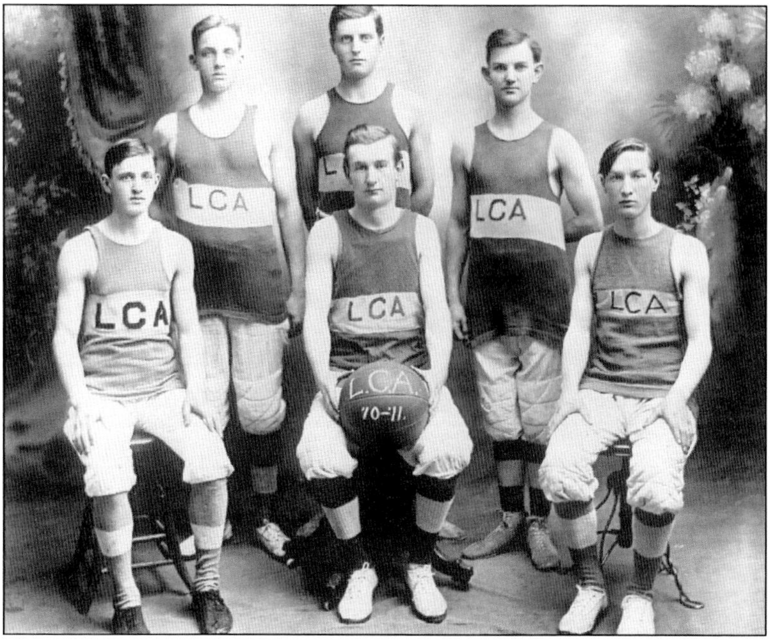

The LCA boys basketball team for 1910–1911 school year is pictured here. Carroll Page is the young man in the center of the second row. (Courtesy of the Page/ McFarland family.)

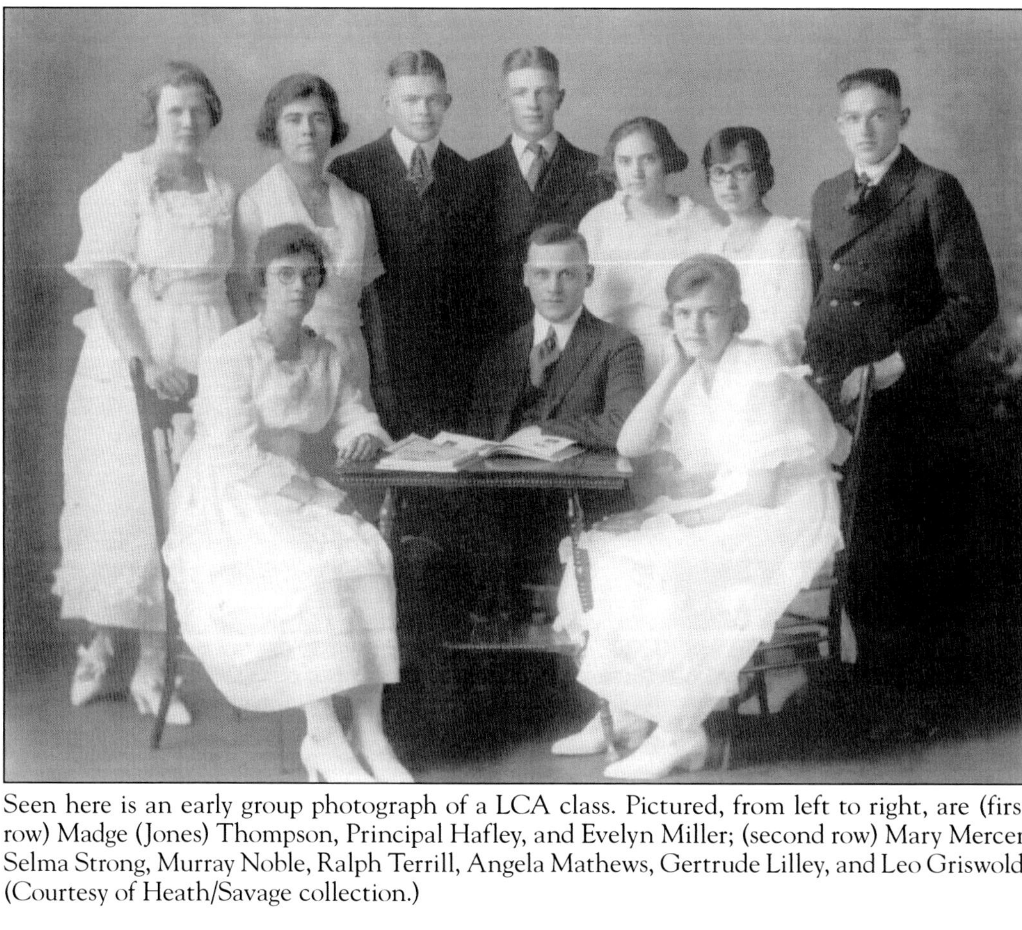

Seen here is an early group photograph of a LCA class. Pictured, from left to right, are (first row) Madge (Jones) Thompson, Principal Hafley, and Evelyn Miller; (second row) Mary Mercer, Selma Strong, Murray Noble, Ralph Terrill, Angela Mathews, Gertrude Lilley, and Leo Griswold. (Courtesy of Heath/Savage collection.)

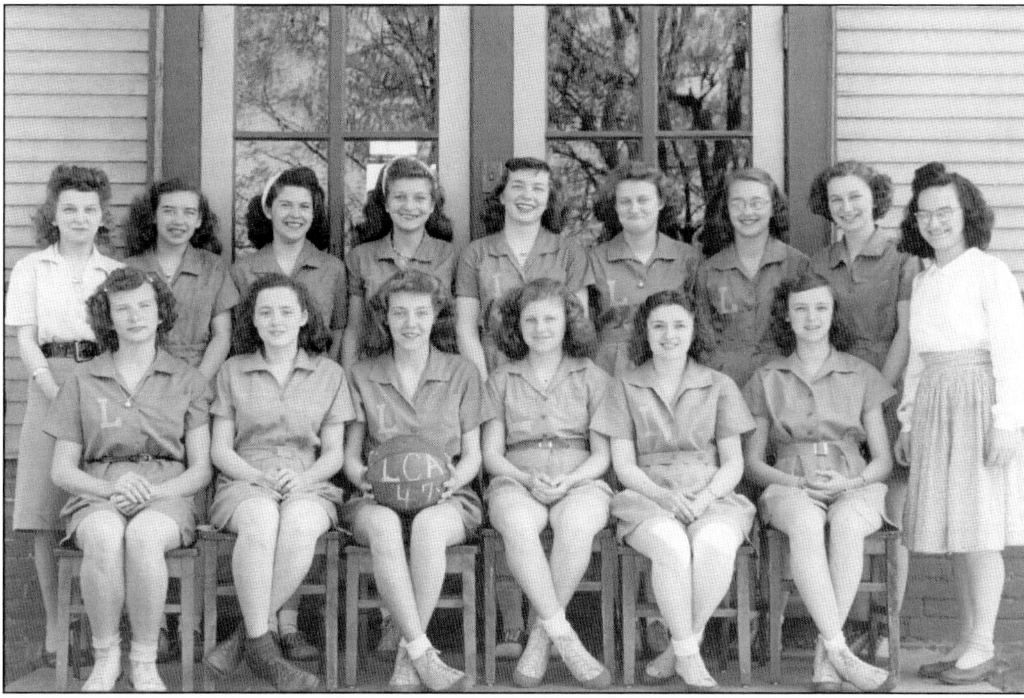

The 1947 LCA girls basketball team is pictured here. Included in the photograph are, from left to right, (first row) Ida Manning, Betty Jones (Chapman), Gladys "Dolly" Dudley (Cubit), Norma Thompson (Savage), Barbara McAllister (Cubit), and Marjorie McAllister (Graves); (second row) Elsie Dunkling (teacher), Viola Stoddard, Jean Goodwin, Jeannette Lanphear, Julie Cook, Mary Mudgett (Adams), Janice Morey (Wallace), Joanne Lanphear (Dewey), and Jeanne Godin. (Courtesy of the Heath/Savage family.)

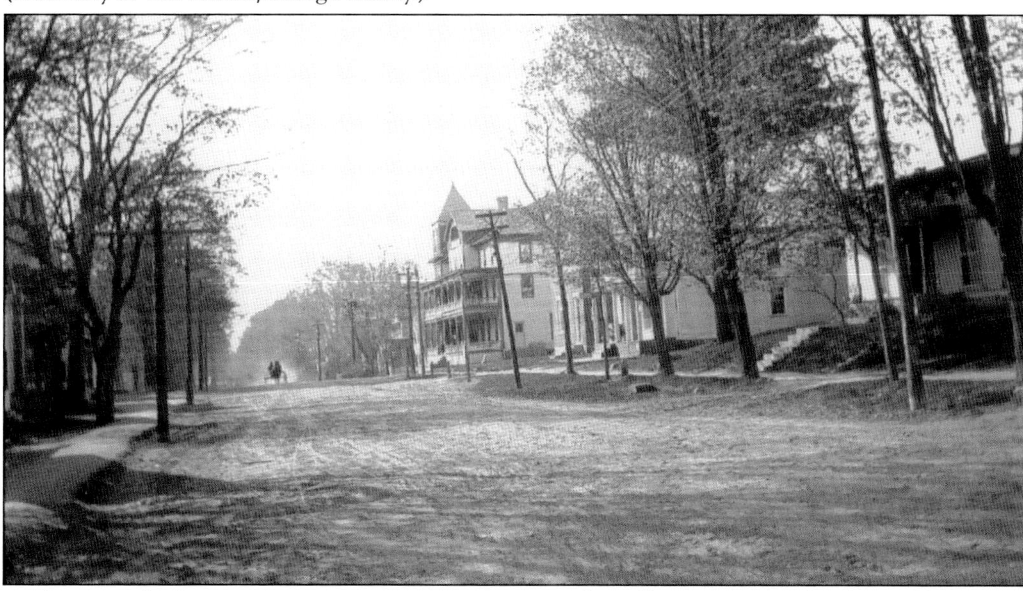

In this view looking west on upper Main Street in the village, one see the days of horse and buggy, with the Hotel Phoenix and Lamoille County Bank visible on the right. (Courtesy of the Page/McFarland family.)

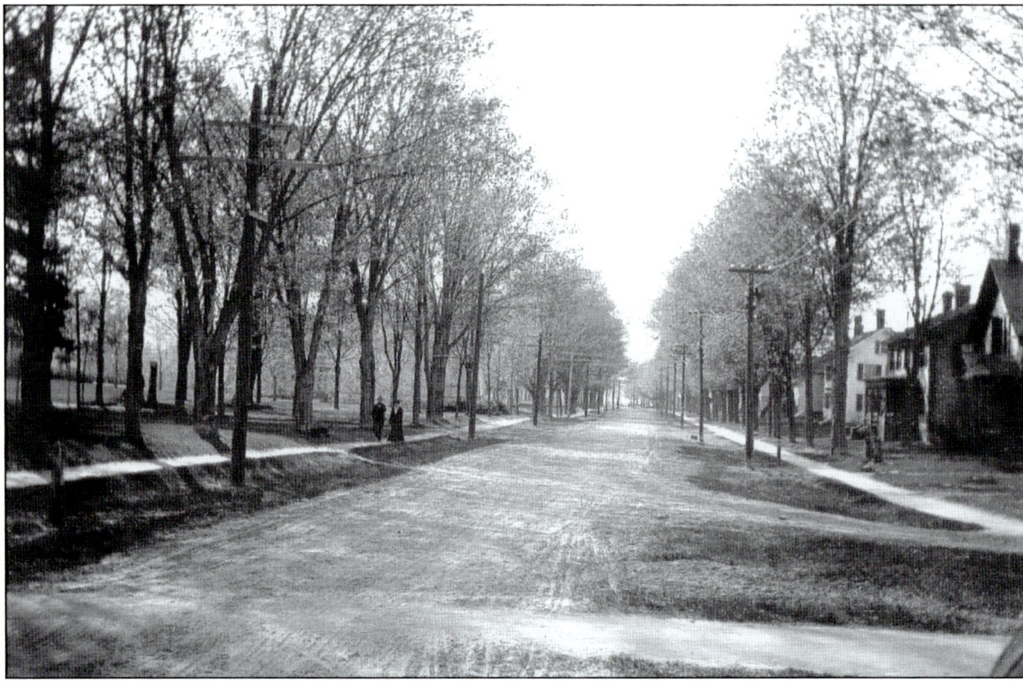

This west-looking view of lower Main Street features the Grant Building on the right. On the left, two people take a leisurely stroll on the sidewalk underneath the large maple trees. (Courtesy of the Page/McFarland family.)

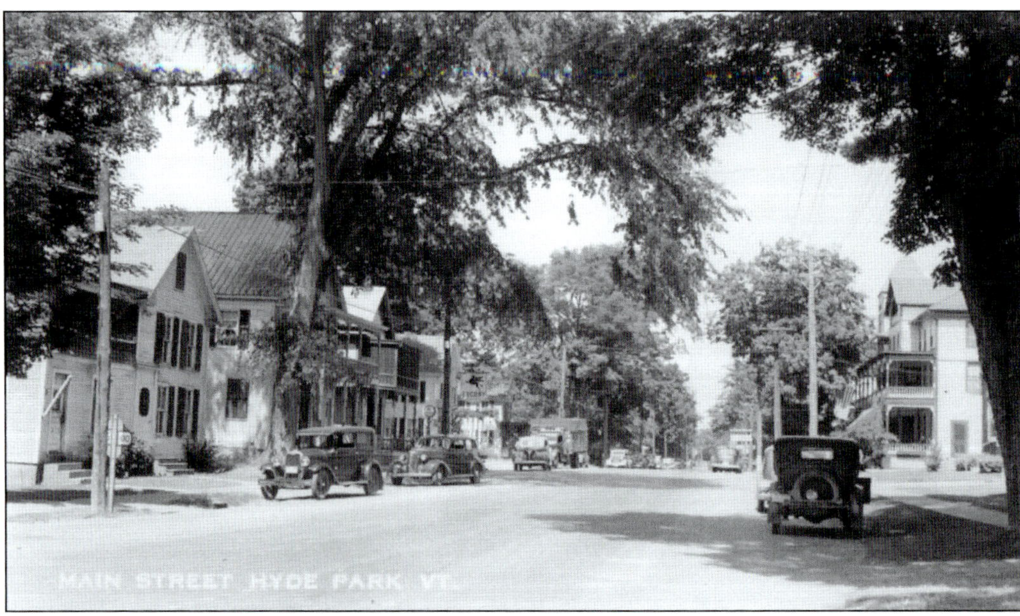

This 1930s photograph with a view looking west was taken in front of the Lamoille County Bank. Notice the change in the village from the photographs of the 1910 fire—the town was enjoying greater prosperity. (Courtesy of the Page/McFarland family.)

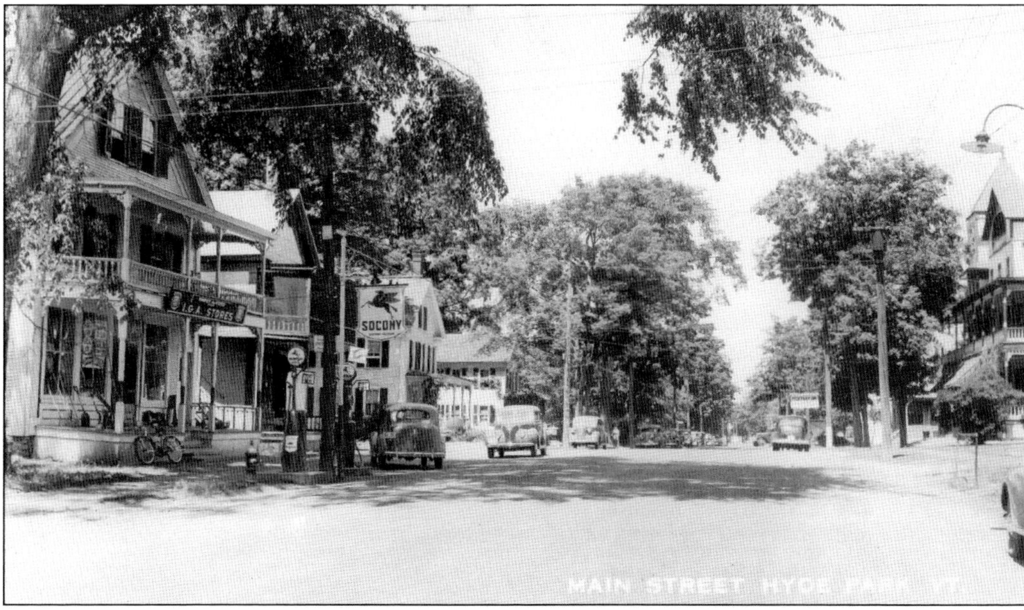

This grand view of Main Street in Hyde Park was captured during the 1940s. On the left is Foss's IGA store, which was purchased from Burt Crane in 1902. (Courtesy of Linda Jones.)

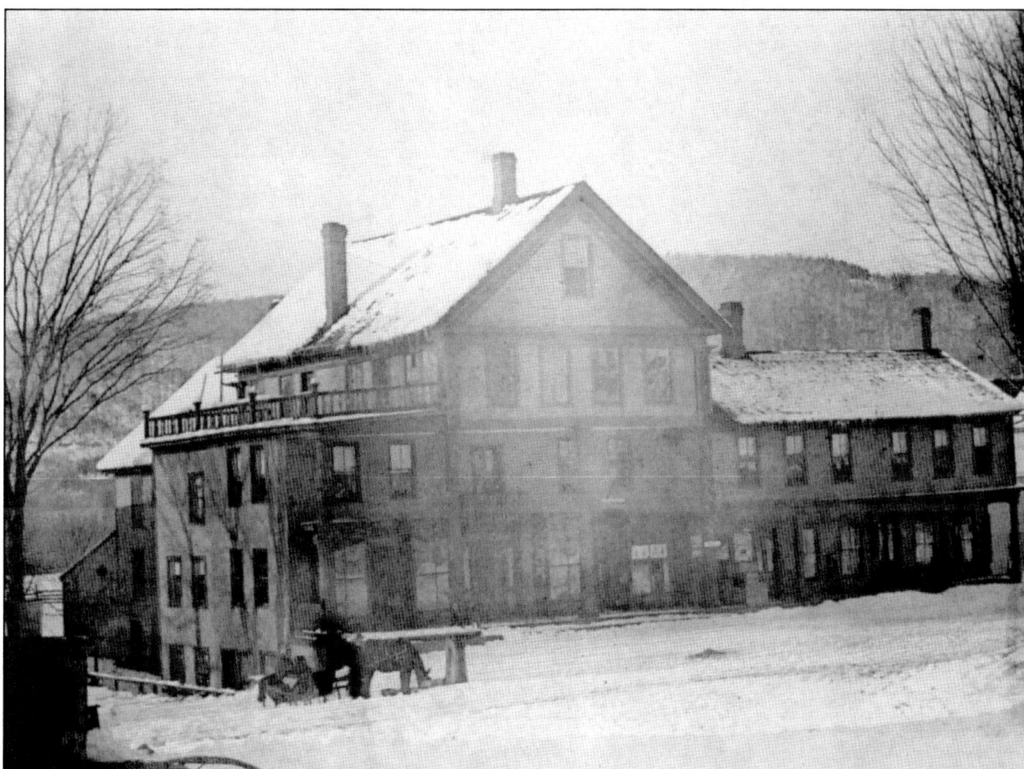

This building was located on the corner of Main and Depot Streets. It is believed to have been a boardinghouse or hotel, although it may have housed other businesses on the main floor. (Courtesy of Francis Favreau.)

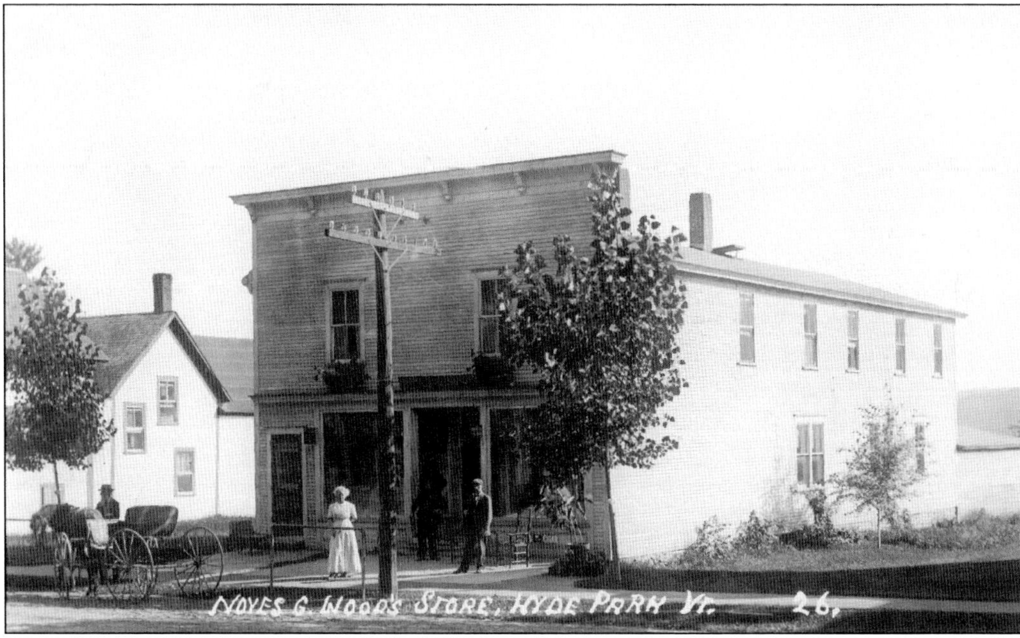

This image of the Noyes G. Wood's Store located on the south side of Main Street in Hyde Park Village was taken around 1915. Many community members remember this store when it was under the ownership of Max Carr. As a side note, Noyes Wood was also the judge of probate in the county courthouse. (Courtesy of the Heath/Savage family.)

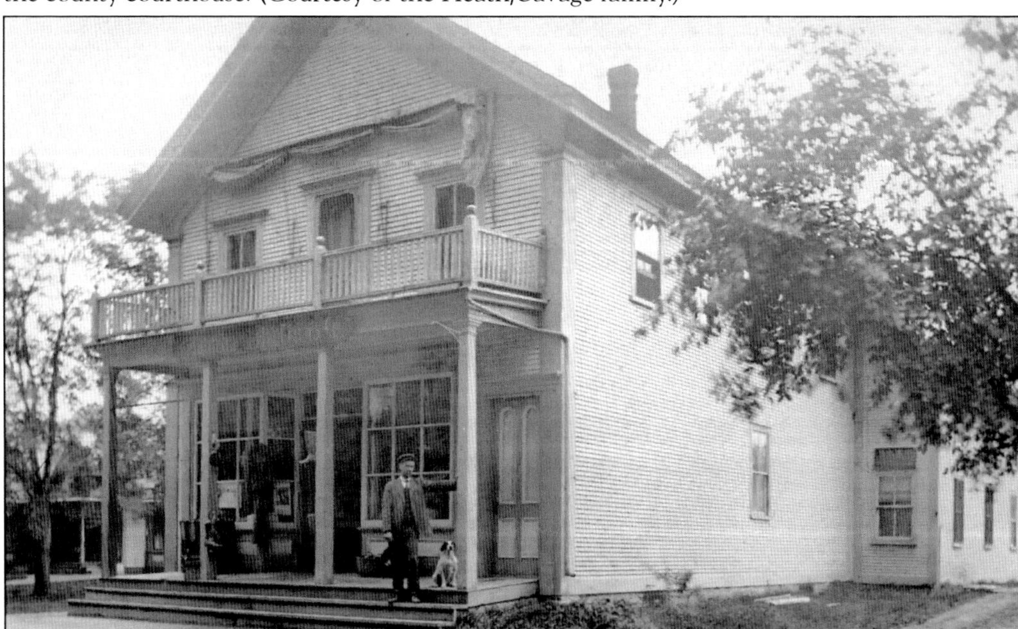

Thomas Brothers Company, formerly known as Wetherby & Page, was a company owned by Charles B. Wetherby and John B. Page, who originally had a location on Main Street in Jeffersonville, Vermont. They were dealers of dry goods, groceries, ready-made clothing, boots and shoes, hardware, general merchandise, plows, harrows, and so forth. The name Wetherby & Page was changed to Thomas Brothers Company in 1894. (Courtesy of Francis Favreau.)

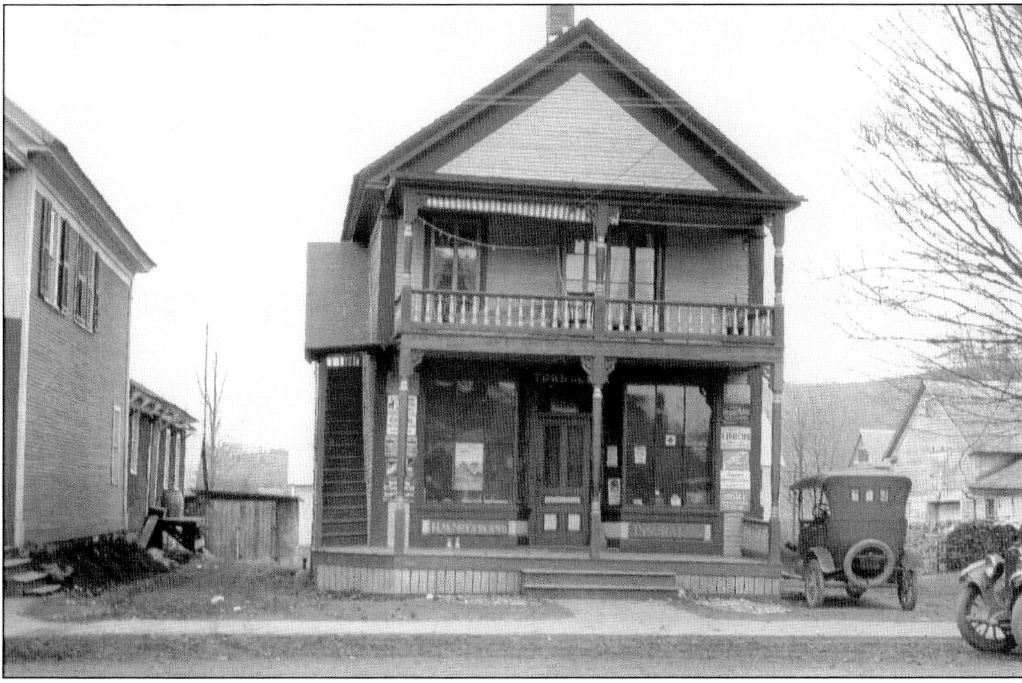

This building was home to the Hyde Park town clerk's office, H.M. McFarland Insurance, and Foss's IGA store, which Harry A. Foss inherited from his father, George Benjamin Foss. (Courtesy of Francis Favreau.)

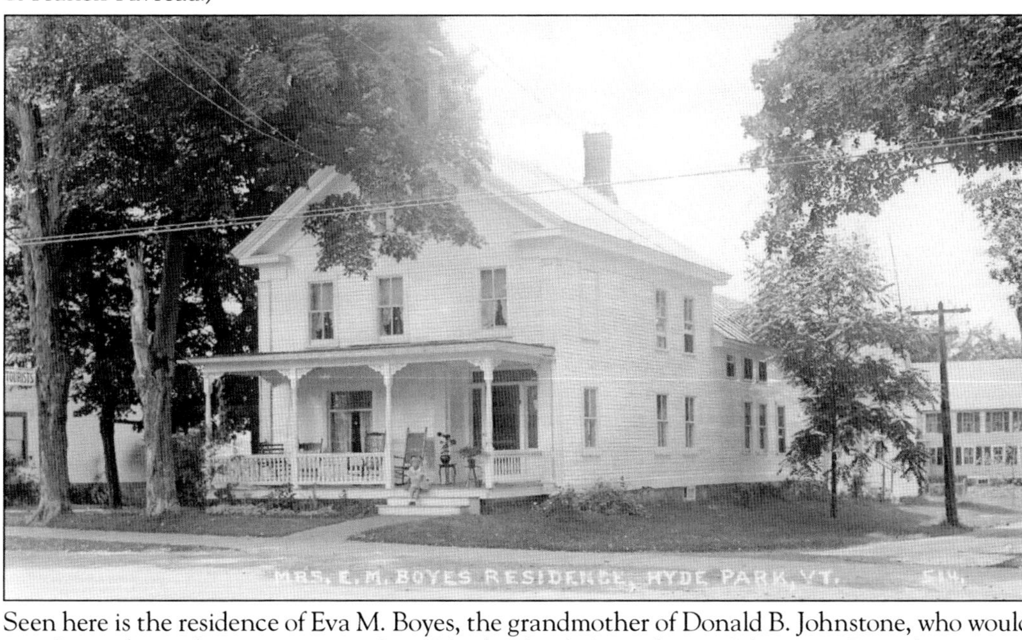

Seen here is the residence of Eva M. Boyes, the grandmother of Donald B. Johnstone, who would visit Boyes during his summer trips from Rhode Island. According to Johnstone, Boyes hung a sign that read "Tourists" on the tree in her front yard. She would charge $1 per person per night. She and the proprietors of the Hyde Park Inn (previously known as the Hotel Phoenix) had a good relationship, and the inn's owners would send overflow patrons to her tourist home. (Courtesy of Donald B. Johnstone.)

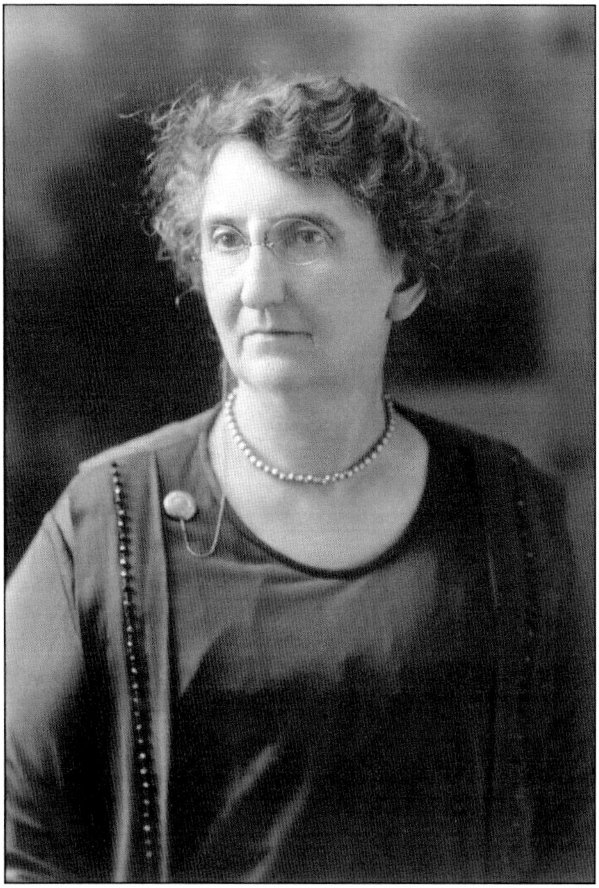

Seen here is a wonderful c. 1920 photograph of Eva M. Boyes. She ran a tourist home on Main Street opposite the Hyde Park Inn. Upon her death in 1937, her house was sold to the Dr. Edward French family. (Courtesy of Donald B. Johnstone.)

In this view looking down Commonwealth Avenue, the house with the turret was purchased from Emeroy Page prior to World War II by Elizabeth and Katharine Beebe, who were from New York City. The Beebes came to Hyde Park as summer residents before the 1920s and enjoyed the village culture, which prompted their move. (Courtesy of Francis Favreau.)

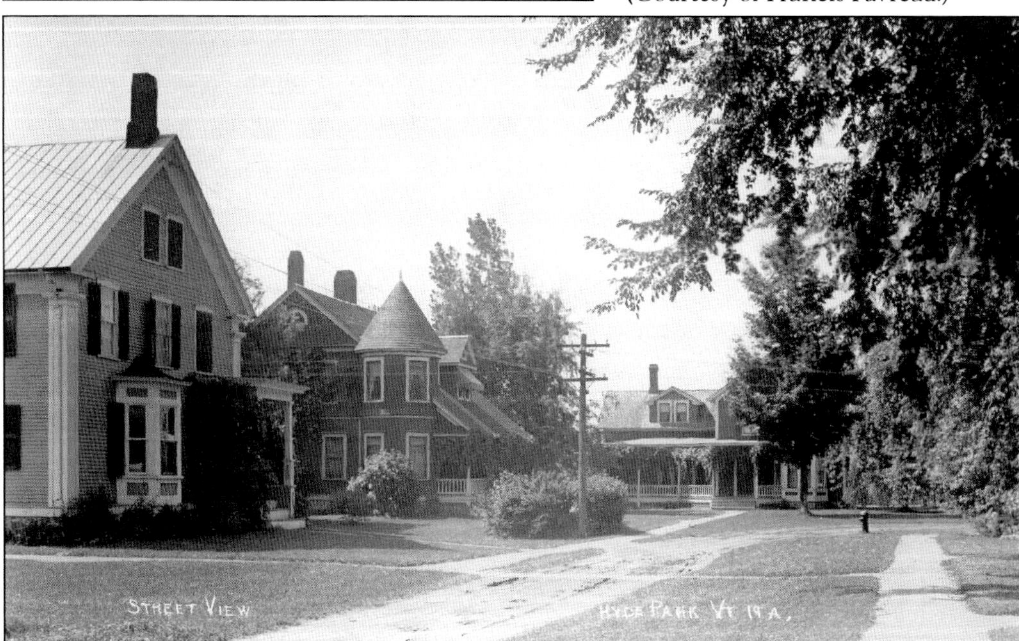

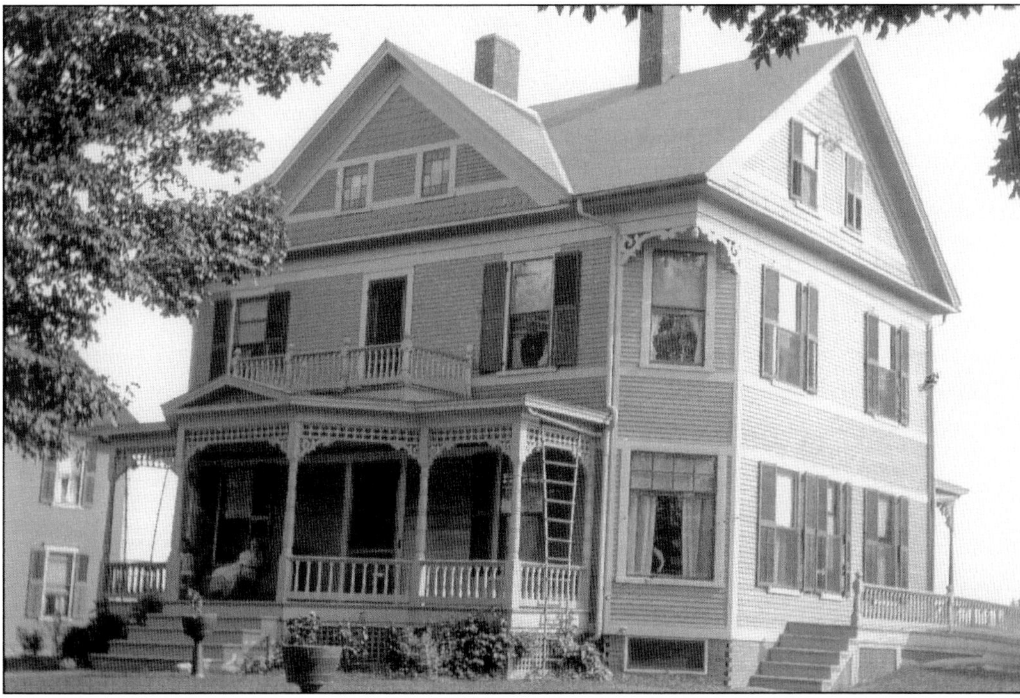

Two ladies take in the warm days of summer on the porch of Andrea Viets's home, located on Commonwealth Avenue. This home is one of many in Hyde Park renowned for its intricate architectural design. (Courtesy of Francis Favreau.)

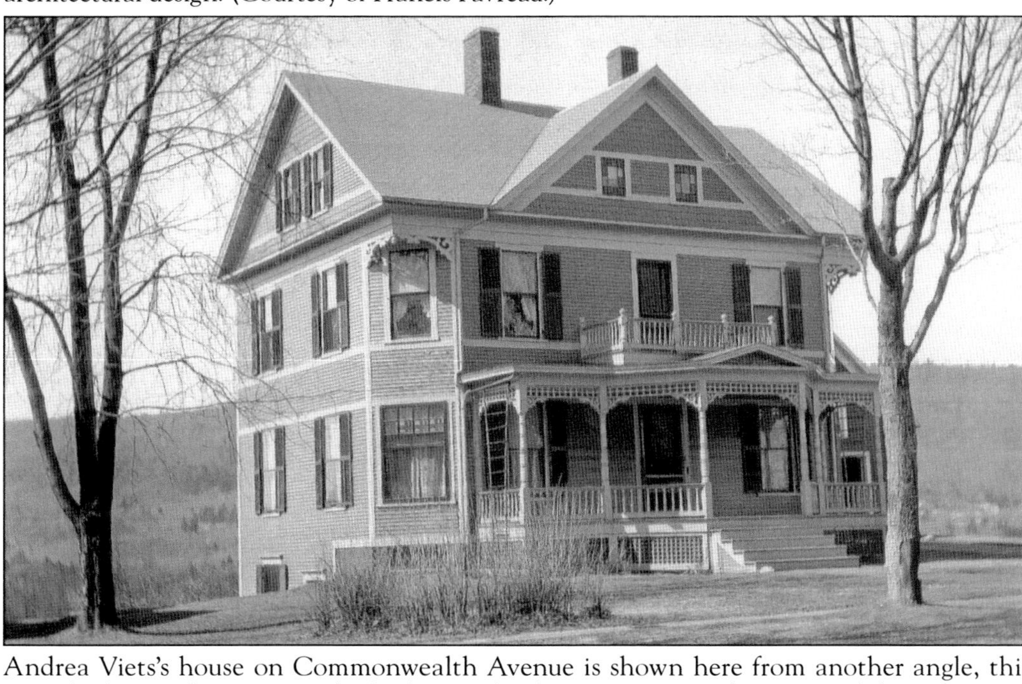

Andrea Viets's house on Commonwealth Avenue is shown here from another angle, this time displaying the views in the background. John B. Viets was the owner of the C.H. Dana Company, which produced livestock tags and was located in Hyde Park Village. (Courtesy of Francis Favreau.)

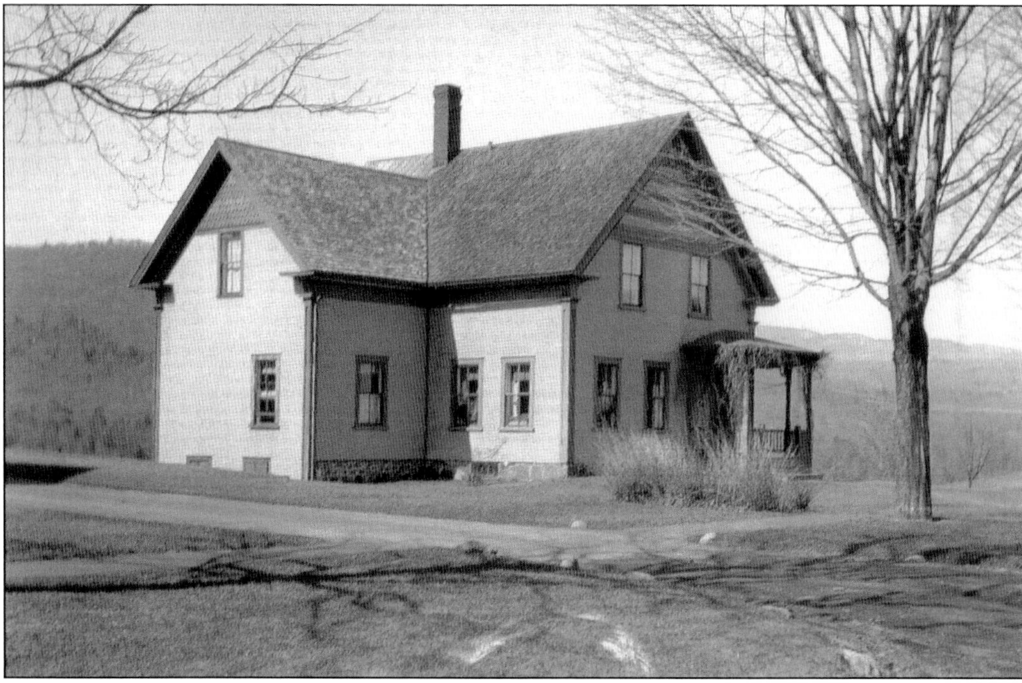

Located on the corner at the end of Commonwealth Avenue, this residence was home to the Stanton family, who, along with the Noyes and Keeler families, were among the very early settlers of Hyde Park Village. (Courtesy of Francis Favreau.)

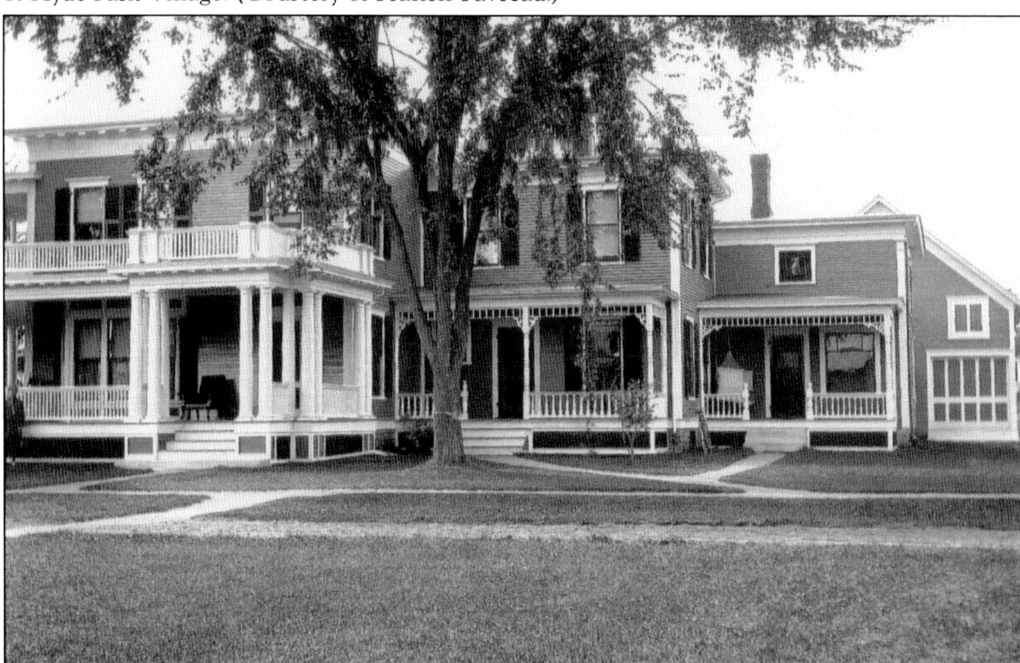

The Emile Hamlin house was located next to the J.A. Childs building on the newly created Commonwealth Avenue. In addition to the details of this wonderfully designed home, notice the dog sitting in the second-floor window on the far right. (Courtesy of Francis Favreau.)

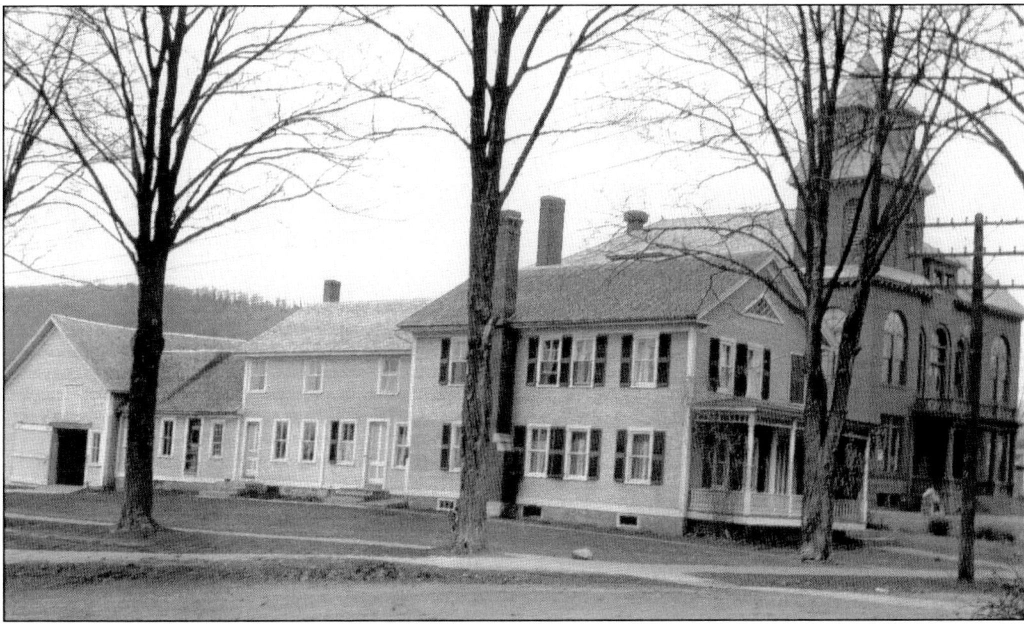

According to the Beers Atlas printed in 1871, this house once belonged to Mrs. J.A. Childs and was located east of the courthouse on the corner of what is now Commonwealth Avenue and Main Street. Commonwealth Avenue did not exist in 1871 and was a field owned by none other than Childs. (Courtesy of Francis Favreau.)

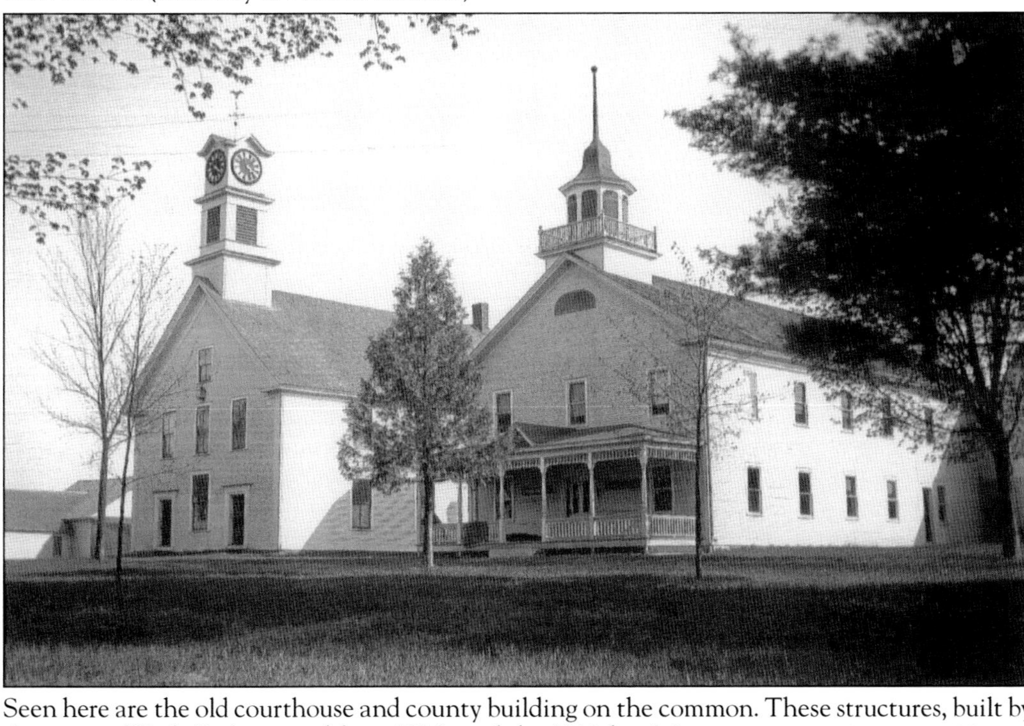

Seen here are the old courthouse and county building on the common. These structures, built by the town of Hyde Park, existed from 1836 until the 1910 fire. Many towns were in competition to inherit the status of becoming the shire town for the newly formed Lamoille County. (Courtesy of the Page/McFarland family.)

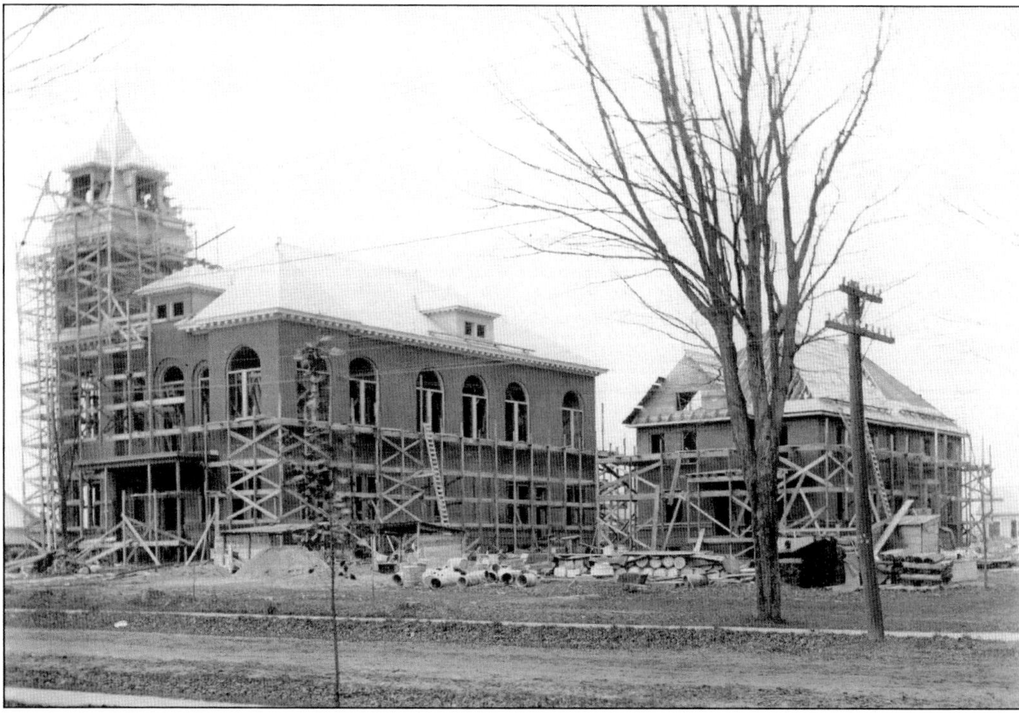

A December 1911 *News & Citizen* reports that "the outside scaffolds are down and the interior will be finished during the winter months, in readiness for the June term of court. It is a handsome structure and stands out in all its glory." (Courtesy of the Page/McFarland family.)

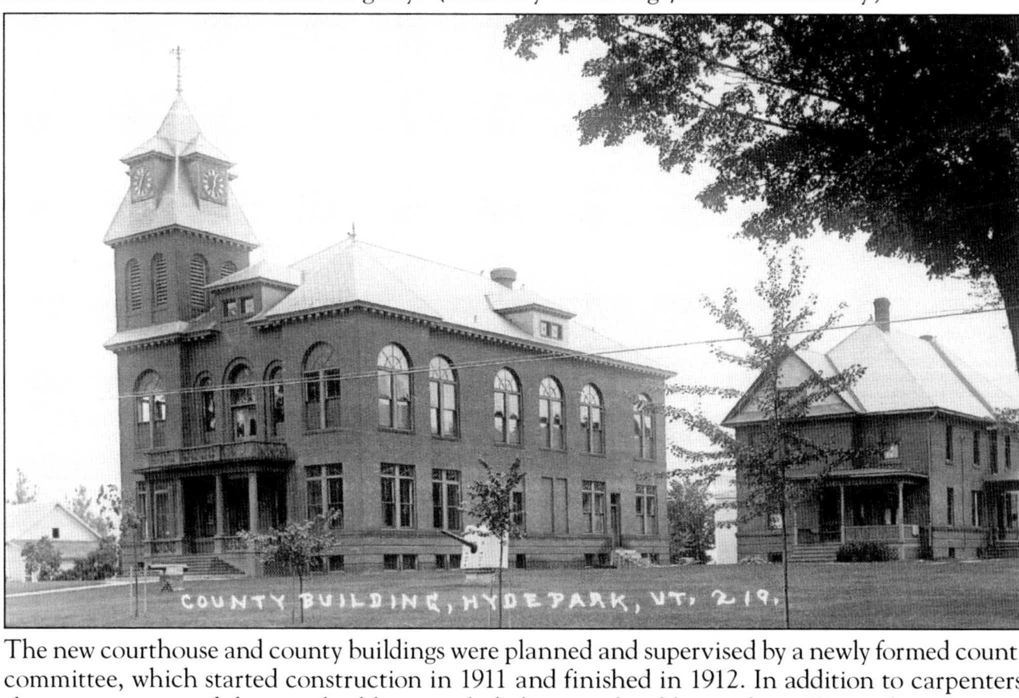

The new courthouse and county buildings were planned and supervised by a newly formed county committee, which started construction in 1911 and finished in 1912. In addition to carpenters, the construction of the new buildings included expert bricklayers from Winooski, Vermont. (Courtesy of Francis Favreau.)

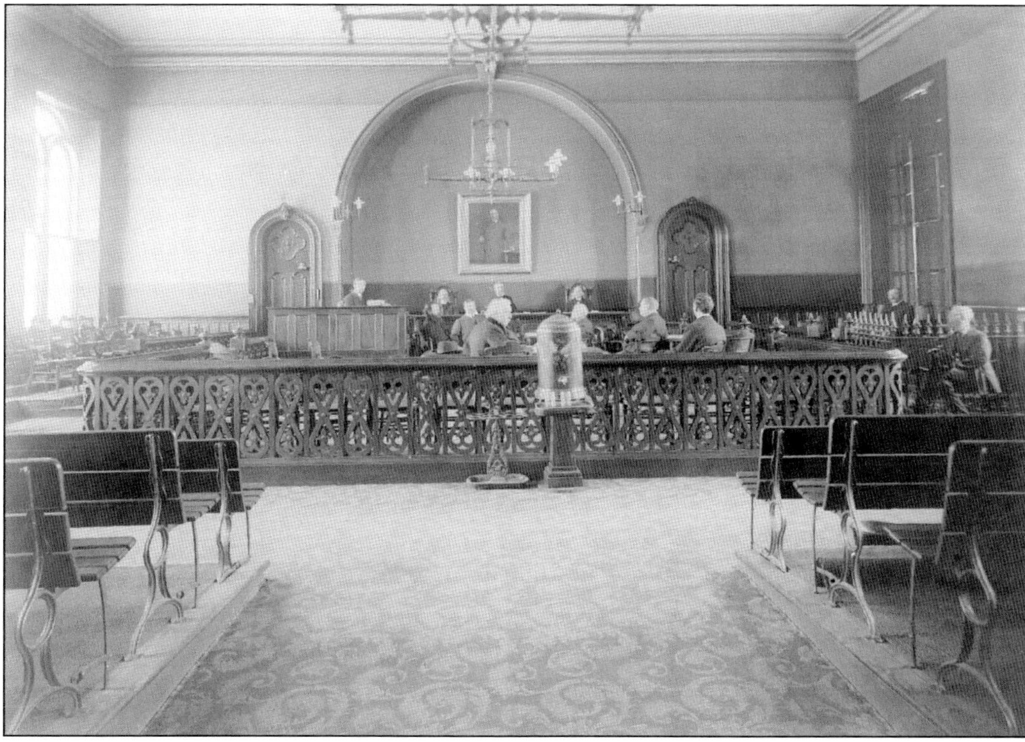

Court is in session in this photograph of the interior of the courtroom. Notice the lighting fixtures suspended from the ceiling and the style of the seating arrangements. (Courtesy of Robert and Caroline Jones.)

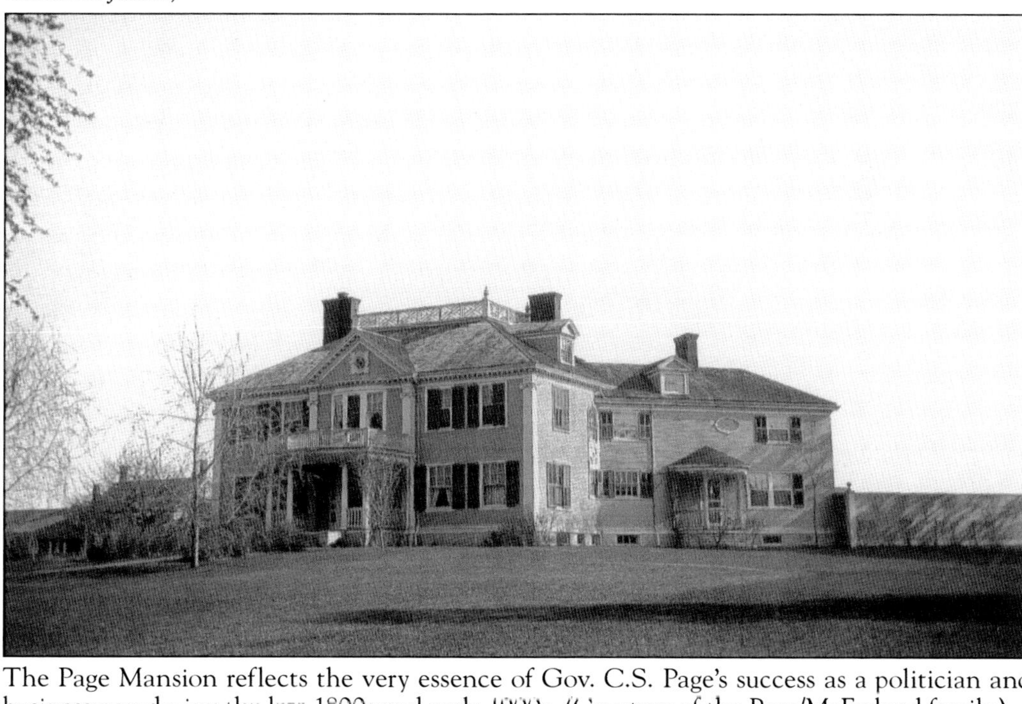

The Page Mansion reflects the very essence of Gov. C.S. Page's success as a politician and businessman during the late 1800s and early 1900s. (Courtesy of the Page/McFarland family.)

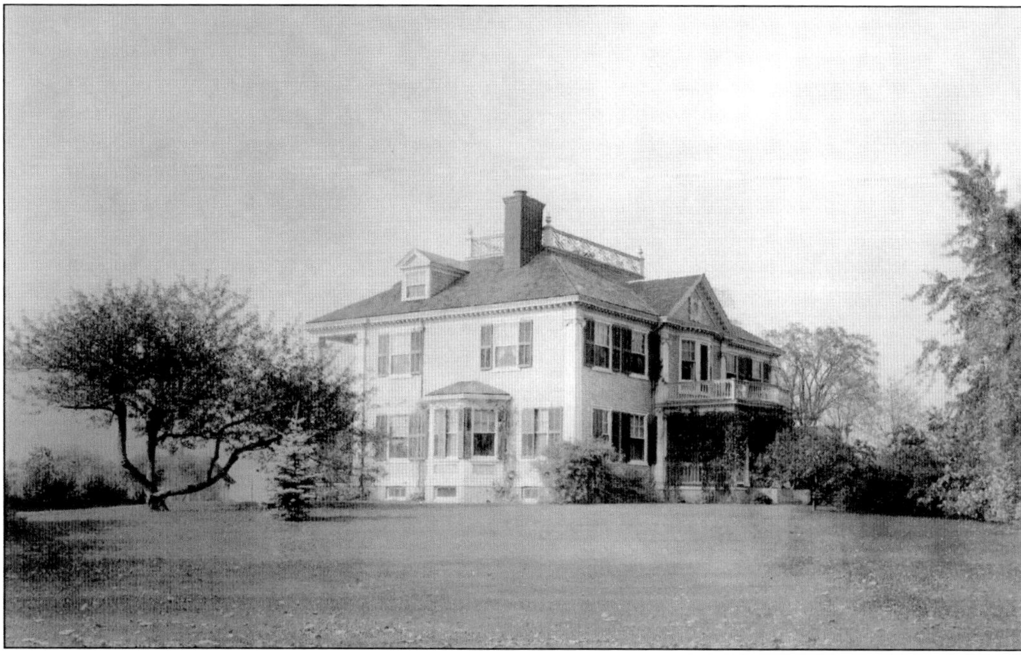

Pictured here is the east side of Page Mansion. Although the estate fell into disrepair during the 1970s, it was later purchased by Mrs. Omer Brosseau, who restored it back to its former state as one of the village's pristine homes. (Courtesy of the Page/McFarland family.)

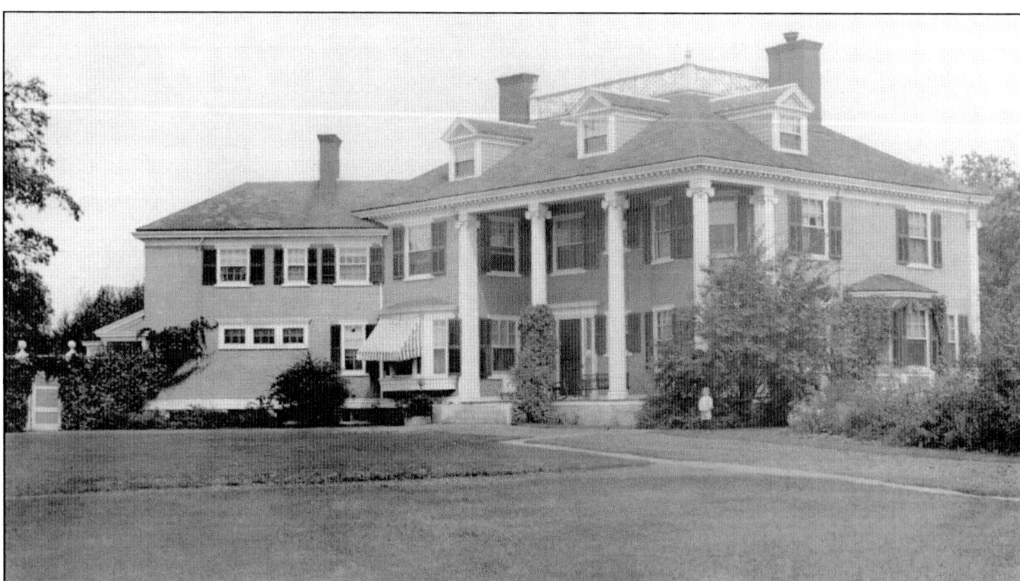

Seen here is the back of the Page Mansion. After the estate was occupied by Alice Page, it changed ownership several times. At one time, it was purchased by Alexander Copley, who considered converting it into a convalescent home. The furnishings of the estate were sold off in a three-day auction at the old Morrisville Fairgrounds. Many of these pieces still exist in local homes today. (Courtesy of the Page/McFarland family.)

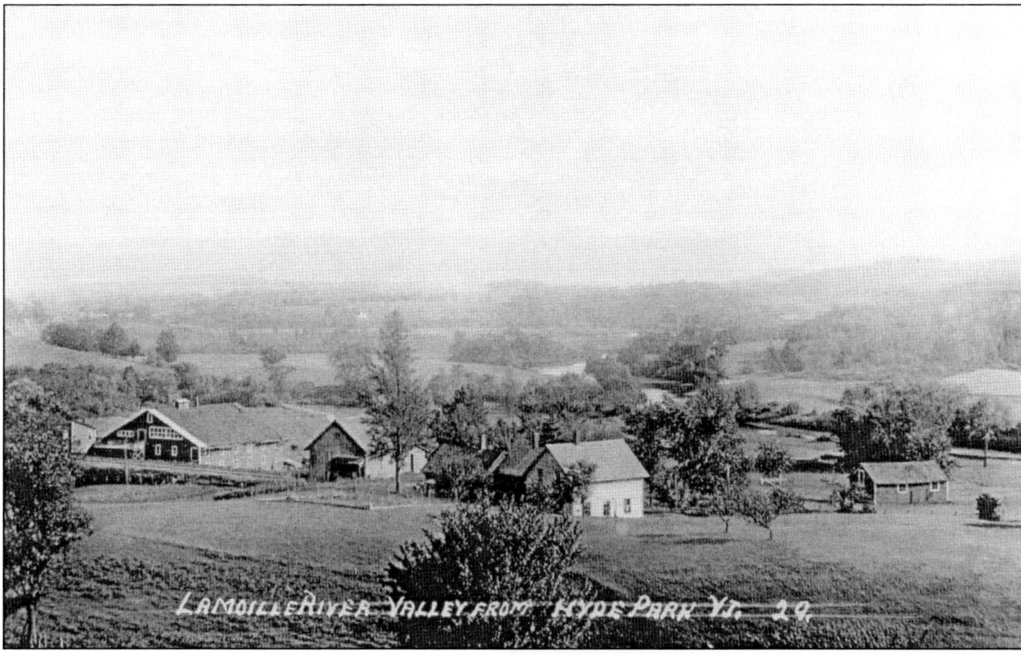

Pictured from behind Page Mansion, this view of the Lamoille River Valley shows the expanse of the great valley, with farmlands, businesses, and homes dotted along its landscape. (Courtesy of Francis Favreau.)

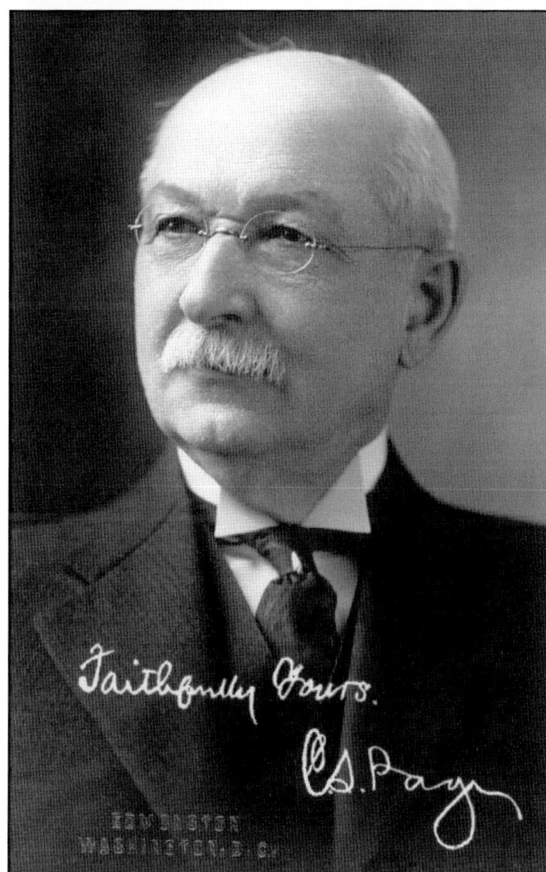

Carroll Smalley Page was born January 10, 1843, in Westfield, Vermont, and died on December 3, 1925, in Hyde Park. He married Ellen F. Patch and had three children. Page held the office of governor from October 2, 1890 to October 6, 1892. It also should be noted he held political office as a legislator for four years, was a Vermont senator for two years, and filled a vacancy in the US Senate, to which he was successfully reelected. (Courtesy of the Page/McFarland family.)

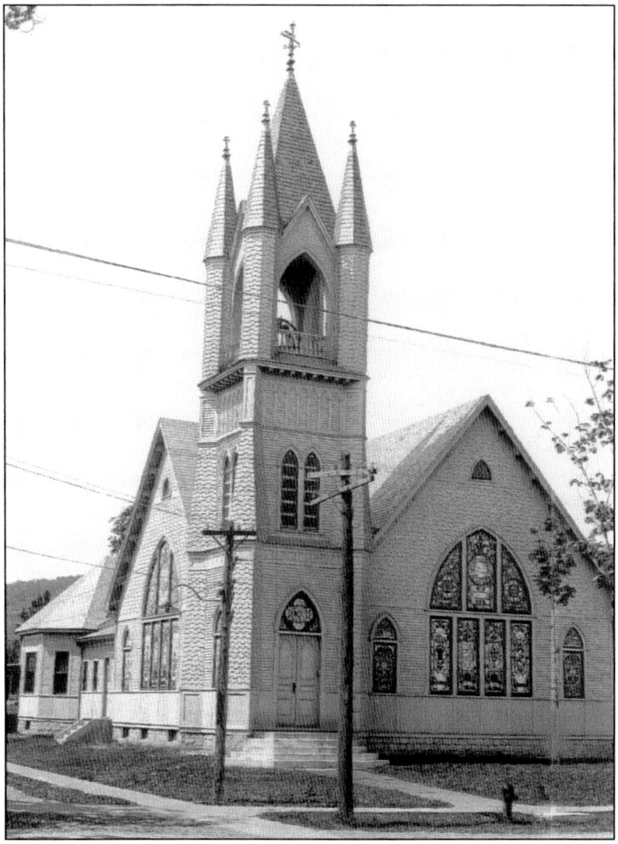

The land of the Second Congregational Church, located on the corner of Prospect and Main Streets, was purchased for the sum of $300 in 1871. A building committee was formed and consisted of H.M. McFarland, H.M. Noyes, L.H. Lewis, and S.B. Waite. On September 20, 1900, there was a dedication for the newly erected church, which burned down in the fire of 1910. (Courtesy of the Page/McFarland family.)

The construction of St. Theresa's Roman Catholic Church at the west end of Main Street was completed in 1872. The land on which the church is located was purchased from Russell S. Page Sr. for $150, with a stipulation that none of the land be used for burial purposes. (Courtesy of the Page/McFarland family.)

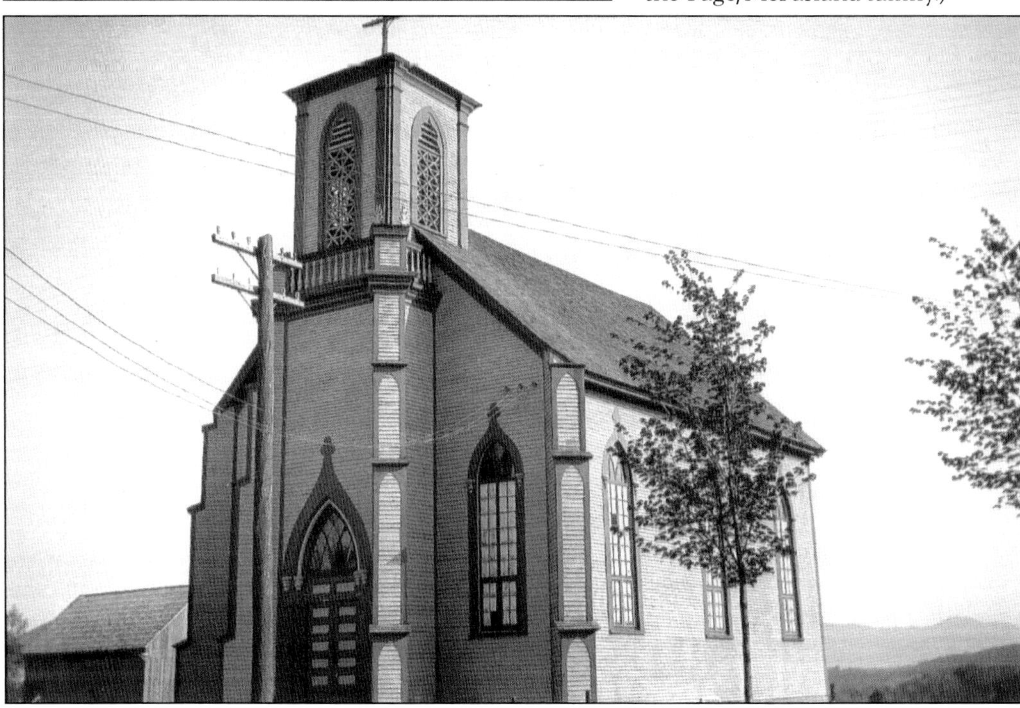

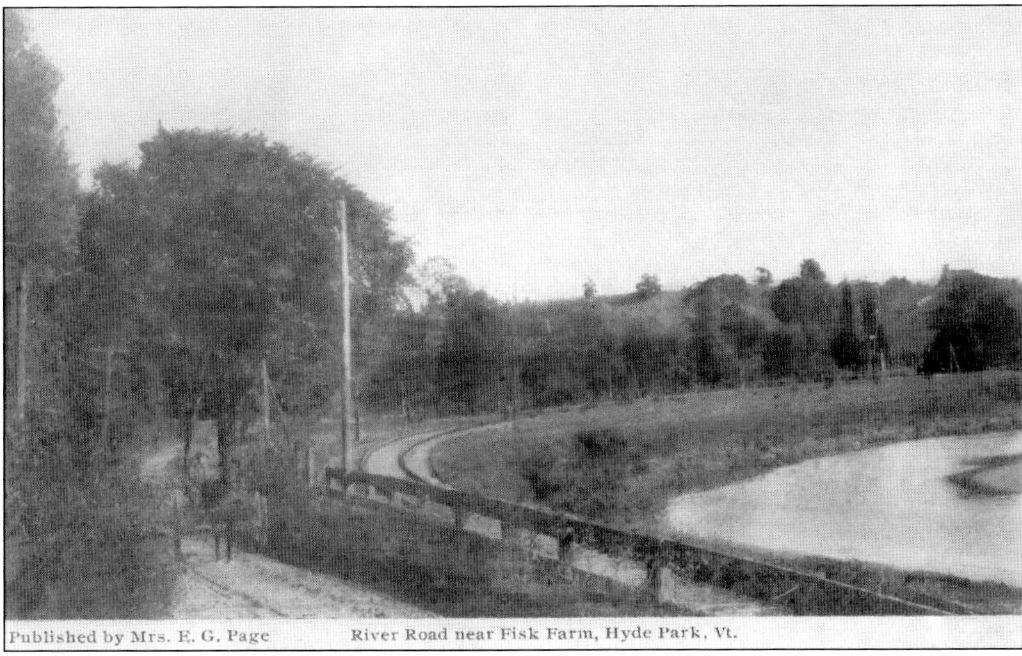

A horse and buggy passes by the Lamoille River at Ten Bends. The river and railroad contributed to the economic development of the town during its early stages. (Courtesy of the Heath/Savage family.)

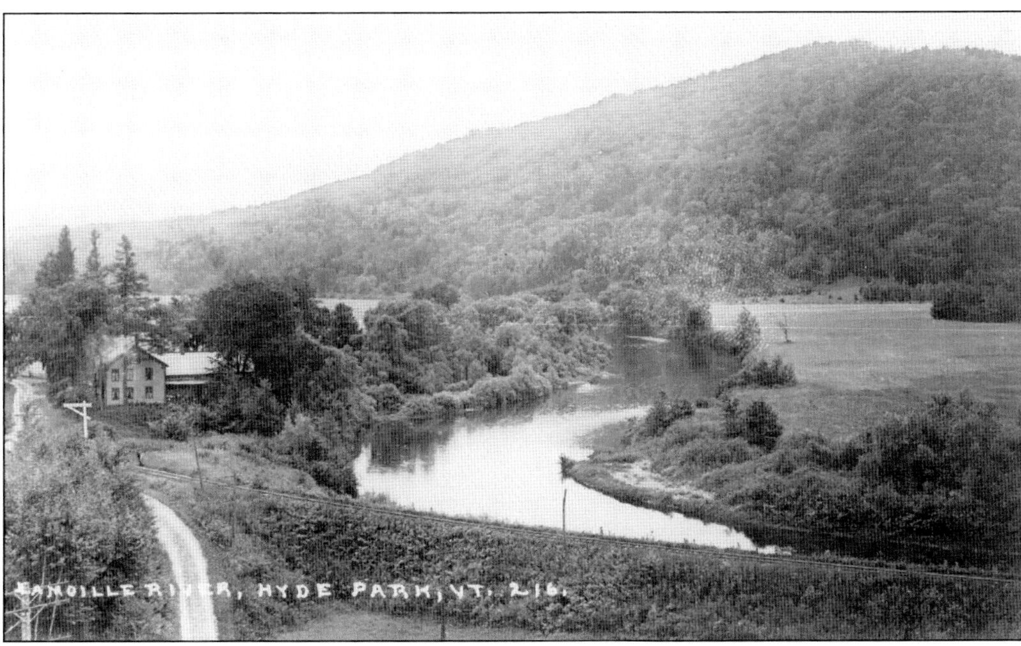

River Road was located near Fisk Farm, now known as Ten Bends. Notice the railroad tracks that run parallel to the road and river that is known as part of the Rail Trail today. Terrill Hill is visible in the background. (Courtesy of Linda Jones.)

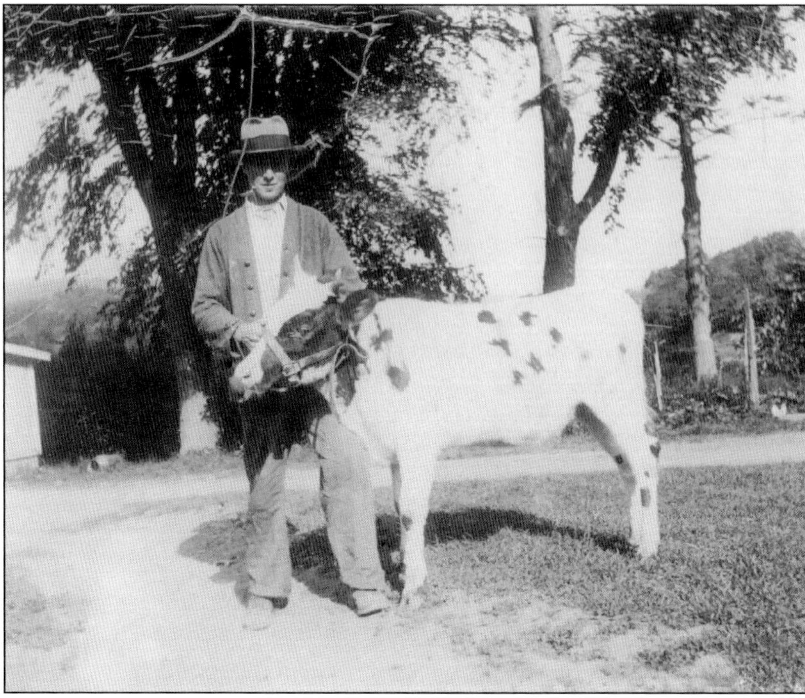

In this 1937 image, Norman Black is pictured at his farm on the northern end of Ten Bends, just outside of Hyde Park Village. The farm's location made it ideal for farming and raising crops. (Courtesy of Robert and Caroline Jones.)

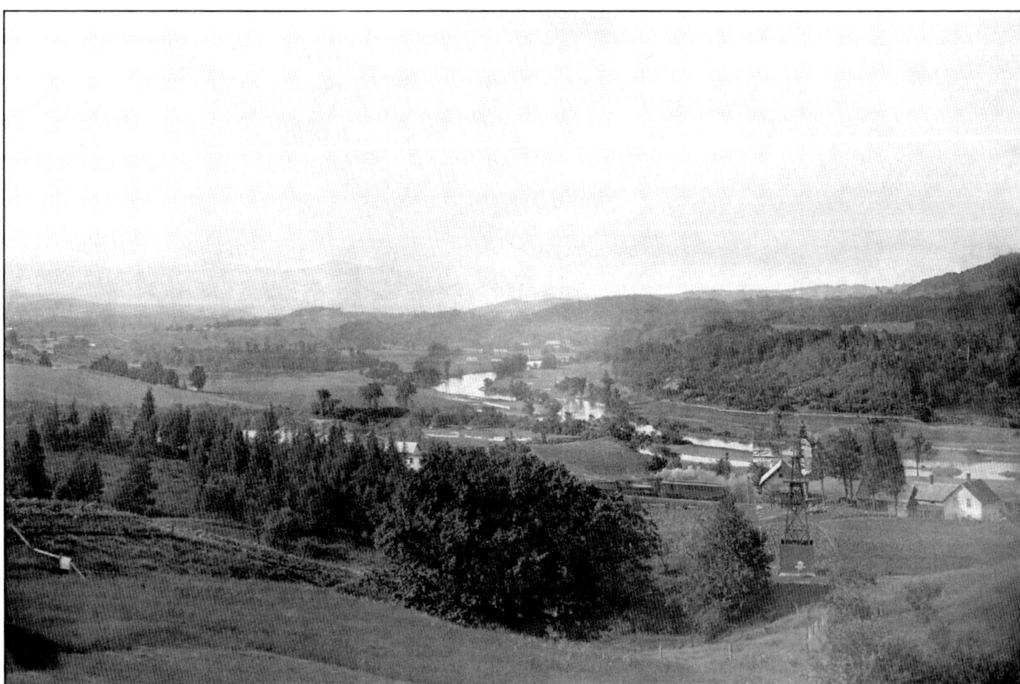

The Lamoille River winds down through the valley in this panoramic view of Ten Bends. The windmill shown here was used to pump water to the village when it was experiencing a shortage in the late 1800s. (Courtesy of Francis Favreau.)

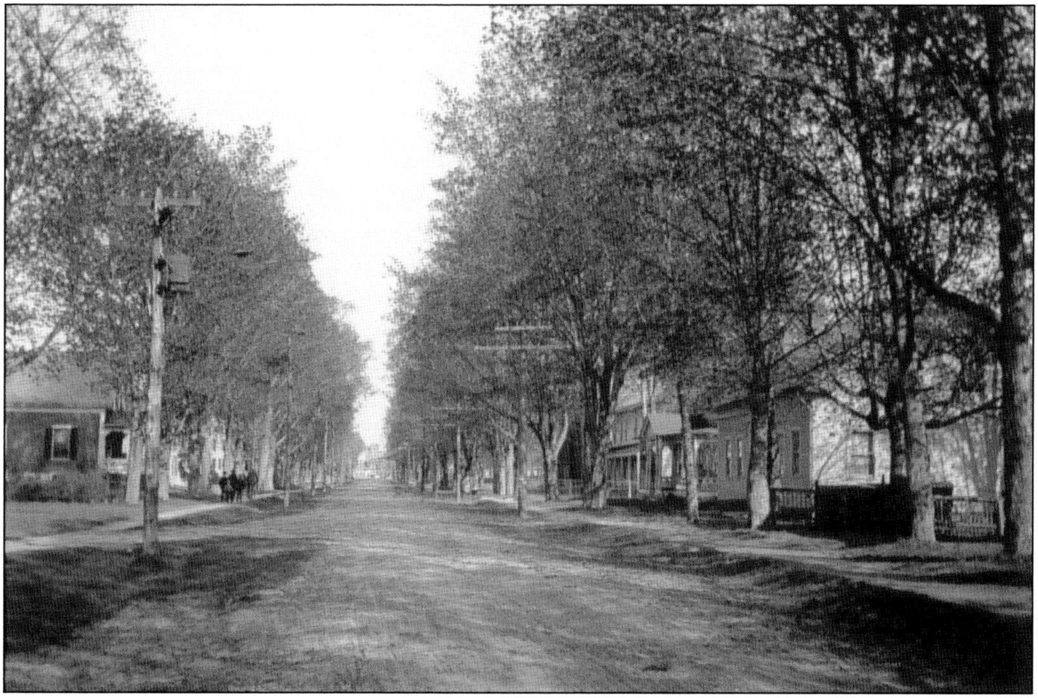

This view of Main Street looks east toward the LCA school building. Looking closely, one will notice that this image was taken prior to the fire of 1910. This dirt road was the main route leading from Johnson to Morrisville. (Courtesy of Linda Jones.)

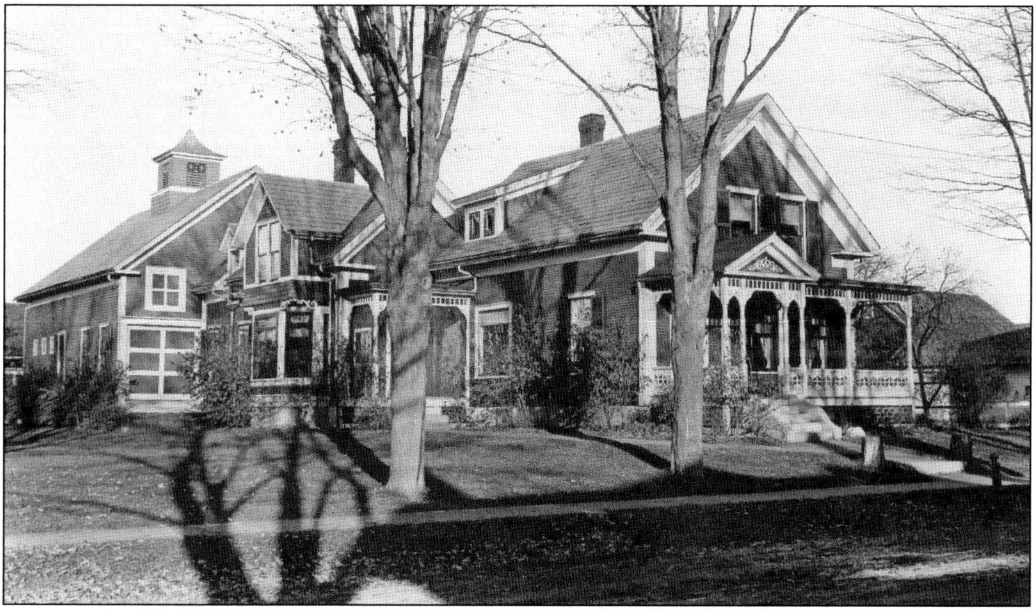

The McFarland House is pictured before it was destroyed in the 1910 fire. H.M. McFarland, who came to Hyde Park from Waterville, was a state attorney and, later, superintendent of schools. An 1878 graduate of the University of Vermont, he was admitted to the Vermont Bar in 1881. (Courtesy of the Page/McFarland family.)

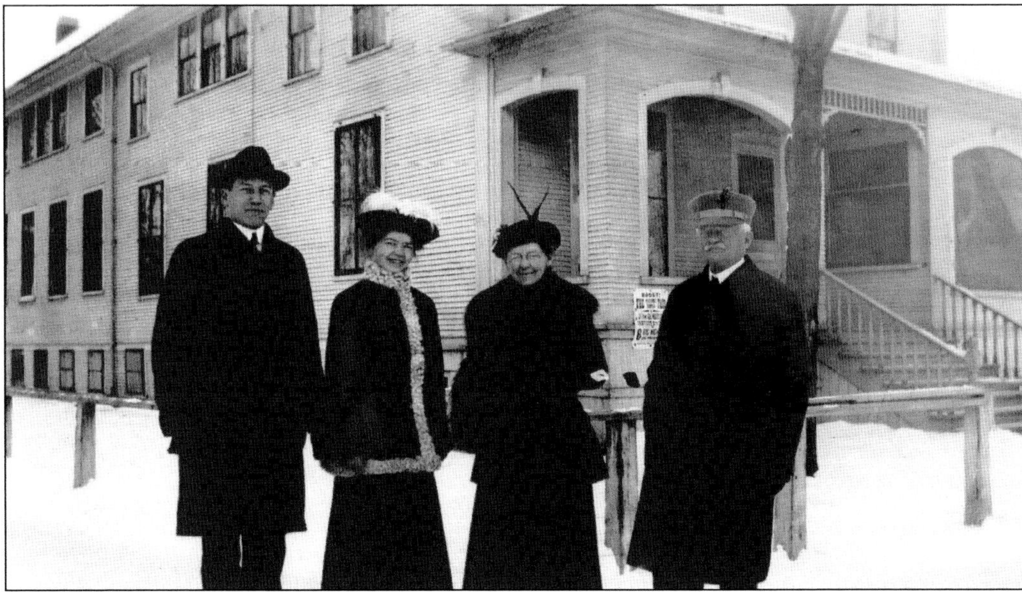

Standing in front of the Page office building, also known as the Lilley House, on Main Street are, from left to right, Ben Douglas, Helen Douglas, Julia McFarland, and Henry M. McFarland. (Courtesy of the Page/McFarland family.)

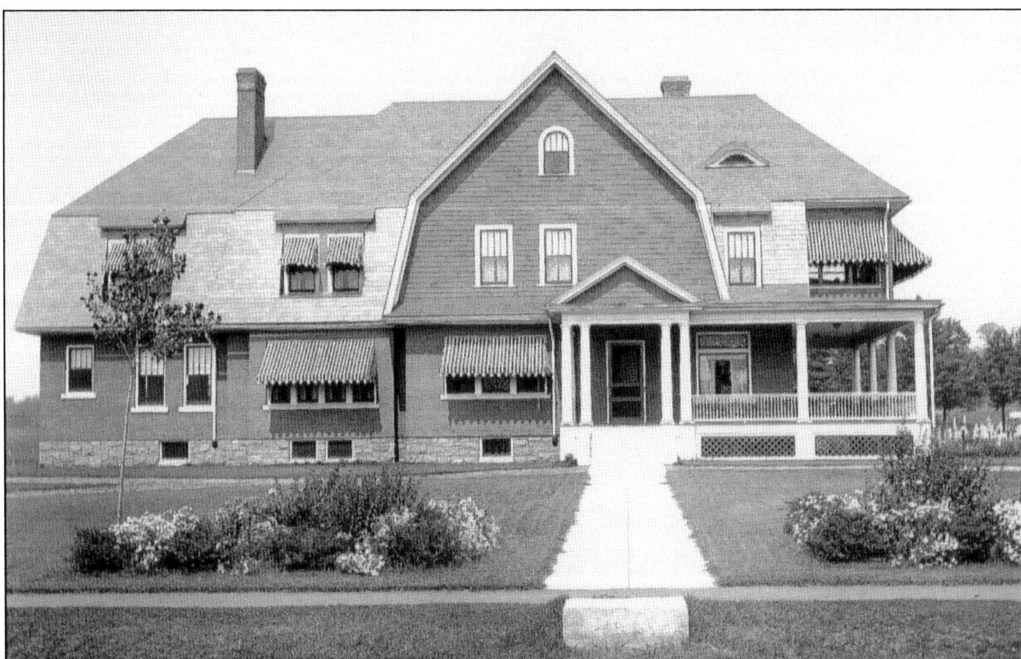

The McFarland House is shown after it was rebuilt following the 1910 fire. Henry Moses McFarland copied a house in Bordentown, New Jersey, when constructing his new home. A quote from *Hyde Park Then and Now* notes that "he was one of the founders of the Lamoille County Bank and was secretary of civil and military affairs under Governor Page from 1890–1892." (Courtesy of the Page/McFarland family.)

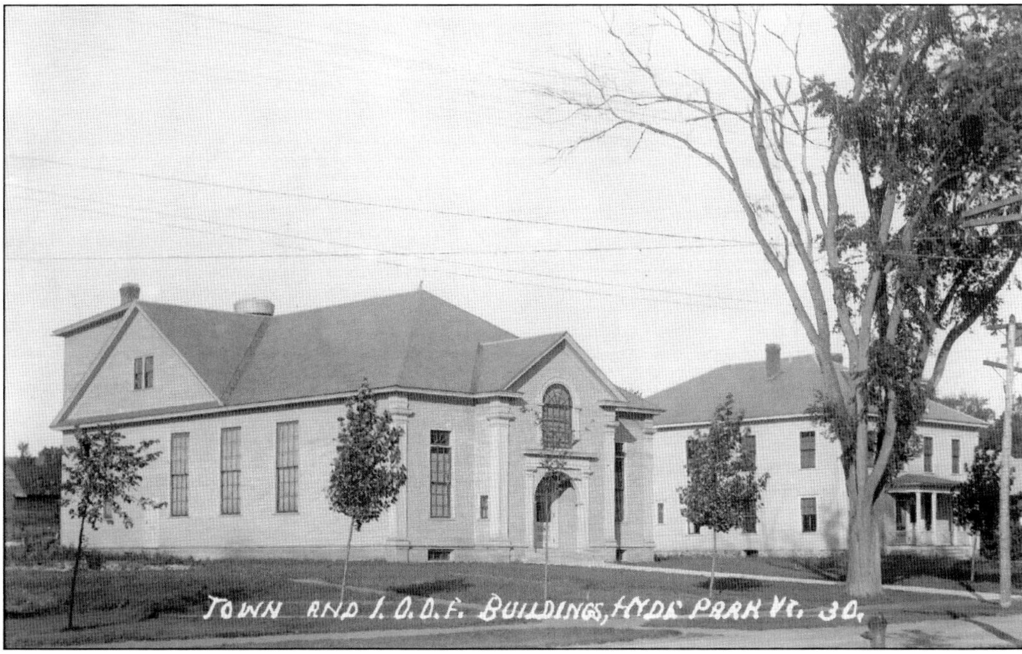

A new town hall was built after the 1910 fire; however, when it was no longer needed as a town hall, it became the home of the Lamoille County Players due to its wonderful structure and acoustics. (Courtesy of Francis Favreau.)

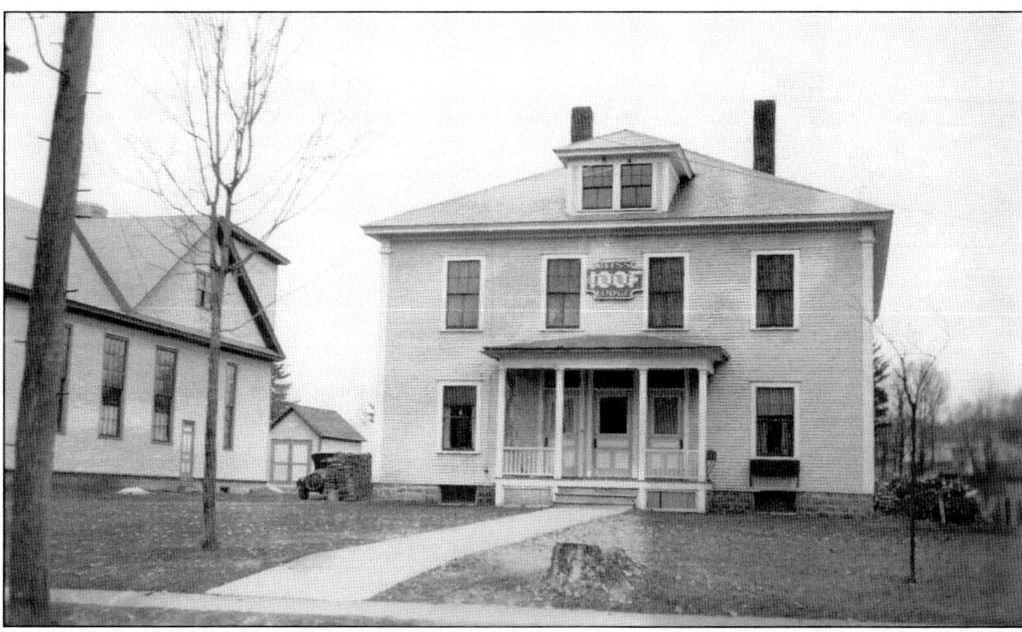

The Independent Order of Odd Fellows (IOOF) building was completed in 1911. The Bliss Lodge, formerly called the Sterling Lodge, was charted on May 29, 1890, and is still an active organization. (Courtesy of the Page/McFarland family.)

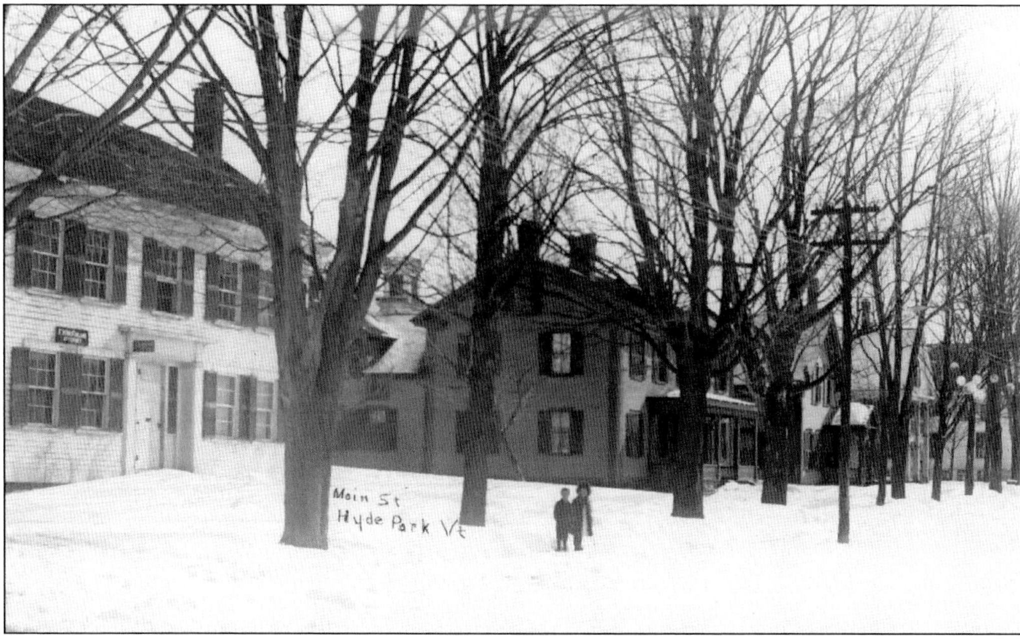

Two young children stand in front of attorney F.H. McFarland's office (located in the building to the far left) during the early winter. (Courtesy of the Page/McFarland family.)

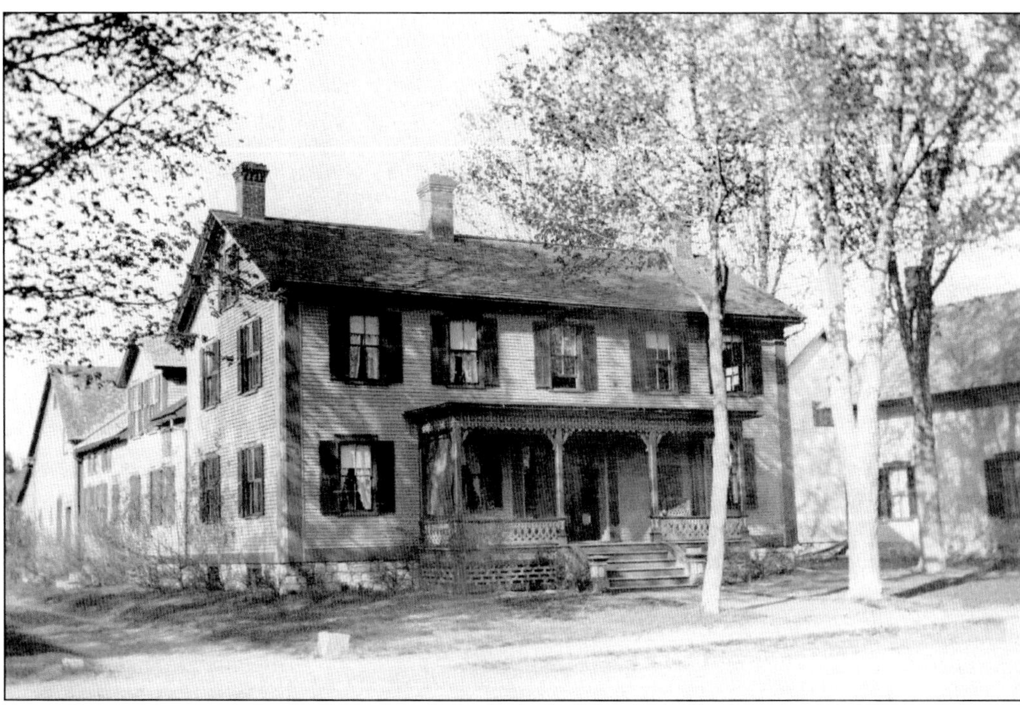

Known as the Grant House, this once large village residence is located on Main Street in Hyde Park. For the past several years, it has been reconstructed for utilization as commercial office space for businesses. (Courtesy of Francis Favreau.)

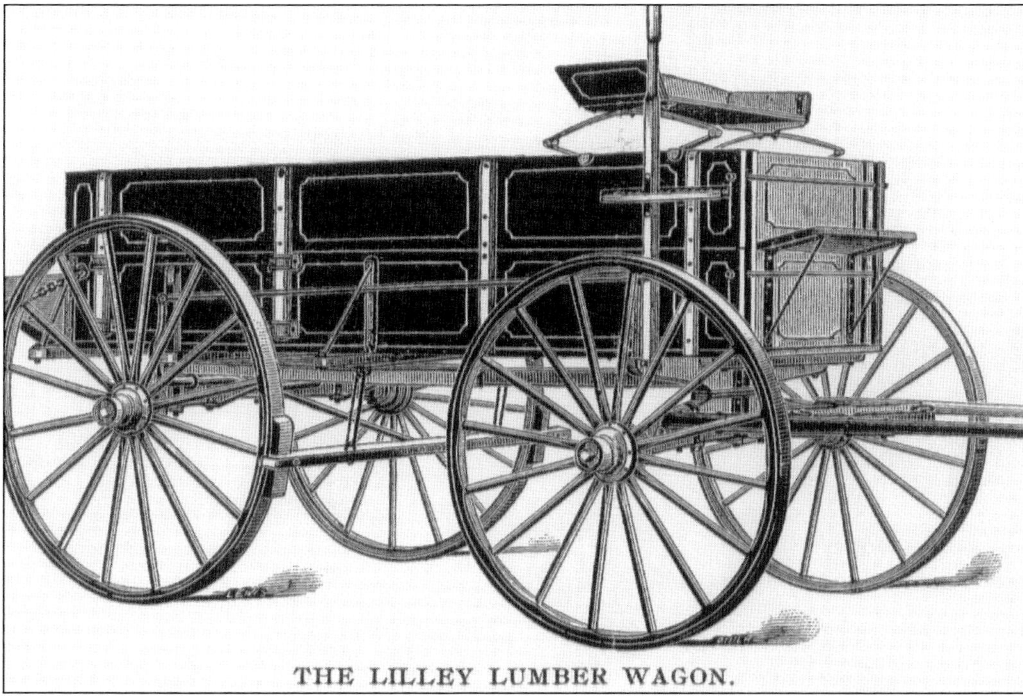

The Lilley Lumber Wagon was made in the shop of the Henry J. Lilley Company, which was building 150 wagons per year at the peak of its business in 1896. (Courtesy of Francis Favreau.)

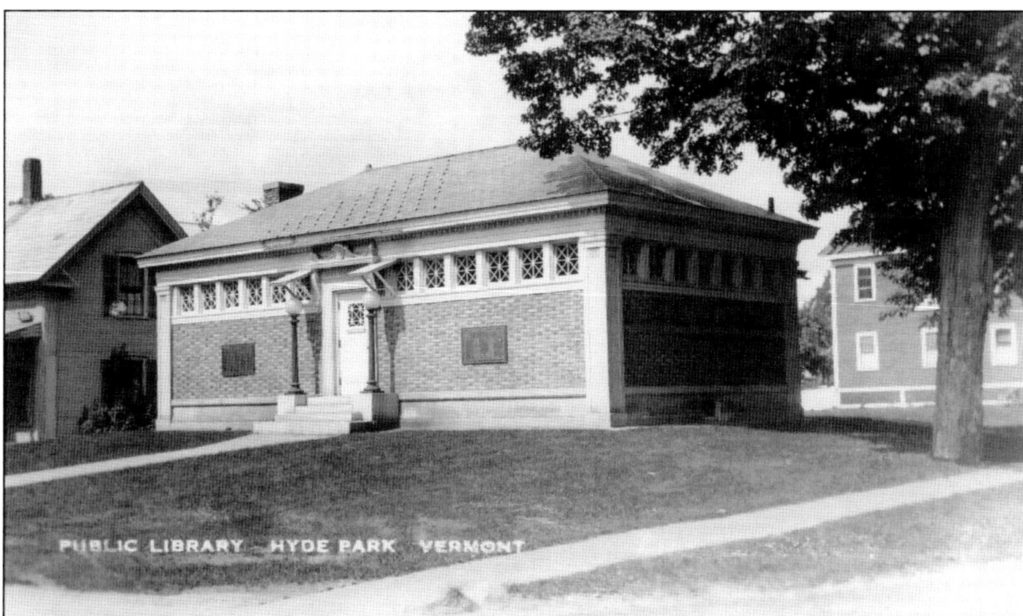

Built in 1916, the Lanpher Memorial Library obtained its name from Loomis H. Lanpher, who willed $5,000 to the town to build the library after his death. (Courtesy of the Page/McFarland family.)

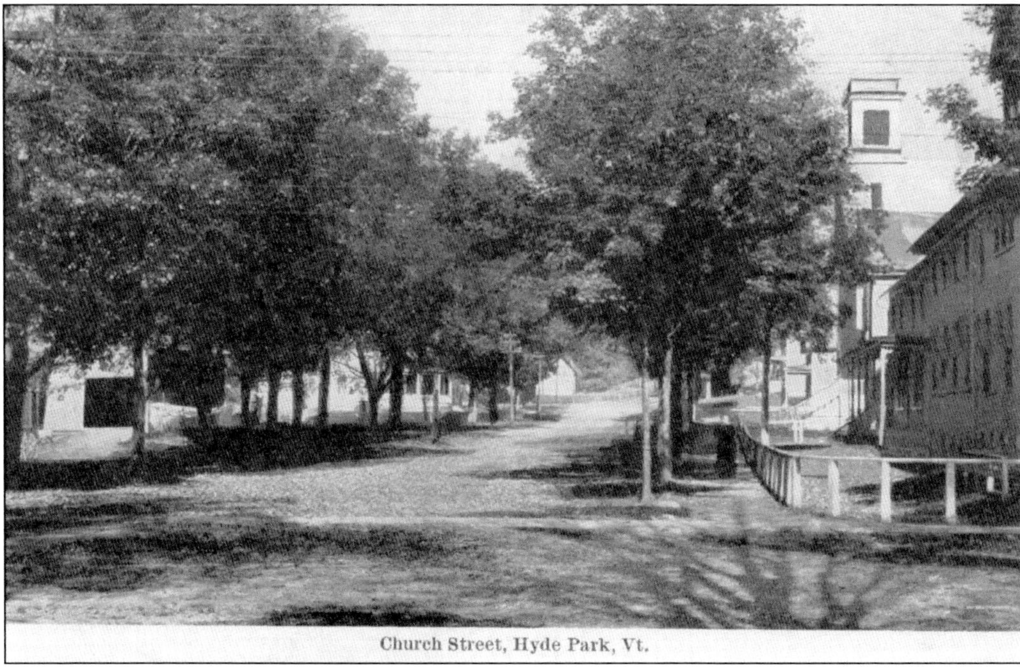

Church Street acquired its name from the Union Church that was built in 1850. The construction of this church was successful due to the hard work of the Hyde Park Union Meeting House Society in 1842. (Courtesy of the Page/McFarland family.)

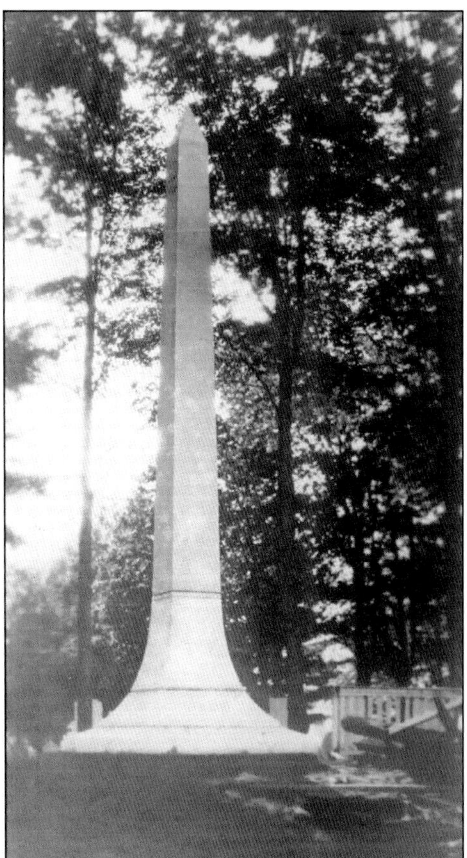

This monument in the Hyde Park Village Cemetery on Church Street honors Governor Page. It is a reminder of the Page family's role in the community and economic development of Hyde Park and the state of Vermont. (Courtesy of the Page/McFarland family.)

Men pose for a photograph on steps of the *News & Citizen* office. H.M. McFarland was a local historian and saw the paper as a valuable source for local history. He gave the Lanpher Memorial Library a bound set of these newspapers dating from 1860 to 1930. (Courtesy of Francis Favreau.)

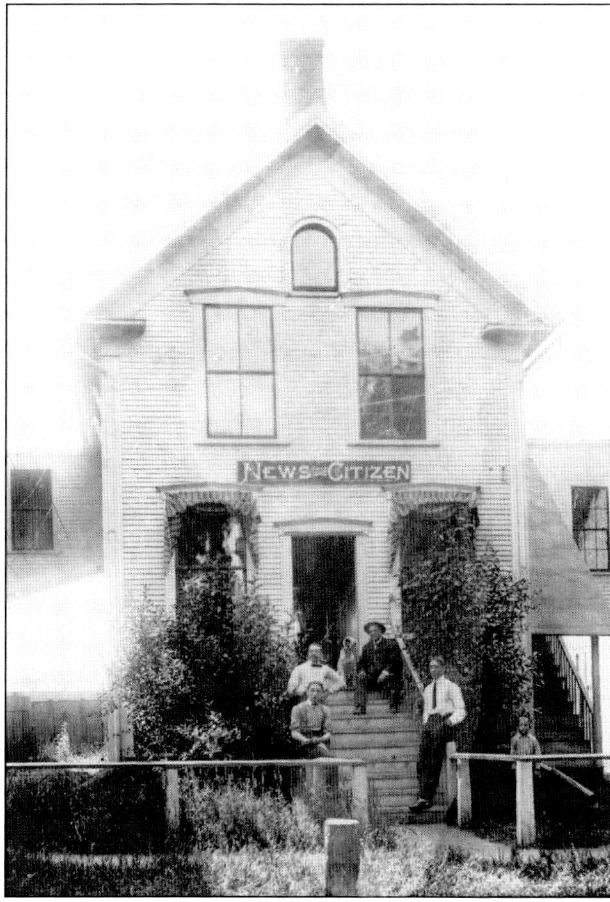

Prior to its location in Morrisville, the *News & Citizen* office was originally located on Church Street in Hyde Park, Two local newspapers, the *Lamoille News* and *Vermont Citizen*, merged together to form the *News & Citizen*. (Courtesy of Linda Jones.)

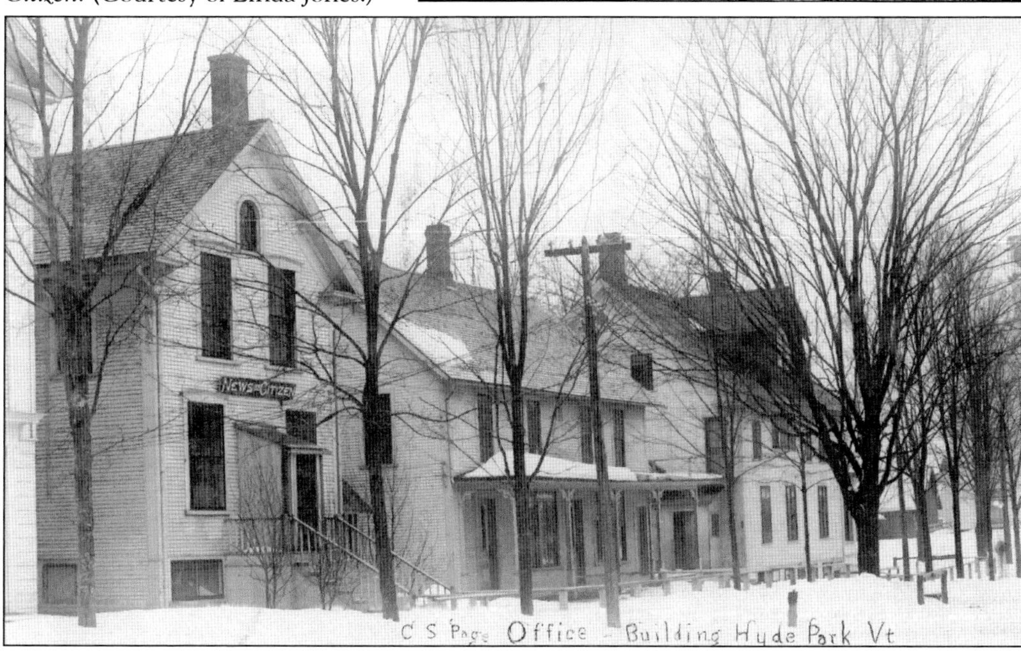

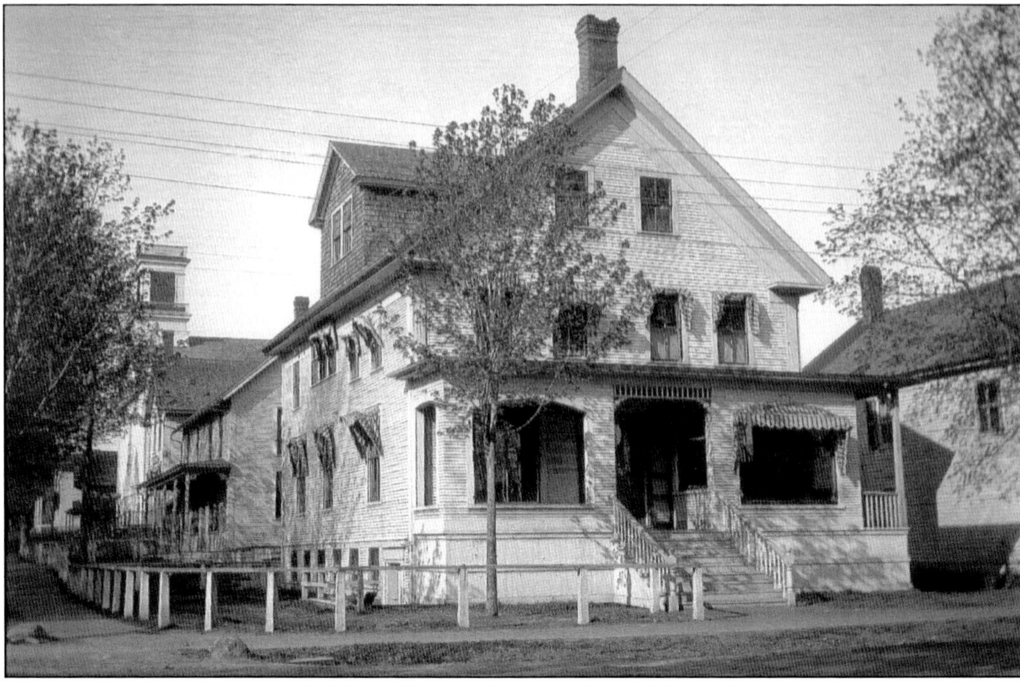

The Page Office building, also known as the Lilley House, was located on the corner of Church and Main Streets. The front part of this building was used for offices that employed up to 25 people. The back part of the building, towards the church, was used for tenants. The front part was later demolished to make room for Fred's Volkswagen Station. (Courtesy of the Page/McFarland family.)

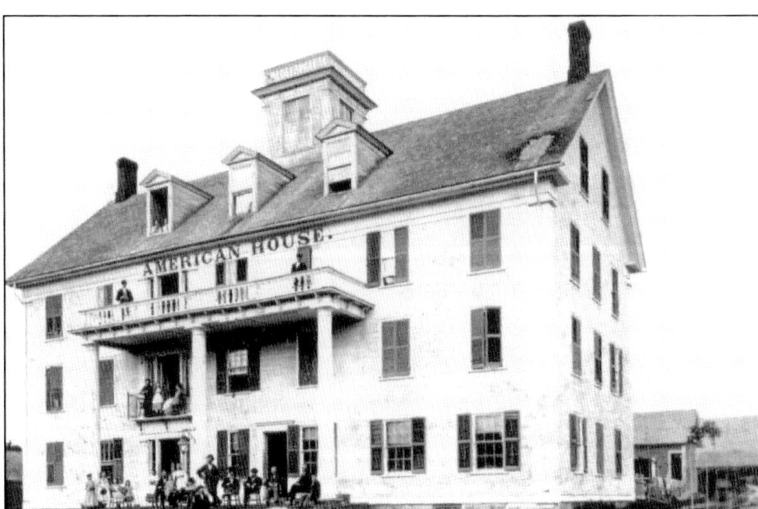

Constructed in 1861, the American House was owned by H.F. Keeler. After being sold and leased several times, the American House was destroyed by fire in 1891. (Courtesy of the Page/McFarland family.)

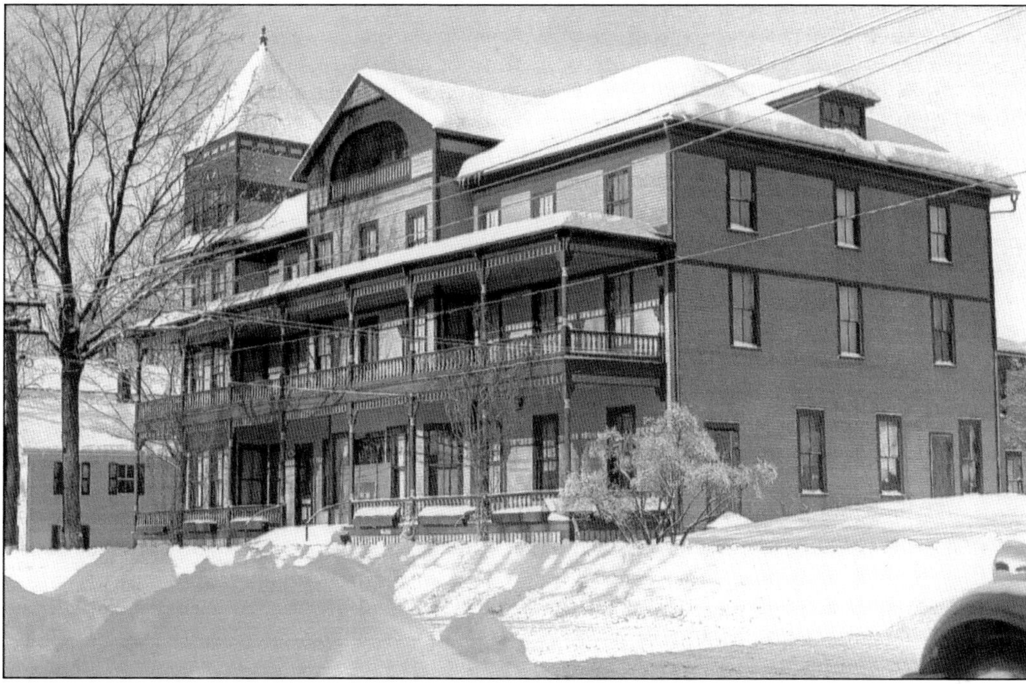

The Hotel Phoenix was built to replace the American House. After its construction, the building was sold to N. Keeler, who later sold it to a proprietor who changed the hotel's name to the Hyde Park Inn. P.H. Edwards Furniture currently occupies this building. (Courtesy of the Page/McFarland family.)

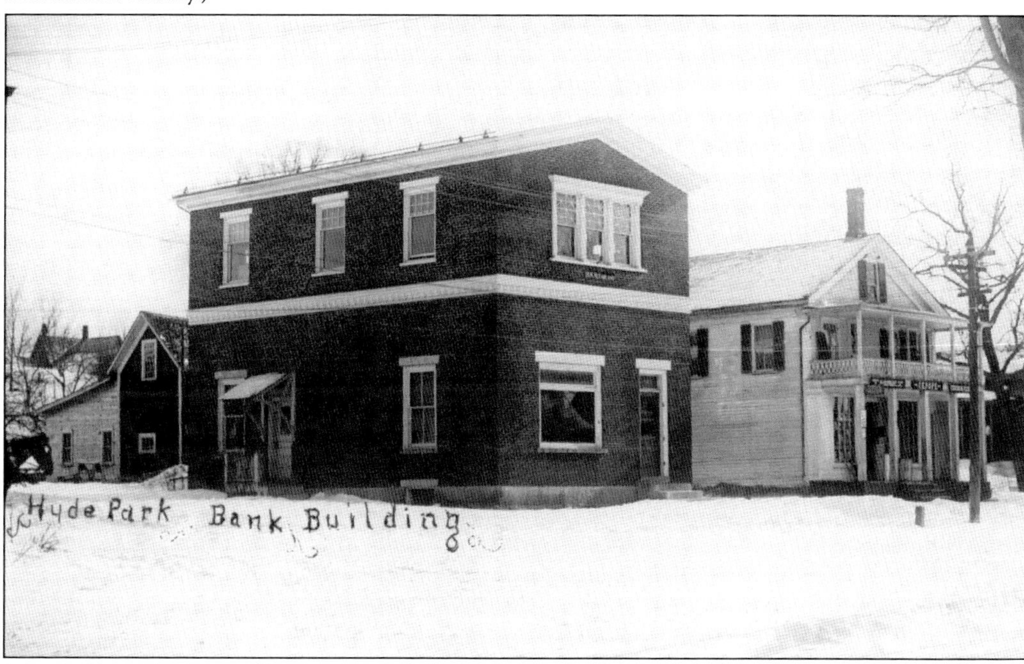

Seen here is the Lamoille County Bank. The name of one of its founders, H.M. McFarland, is displayed on a sign on the front of the bank. The building to the right was known as Sherwin's Drugstore and later became the C.H. Dana Company. (Courtesy of Francis Favreau.)

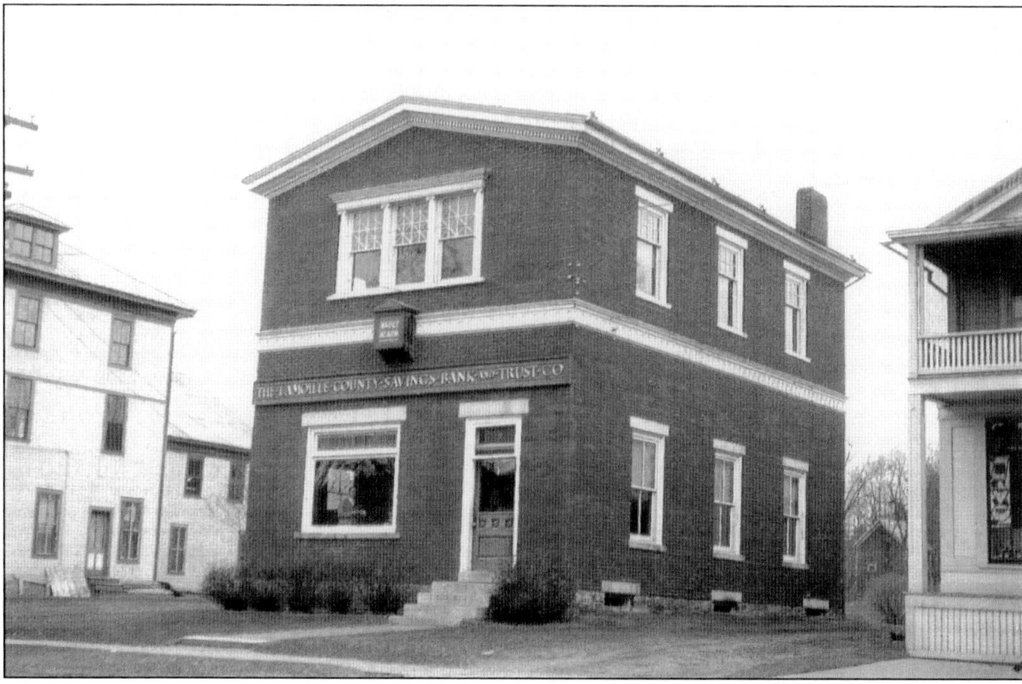

In 1899, the Lamoille County Bank was reorganized by Carroll Smalley Page and named the Lamoille County Savings Bank and Trust Company. The first floor of the building was constructed in 1868, and the second floor was added in 1898. (Courtesy of Francis Favreau.)

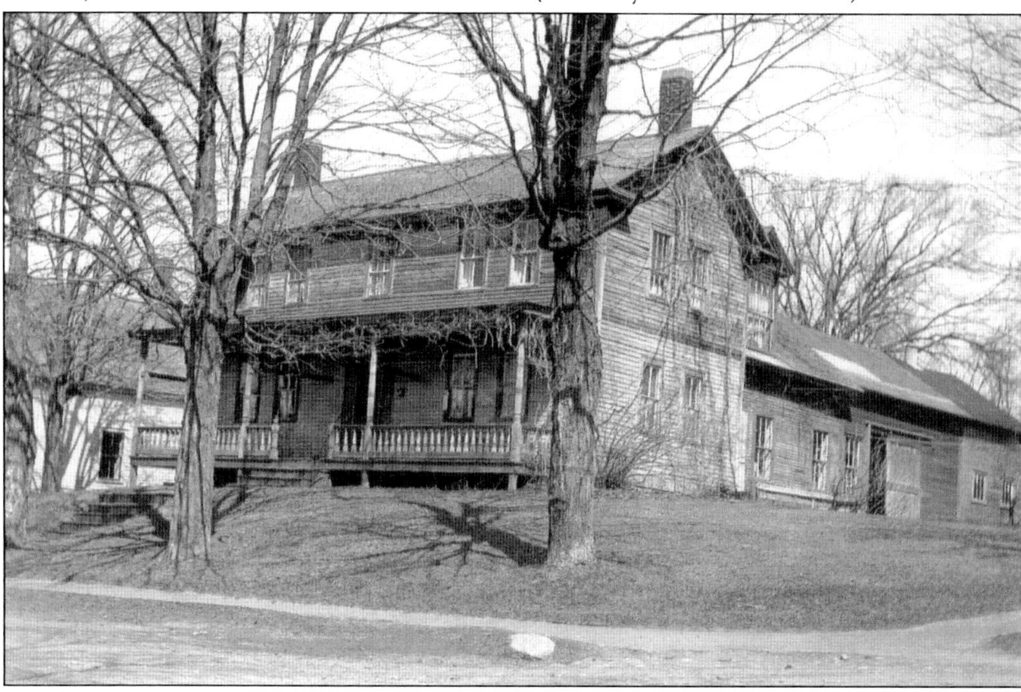

The Colonel Sawyer house is located on the west corner of Eden and Main Streets. The oldest home in Hyde Park Village, it is currently owned by Girdon Deuso. (Courtesy of the Page/McFarland family.)

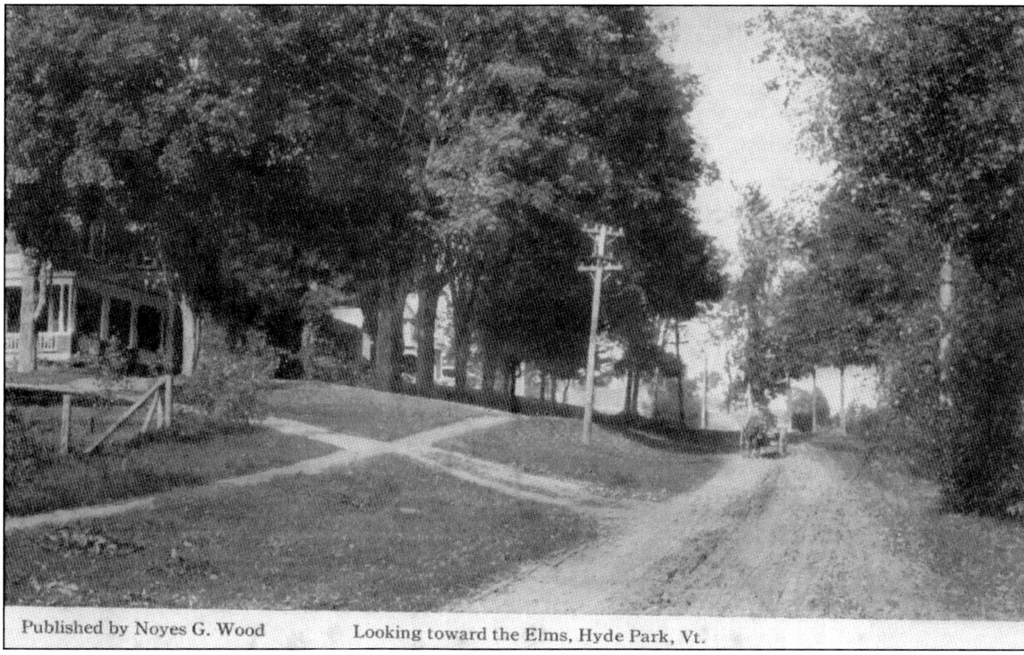

In this view looking north on Eden Street, one can see a horse and buggy coming into town. In years past, Eden Street going north led up Fitch Hill, which continued on as the main road to the North Village. (Courtesy of Francis Favreau.)

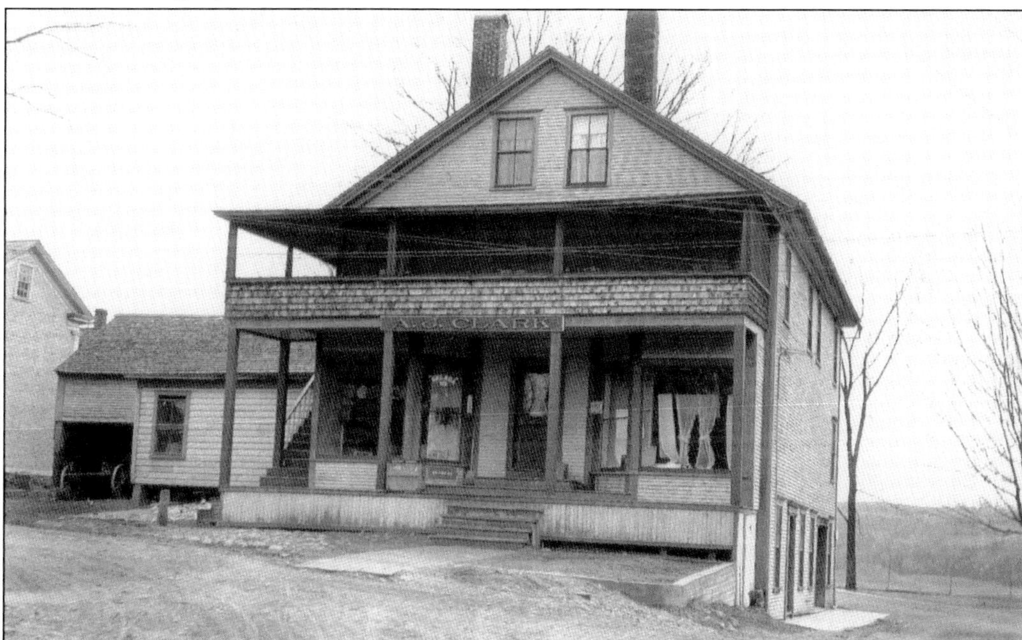

This photograph of A.J. Clark's store, located on the east corner of Eden and Main Streets, was taken across the road from the Sawyer house. The Noyes family erected this corner building in 1840, with their home adjacent to the corner business. Due to the heavy flow of traffic coming through town, the Village of Hyde Park decided to purchase and then tear down the corner building as it proved to be a traffic hazard. (Courtesy of the Page/McFarland family.)

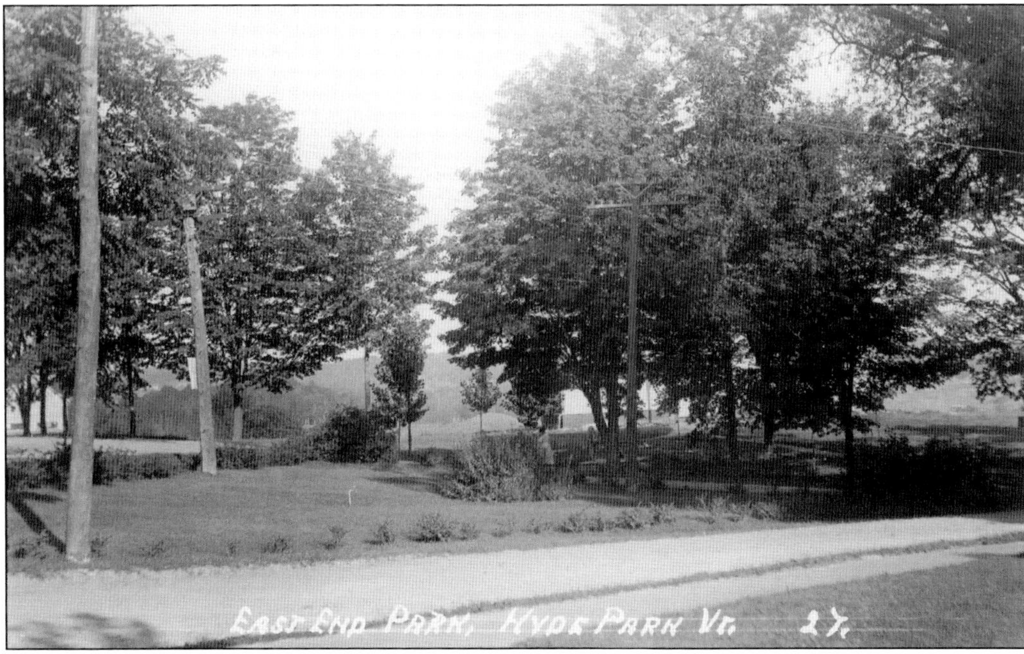

East End Park is pictured from in front of LCA, where the roads fork. Like many parks, this small park served as both a place for families to gather and as a refuge for a quiet stroll. (Courtesy of Francis Favreau.)

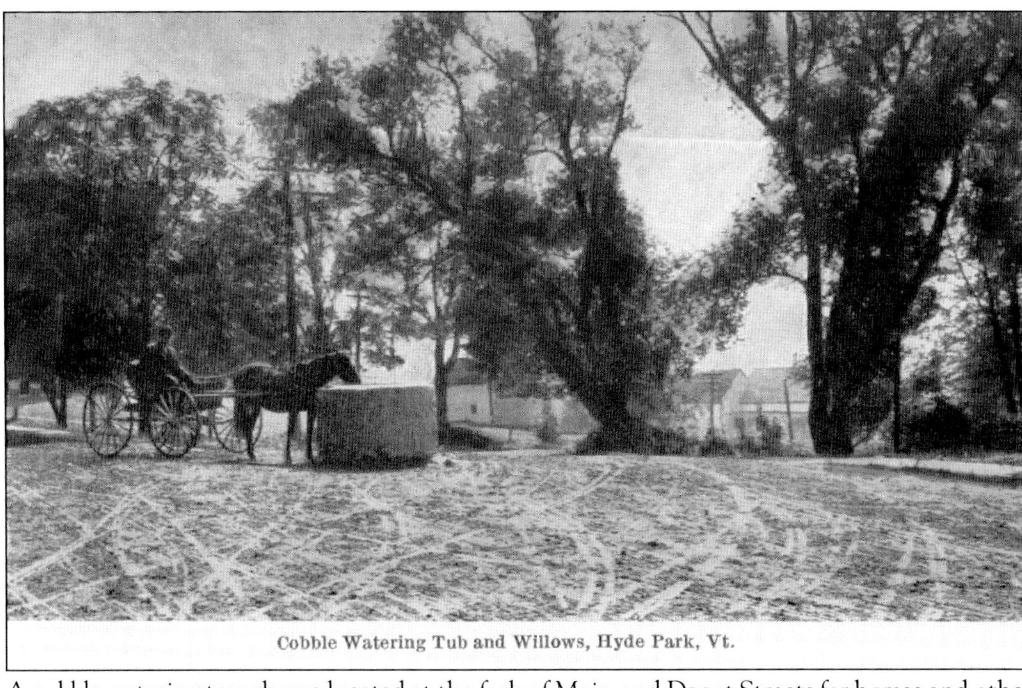

Cobble Watering Tub and Willows, Hyde Park, Vt.

A cobble watering trough was located at the fork of Main and Depot Streets for horses and other livestock coming through town. Albert Heath was one of the men who helped build the watering trough. (Courtesy of the Heath/Savage family.)

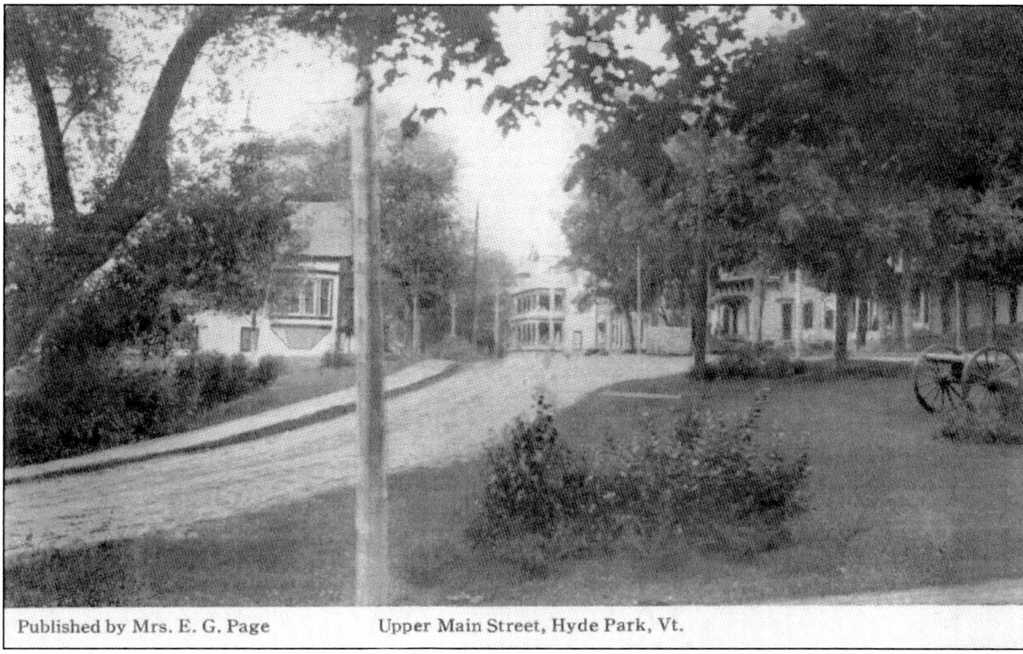

In this view looking down Depot Street, East End Park is on the left. A cannon that was used in the Civil War is on display. When viewing this photograph, one cannot help but wonder what happened to this cannon when it was removed. (Courtesy of Francis Favreau.)

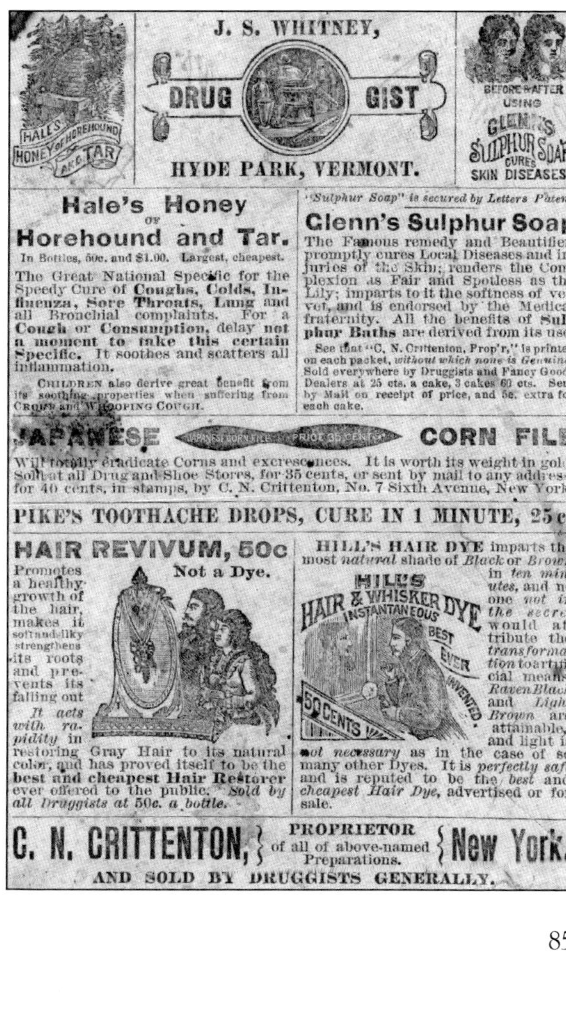

Seen here is an ad for druggist J.S. Whitney, who operated a business in Hyde Park Village in the early 1900s. Ads of this nature were commonly used during this time period to promote business. (Courtesy of Linda Jones.)

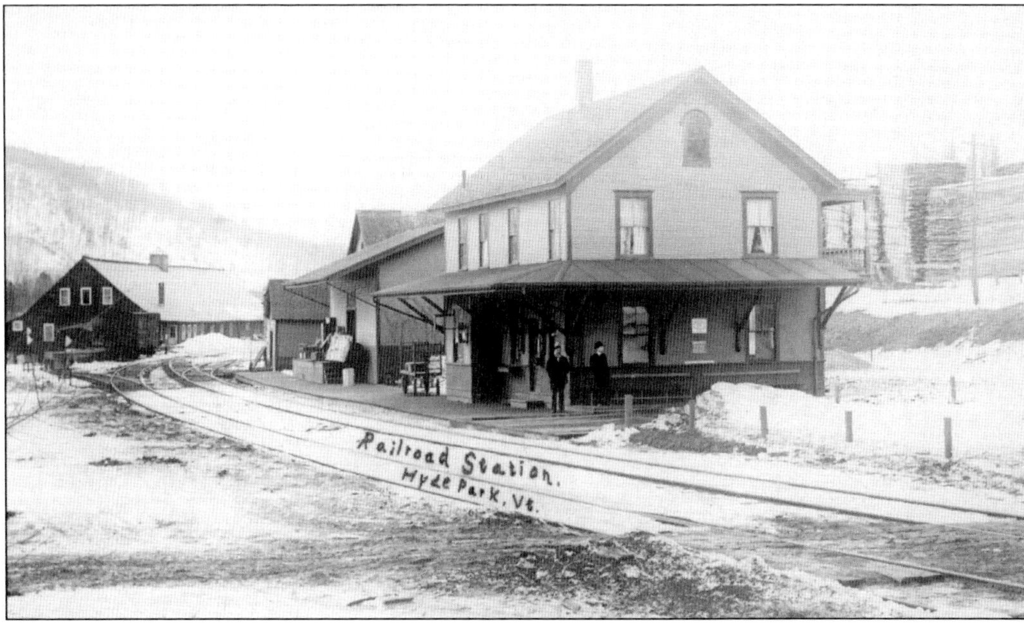

Seen here is an image of the railroad station located on Depot Street in Hyde Park. The station in this image actually stood on the other side of the tracks. It was moved to its present location for safety and the ease of loading goods onto the train, as the businesses were also located on this side of the tracks. (Courtesy of Francis Favreau.)

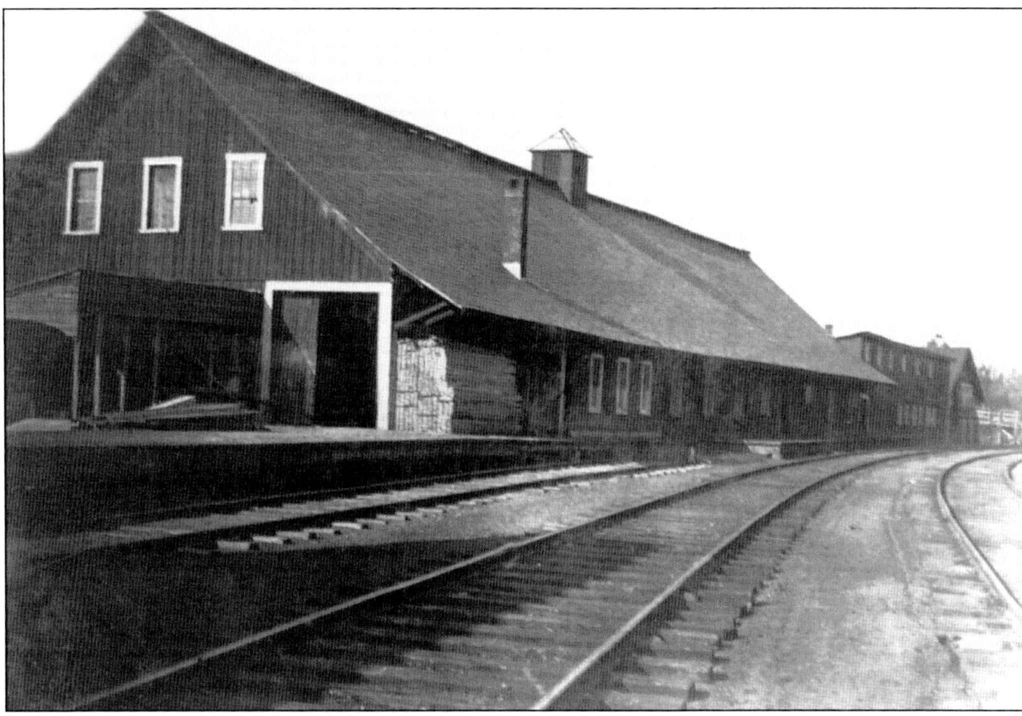

C.S. Page's calfskin plant was located next to railroad tracks—a great location for his business to ship goods out to various parts of the country. At the peak of its operation, the plant building covered two acres. (Courtesy of Francis Favreau.)

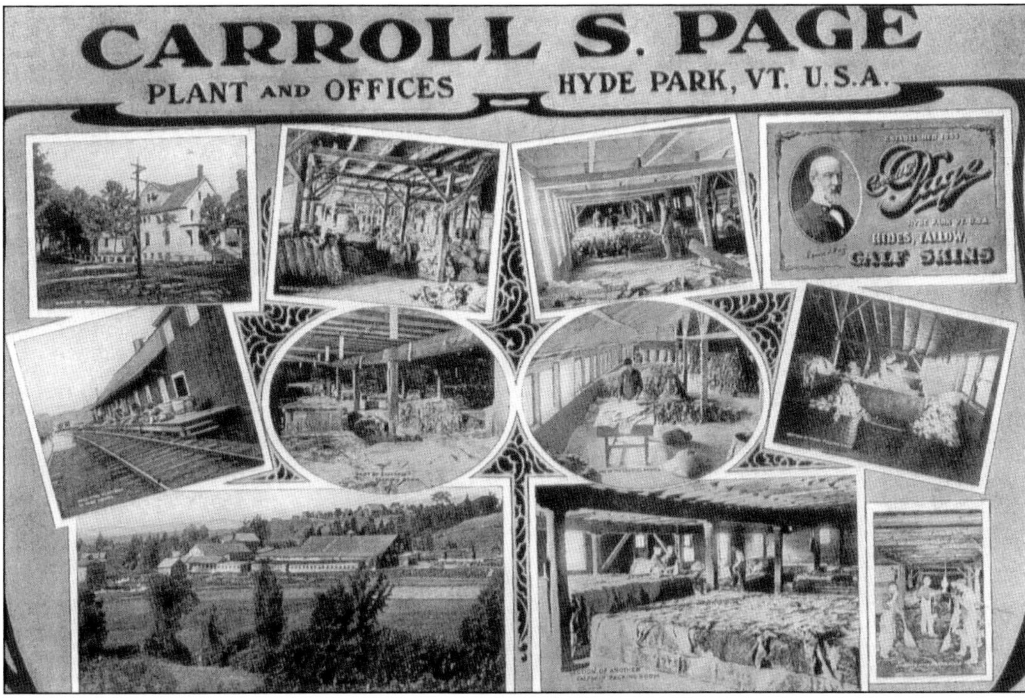

This C.S. Page advertisement is rather unique as it shows the many different processing areas inside the plant, a panoramic view of the plant, and a photograph of Carroll Smalley Page in the upper right-hand corner. (Courtesy of Francis Favreau.)

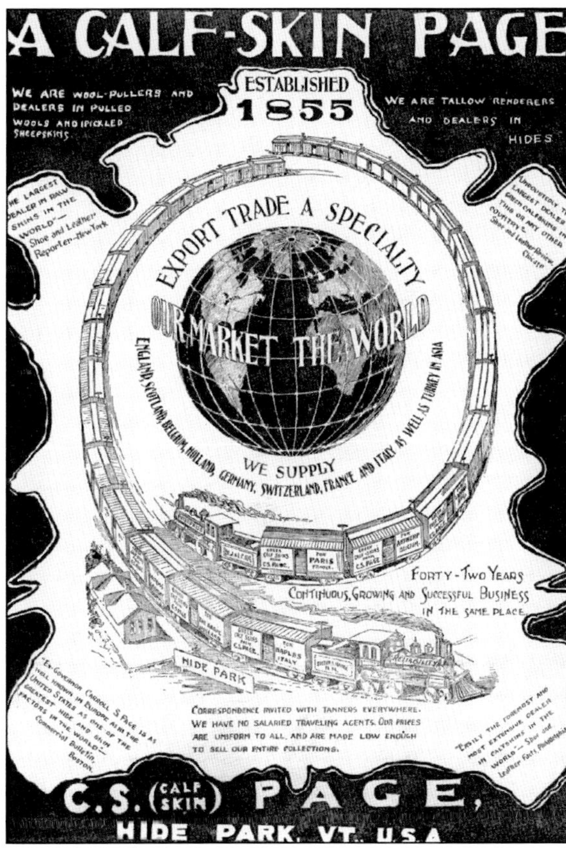

This C.S. Page advertisement shows when the hide plant was established and how it exported its goods worldwide. It is evident that this card was printed in 1897 because it proudly says that it has been in business for 42 years. (Courtesy of Francis Favreau.)

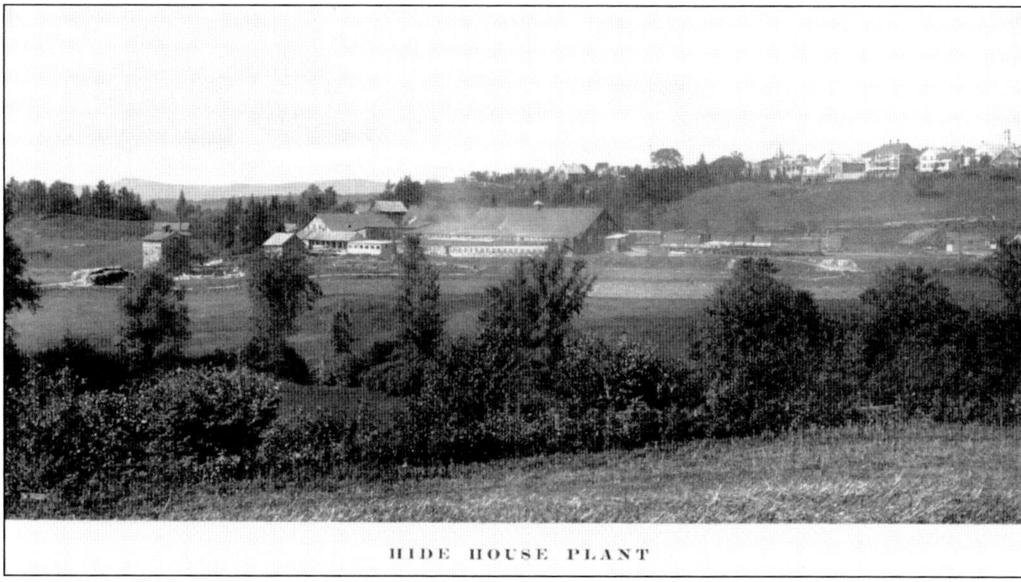

Seen here is a broad view of the C.S. Page hide plant, with Hyde Park Village in the background. Looking closely, one can see Governor Page's mansion on the hill that rises behind the plant. (Courtesy of Francis Favreau.)

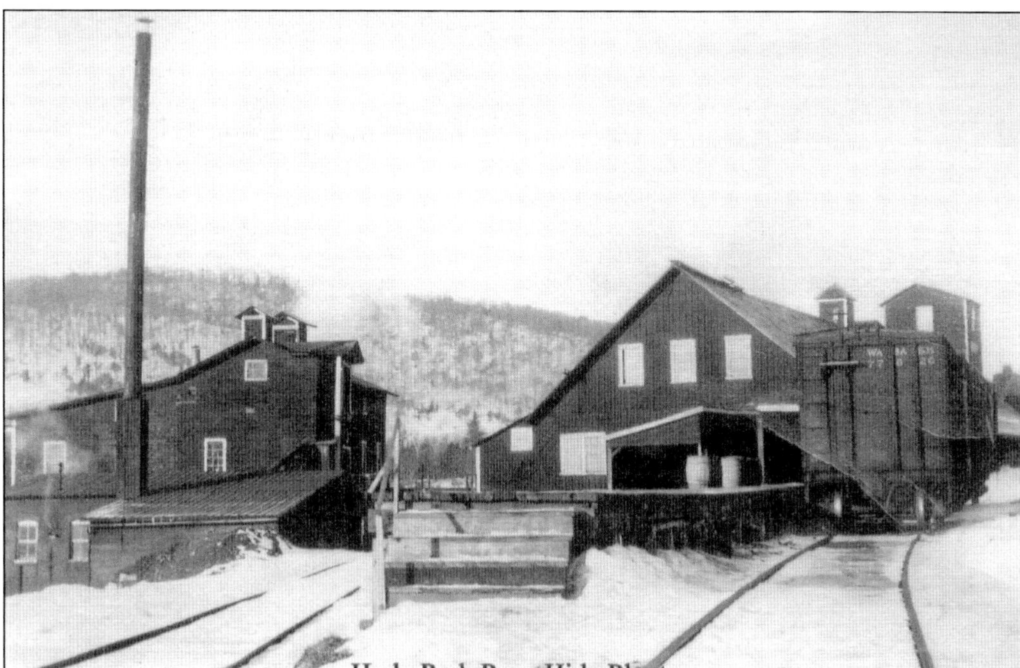

This is a great shot of the hide plant at its location next to the railroad tracks. Notice how the railroad track divides to both sides of the loading dock and building: This made loading and shipping much easier by accessing the train bed from both sides. (Courtesy of Francis Favreau.)

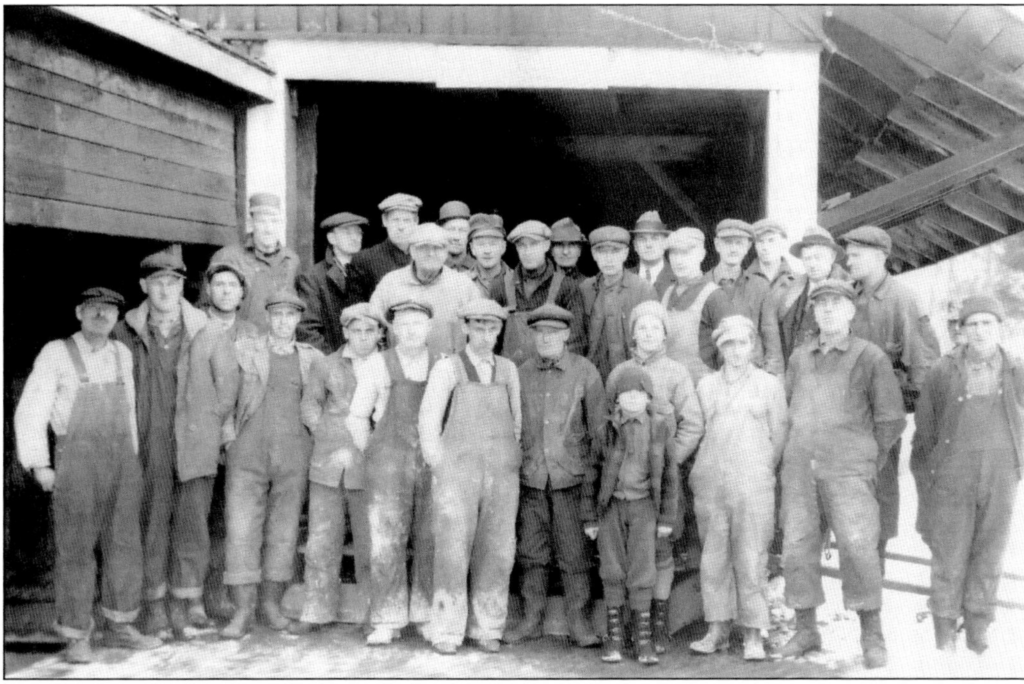

Workers at the C.S. Page hide plant pose on their last day of work around 1926. (Courtesy of Francis Favreau.)

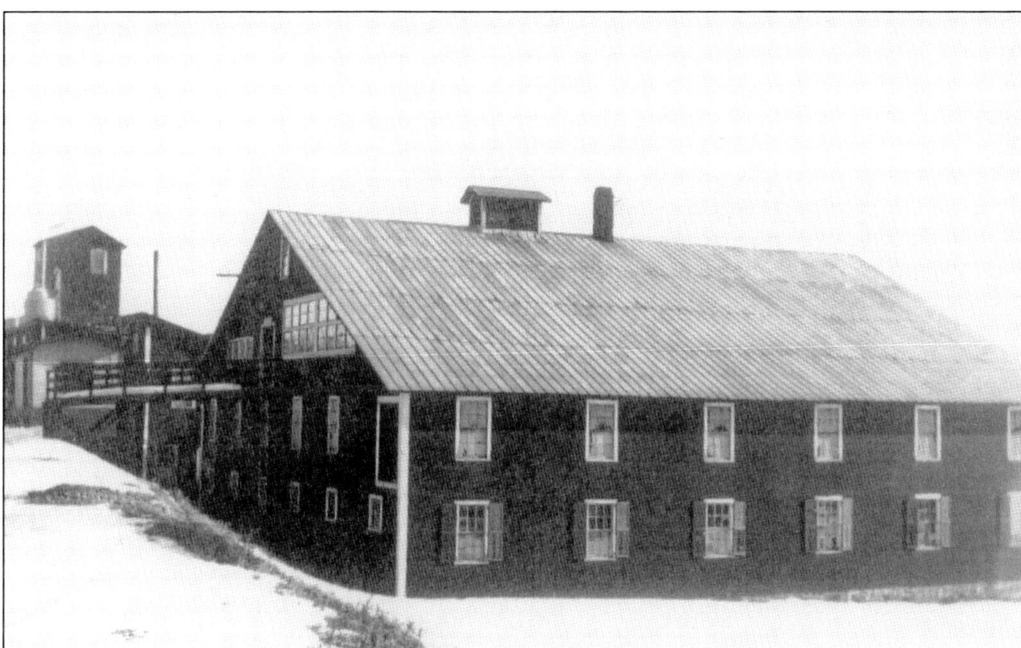

Shown here is the C.S. Page wool processing plant that sat beside the railroad tracks in Hyde Park. This business shipped 30 distinct selections of wool to Boston. (Courtesy of Francis Favreau.)

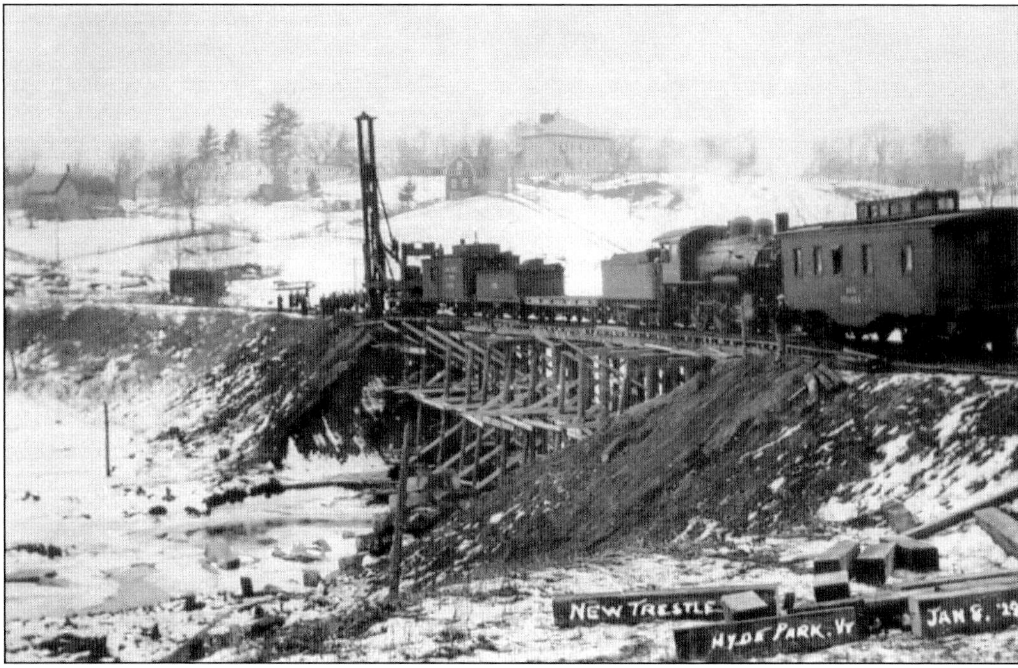

The railroad was incredibly important in the transportation of goods and passengers for long distances before the roads in Vermont were fully developed. Located southeast of Hyde Park Village, this railroad trestle was destroyed in the flood of 1927 and is seen here being rebuilt in 1929. (Courtesy of the Page/McFarland family.)

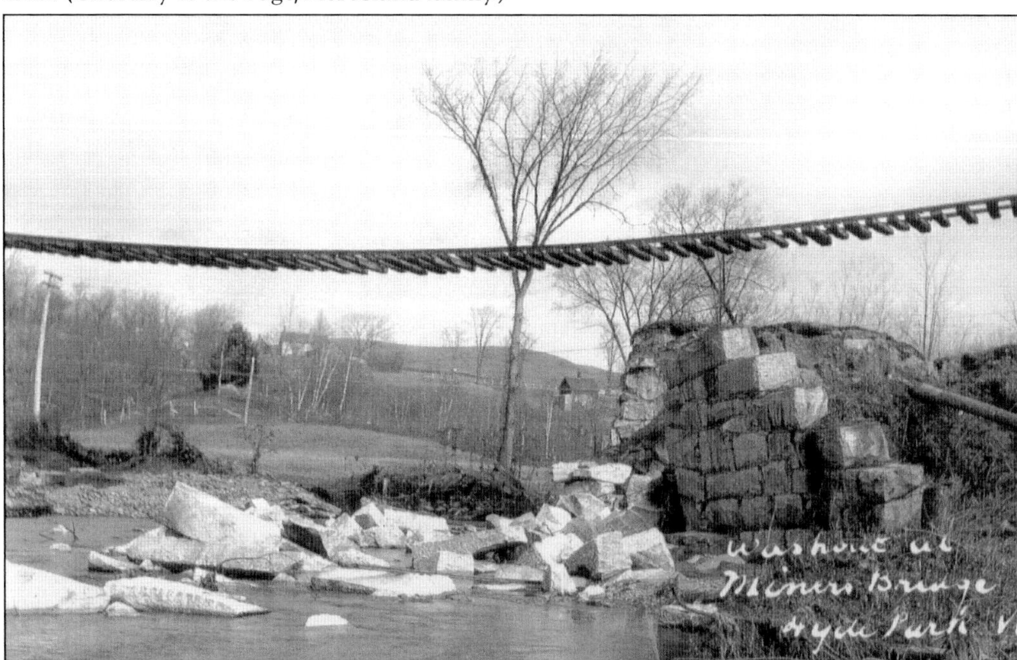

This suspended railroad track at Miner's Bridge had its supports washed out in the flood of 1927. Scenes like this were typical around the state. (Courtesy of Francis Favreau.)

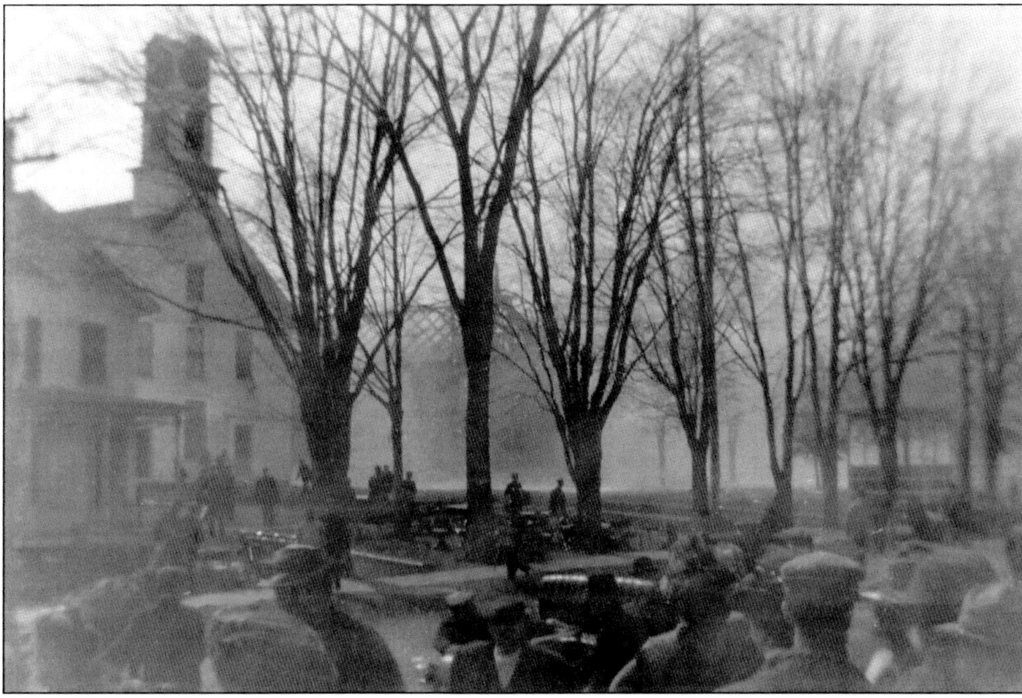

A crowd gathers to see what was still standing after the massive fire that consumed many buildings and homes on Sunday, April 17, 1910. The fire started when two inmates in the sheriff's office built a fire in the stove. The stovepipe became too hot and set the building on fire. The wind, being very strong that day, fanned the sparks and embers onto the adjacent buildings as it grew out of control. (Courtesy of the Page/McFarland family.)

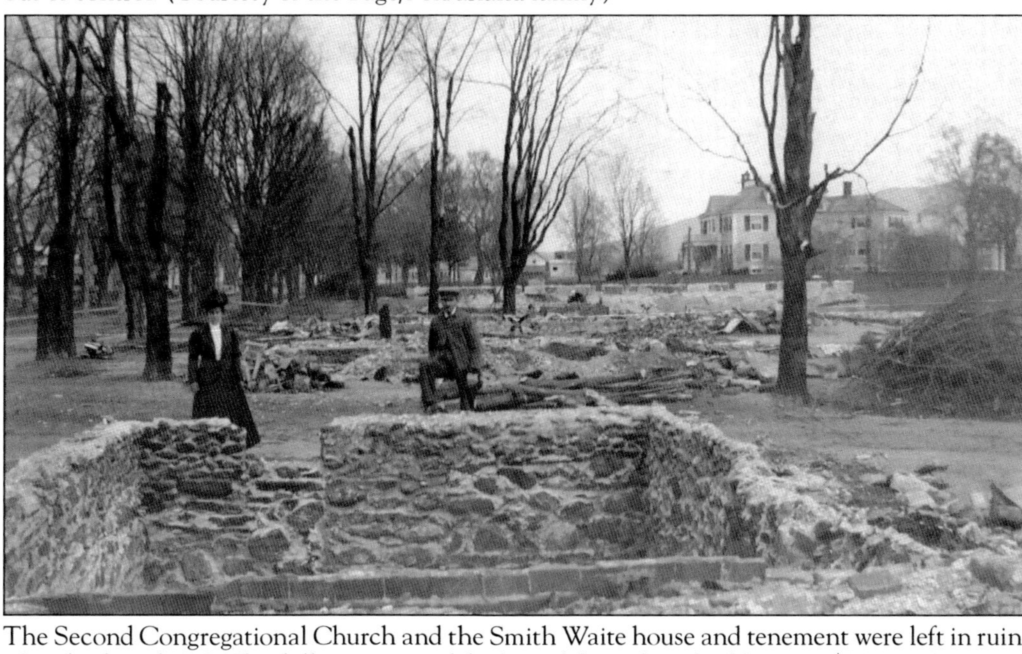

The Second Congregational Church and the Smith Waite house and tenement were left in ruins after the fire of 1910. The dollar amount of the loss of these three building was $20,000. (Courtesy of the Page/McFarland family.)

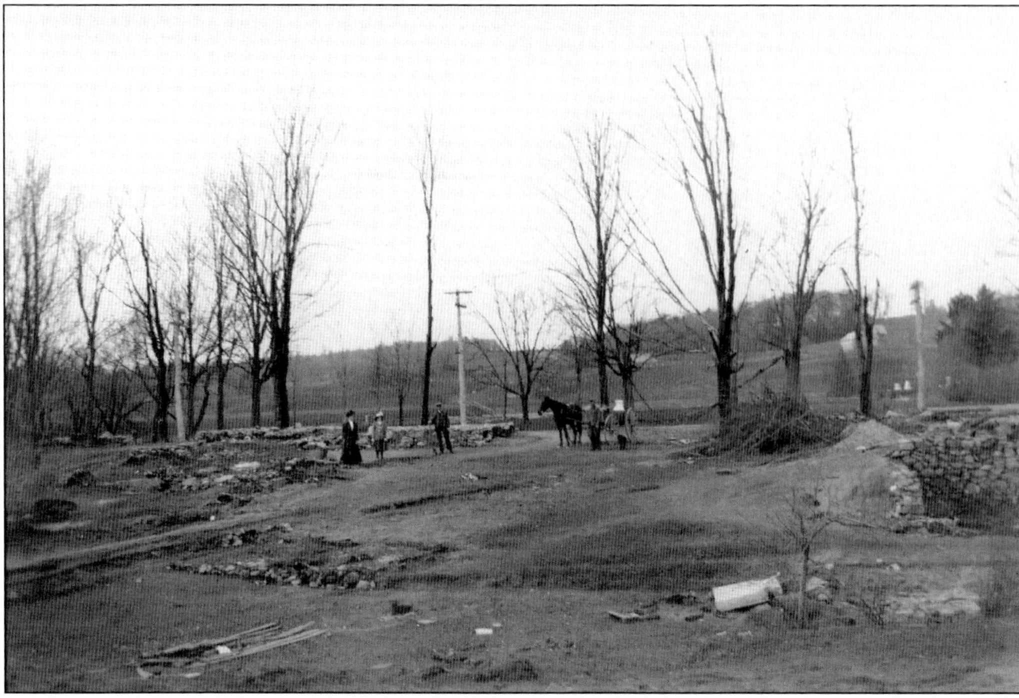

The fire of 1910 left parts of the western end of town, near the Second Congregational Church, in ruins. To the right of the telephone poles in this photograph is the Hyde Park Village Cemetery. (Courtesy of the Page/McFarland family.)

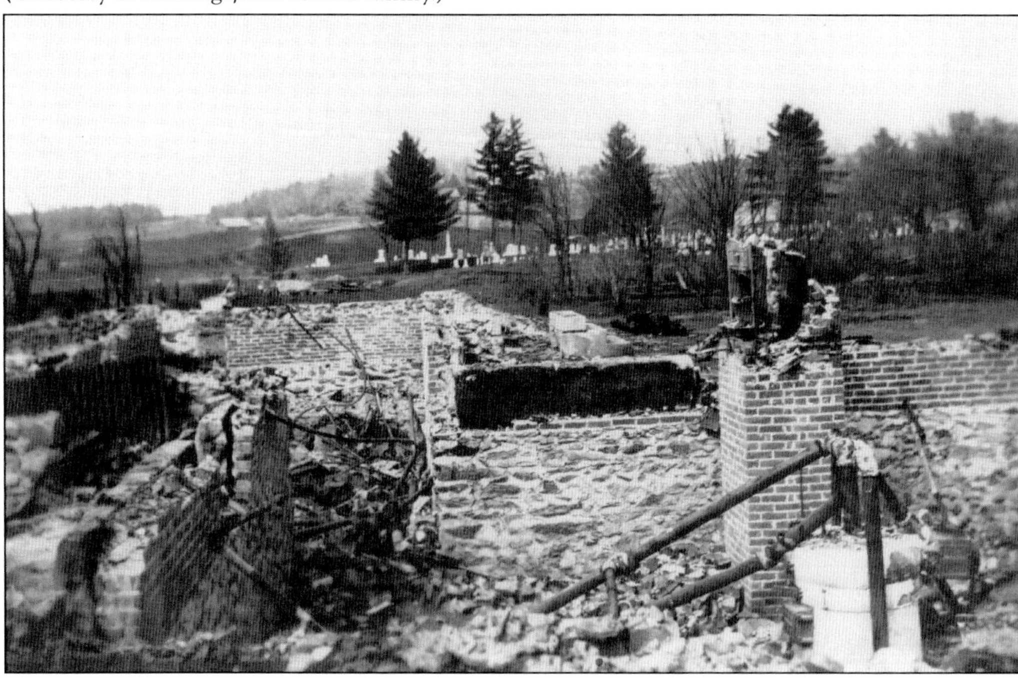

Seen here are the ruins of the McFarland residence. McFarland was known for his home, which was one of the more elaborate structures in town. Notice the Hyde Park Village cemetery in the background. (Courtesy of the Page/McFarland family.)

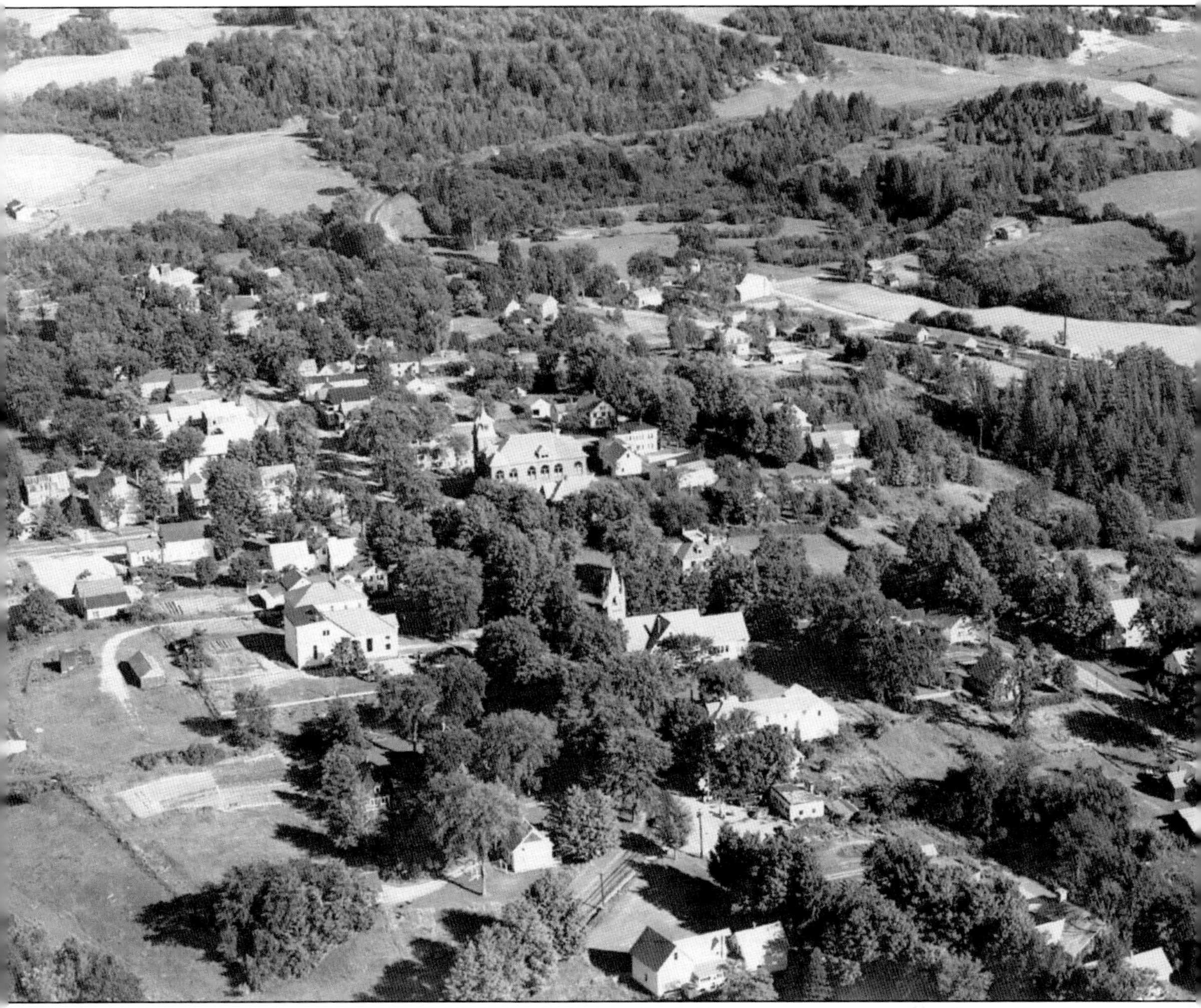

This westerly aerial view of Hyde Park Village shows the village in its entirety. Looking closely, one can see the courthouse, school, church, and businesses that make up the community of Hyde Park Village. Notice the train station in the upper right-hand portion of this image. (Courtesy of Francis Favreau.)

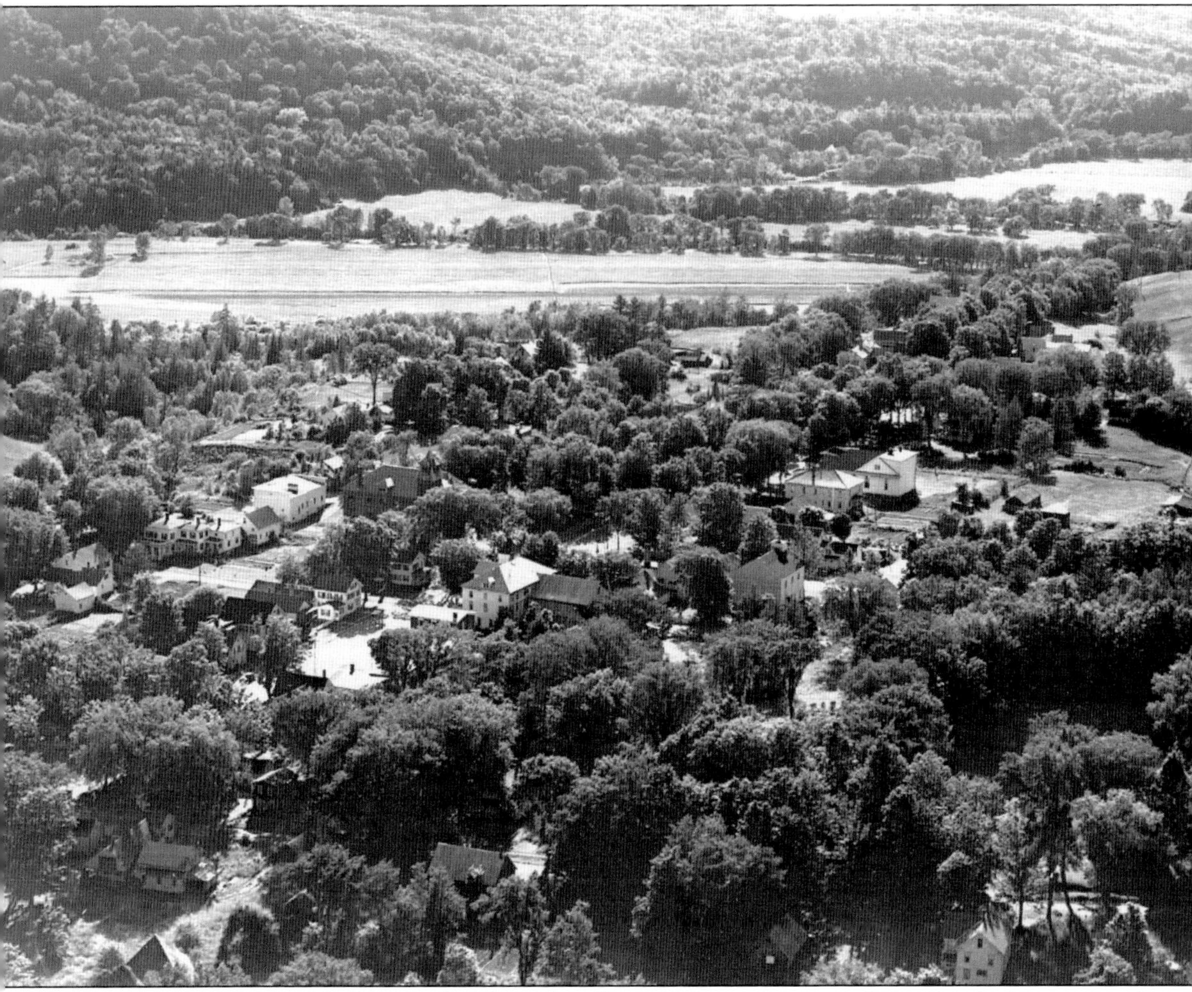

Shown here is an aerial view of Hyde Park Village, looking east toward Ten Bends. (Courtesy of Francis Favreau.)

Three

Rural Hyde Park

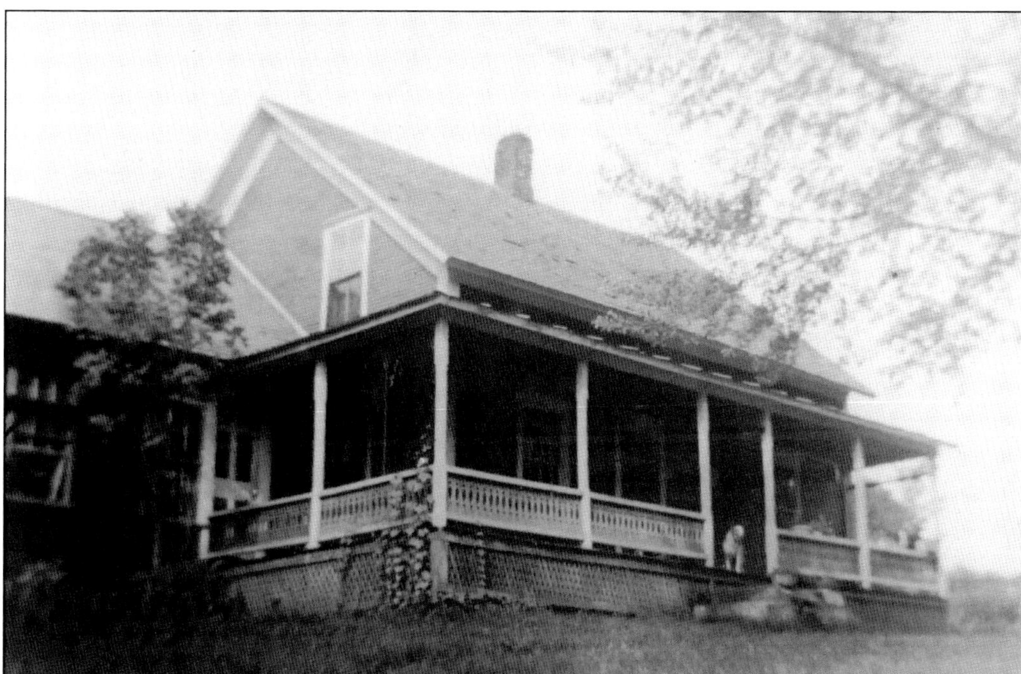

Gil and Maude (Parrin) Hogaboom lived in this home on Thompson Hill. It was originally owned by Jonas and Rosalba (Robinson) Thompson of Williston, Vermont, who came to live there in 1860. (Courtesy of Loren and Jeanne Aither.)

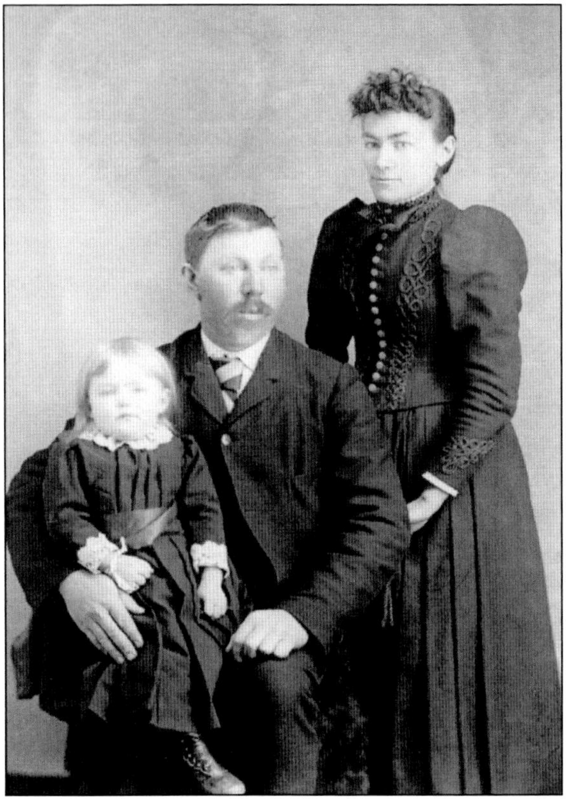

Seen here, from left to right, are Ethel Thompson, her father, John Thompson, and her mother, Ellen "Nellie" (Smith) Thompson. John, the son of Jonas and Rosalba Thompson, continued to farm on Thompson Hill well into his 80s, when his son Guy Thompson took over the farm in the 1940s. John was well known for his trained oxen, which no one else could get to move out of their tracks. Nellie was a teacher at the McKinstry Schoolhouse. (Courtesy of the Heath/Savage family.)

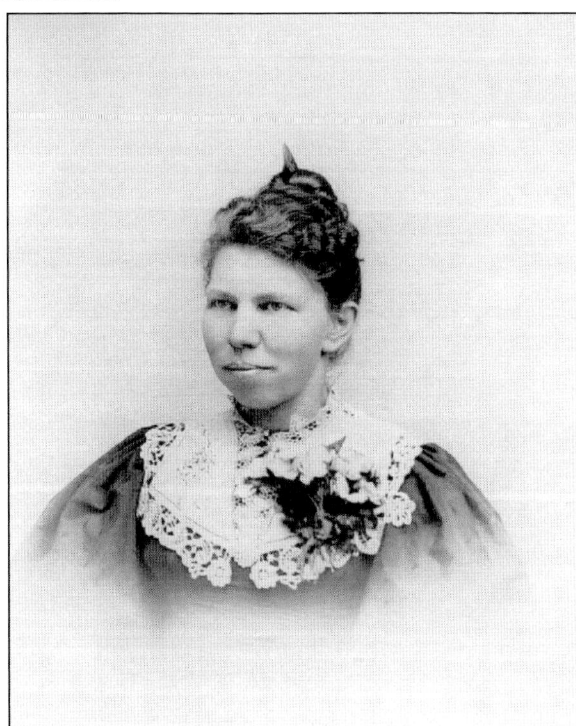

Martha A. Thompson, the daughter of Jonas and Rosalba Thompson, graduated in 1879 with a teaching degree from the Johnson Normal School. She taught at local schools in Lamoille County and in Sac City, Iowa. Thompson moved to Oakland, California, and became the owner of Occidental Publishing. She lectured extensively on women's rights in Vermont, Massachusetts, and New York during her visits to the East Coast. (Courtesy of the Heath/Savage family.)

Located on Thompson Hill, Thompson Falls was a favorite spot for many fishermen, both young and old. These natural falls are a part of Beaver Meadow Brook, which is named after the water source of the three beaver dams that feed into it. (Courtesy of the Heath/Savage family.)

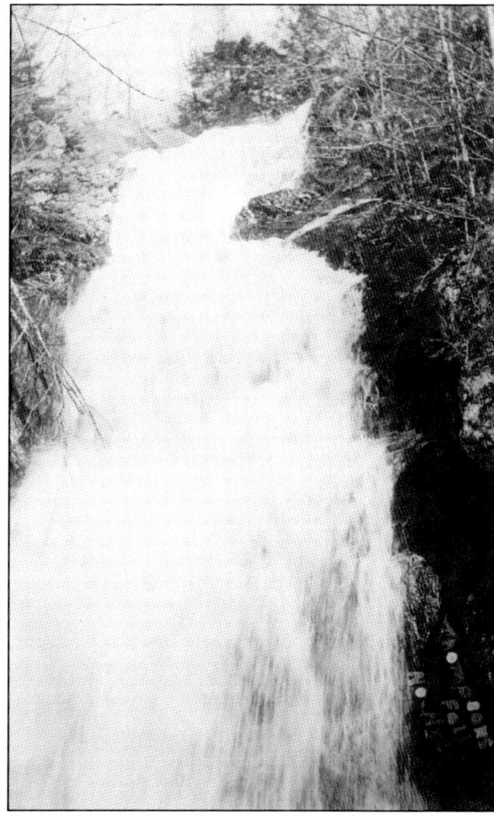

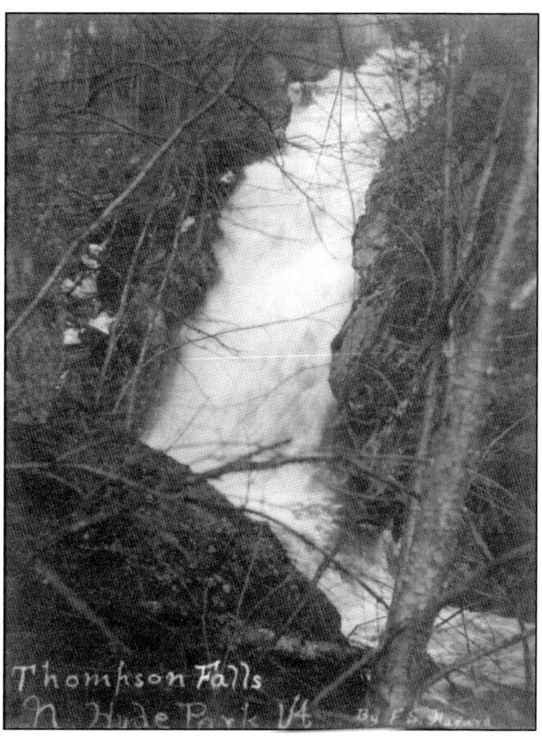

The history of Thompson Falls comes from the Thompson family, who settled in this area. John Thompson, who grew up where Irene Morin now lives, owned and operated a water-powered sawmill across the road from his house. A dam was built above the mill to maintain a water supply to power the mill. Remnants of this dam still exist today on property owned by his great-granddaughter Monica Heath. (Courtesy of the Heath/Savage family.)

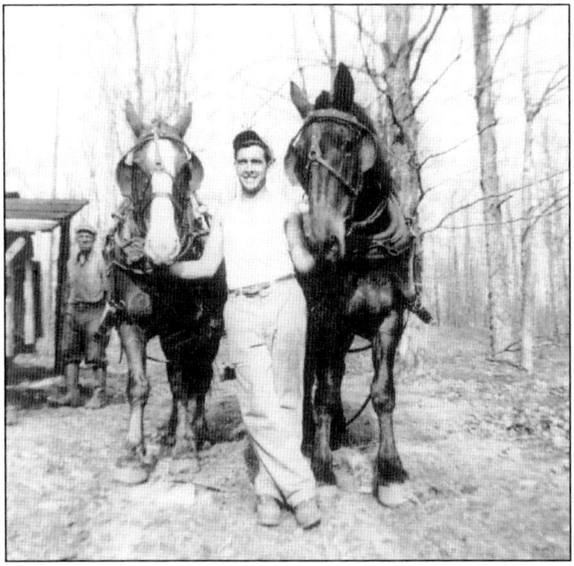

Sugaring in the early days was a little different than it is today. Drilling holes in the trees by hand, tapping in the spouts, hanging the buckets, and, on the days the sap ran, snowshoeing to each tree to empty the buckets into the gathering tanks was comparatively harder than running lines that let the sap flow to the tanks, as is the practice today. It required a lot of physical stamina and strength to sugar. Here, Elliott Savage works with his father-in-law Ralph Thompson's team of horses in 1948, with Ralph in the background. Teams of horses were often used to pull the gathering tanks to the sugarhouse so their contents could be dumped into the holding tanks. (Courtesy of the Heath/Savage family.)

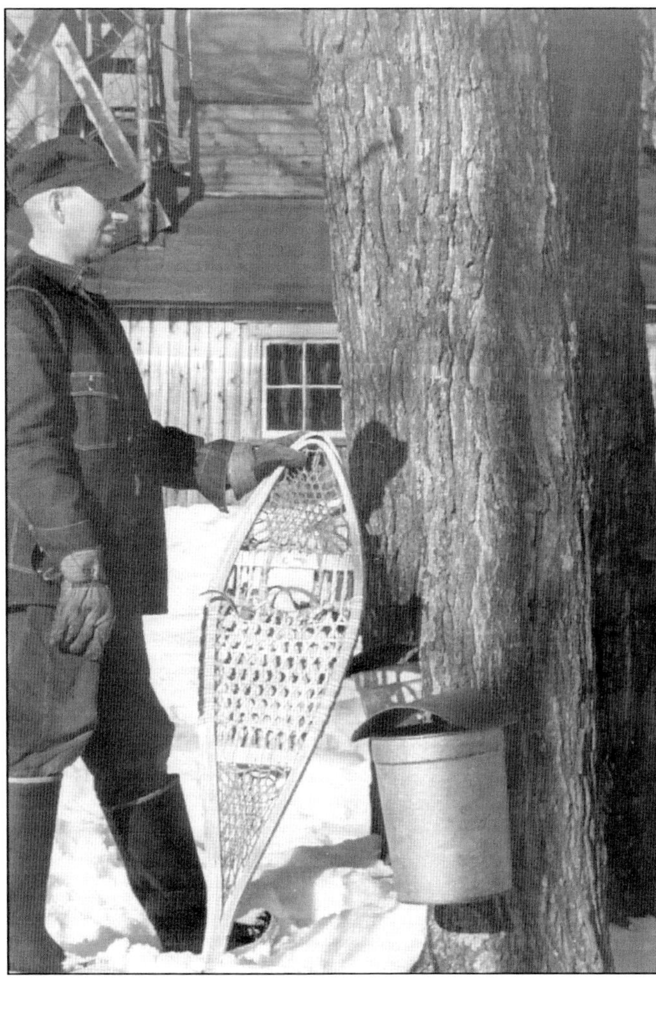

Guy Thompson leans his snowshoes against a maple tree at his sugar place on the old homestead after gathering sap. Thompson owned and operated a small sugar bush across the road from his home on Thompson Hill. (Courtesy of Arland "Bud" Ploof.)

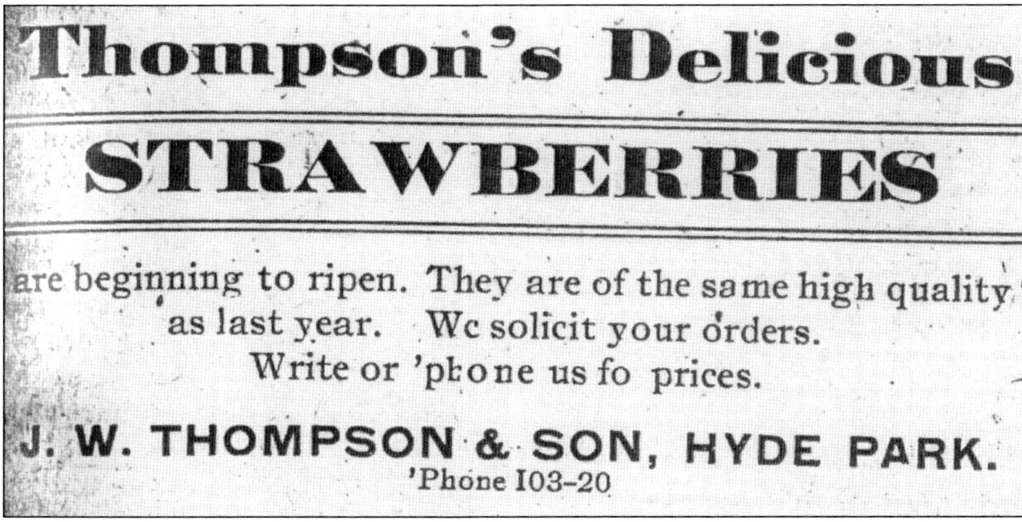

Shown here is an ad for Thompson Strawberries in the *News & Citizen* from June 8, 1921. John Thompson was noted for his strawberries and other produce, which he would sell to the residents of Hyde Park and surrounding areas. Besides strawberries, John sold sweet corn, beans, squash, maple syrup, and firewood. He also built the Thompson Sawmill and sold lumber and shingles. (Courtesy of the Heath/Savage family.)

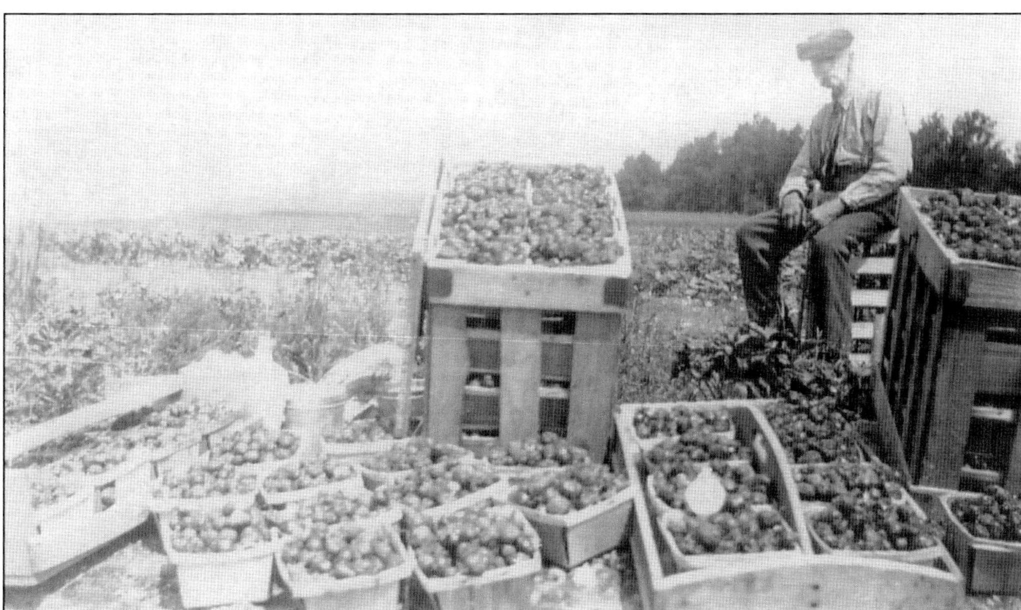

Basketfuls of Thompson's Catskill strawberries are ready to be shipped out. John Thompson's father-in-law, John Smith of Waterville, helped out with the day's harvest. Many locals gladly joined John and his family in the strawberry field to pick their own. (Courtesy of the Heath/Savage family.)

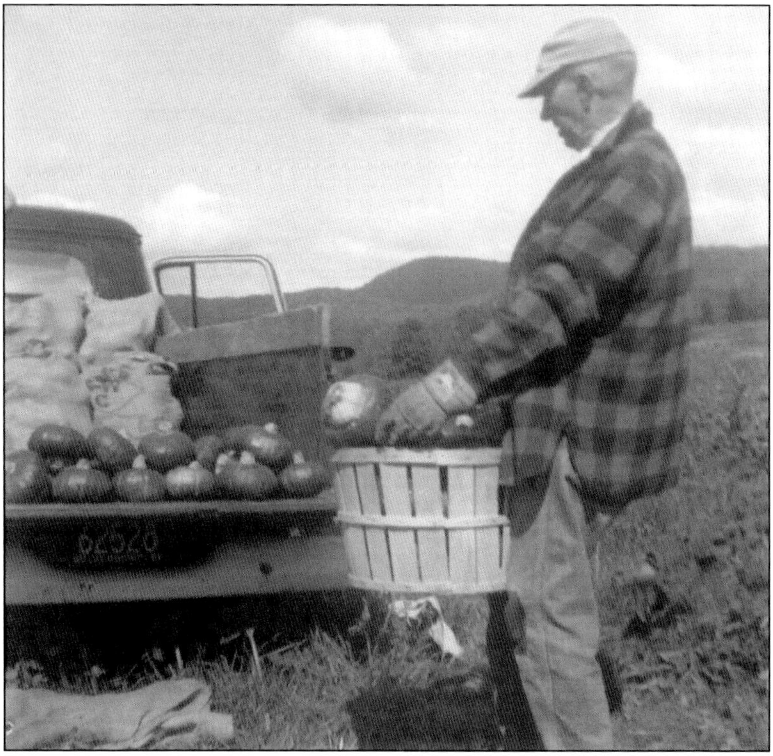

Guy Thompson is seen here loading buttercup squash in his truck. Like his father, John, Guy spent the seasons of the year producing products to sell, such as fruits and vegetables in the summer and maple syrup and firewood in the spring. (Courtesy of Arland "Bud" Ploof.)

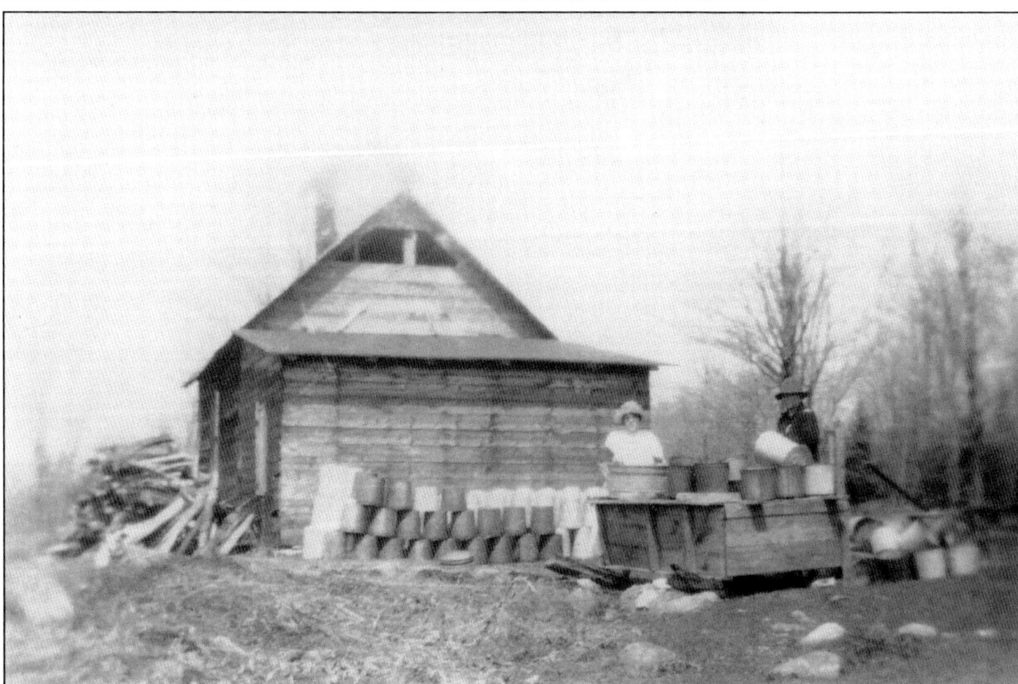

Gil and Maude Hogaboom's sugar place was located on Thompson Hill Road (formerly known as the Stage Coach Road to Eden). Here, Maude and Gil wash sap buckets before putting them away for the next sugaring season. (Courtesy of Loren and Jean Aither.)

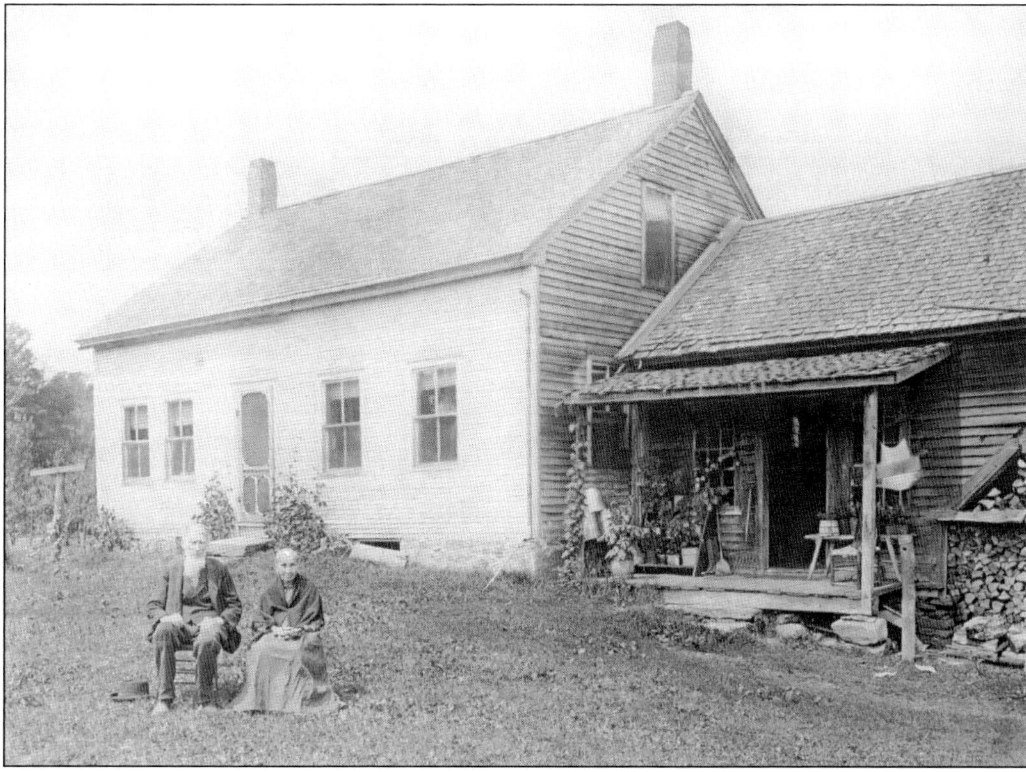

Frederick and Lenora (Warren) Whitcomb sit in front of their home. They had 10 children, from whom many of Hyde Park's residents are descended today. Around 1929, the children of Frederick and Lenora began meeting yearly for a family reunion in honor of their mother and father. This reunion continues today, with many of their descendents attending each year at Robert and Carolyn Jones' home on Jones Road. (Courtesy of the Heath/Savage family.)

Lewis and Elizabeth (Warren) Whitcomb sit in front of their home with their children, from left to right, Sydney, Adna, and Ella. Lewis was a fifer in Company A of the 8th Regiment of the Vermont volunteers. He was home on furlough from the Civil War when this photograph was taken. (Courtesy of the Heath/Savage family.)

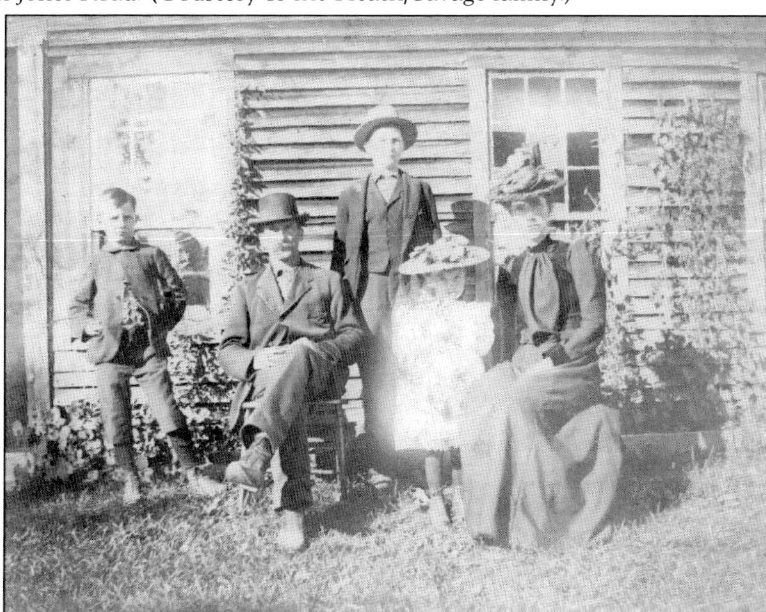

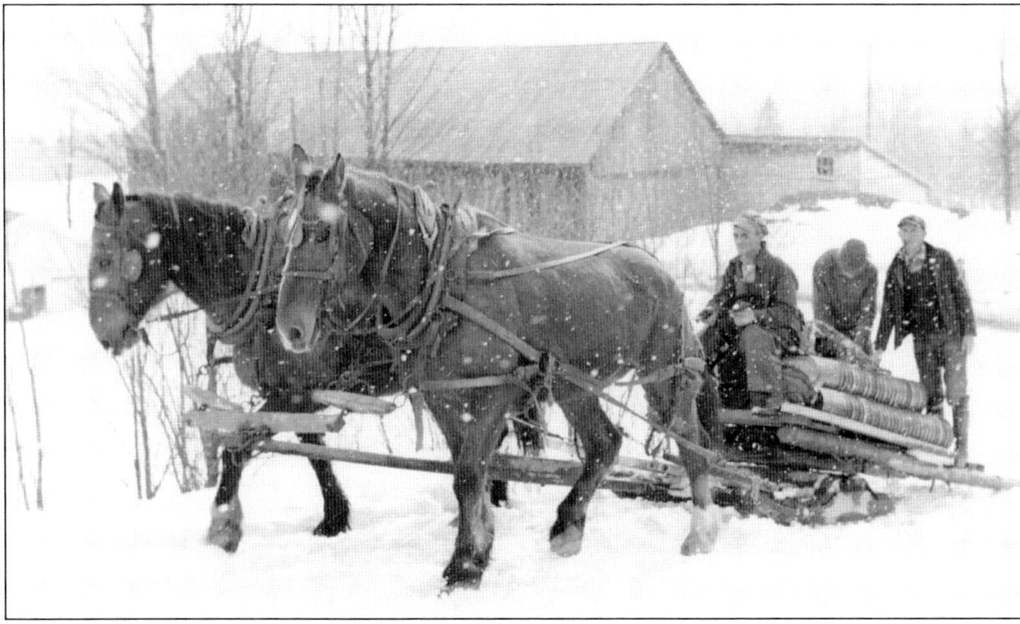

Raymond Jones, the son of Alford and Delia Jones, drives a team of horses on the old Whitcomb farm. The number of sap buckets on the draw sled indicates that sugaring season is about to begin. (Courtesy of Robert and Caroline Jones.)

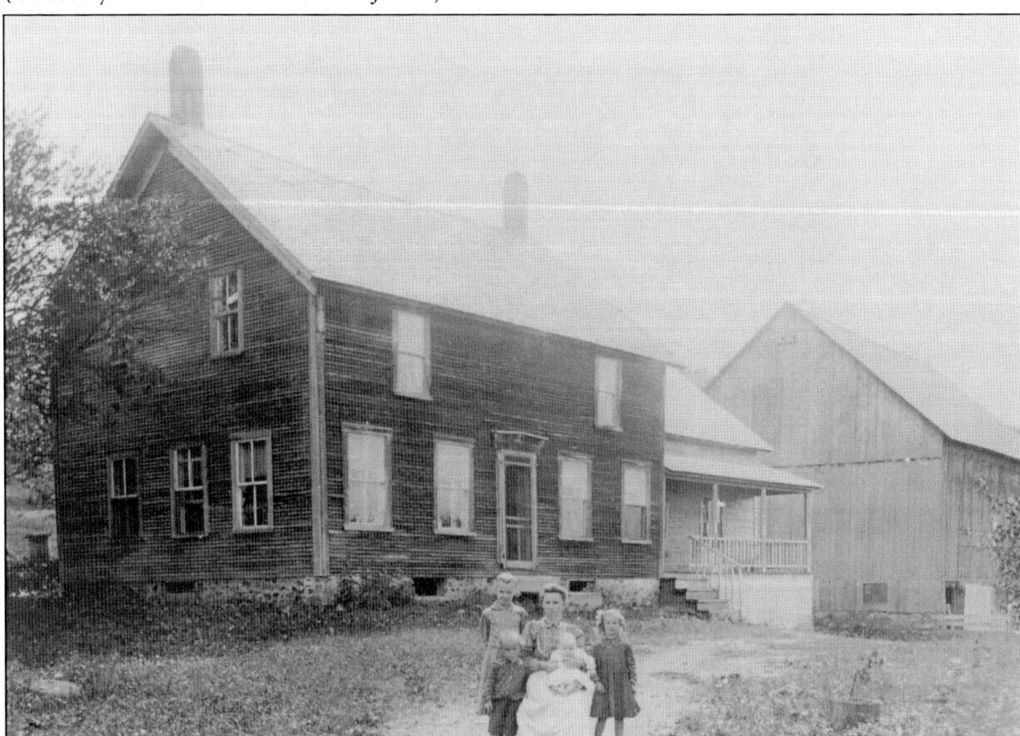

This is an older photograph of the farmhouse in which Robert and Caroline Jones once lived. It is now occupied by their son Brian Jones and his family. (Courtesy of Robert and Caroline Jones.)

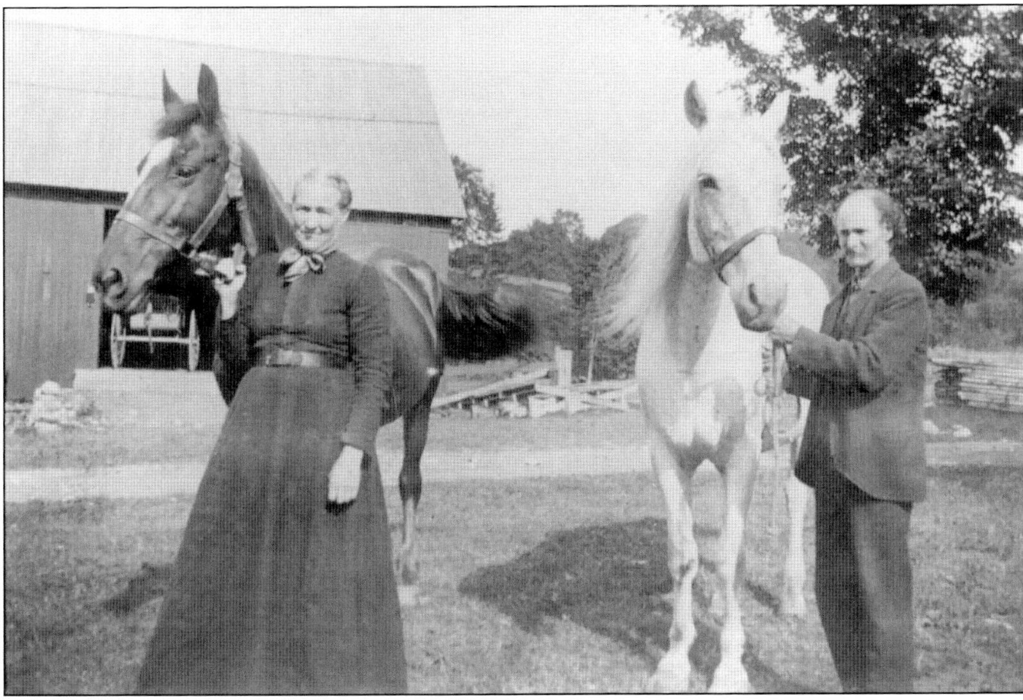

Alford and Delia Jones are the great-grandparents of Robert Jones. The barn in this photograph was located directly across from the old farmhouse. The family farm still exists today but has changed to reflect its modern operation. (Courtesy of Robert and Caroline Jones.)

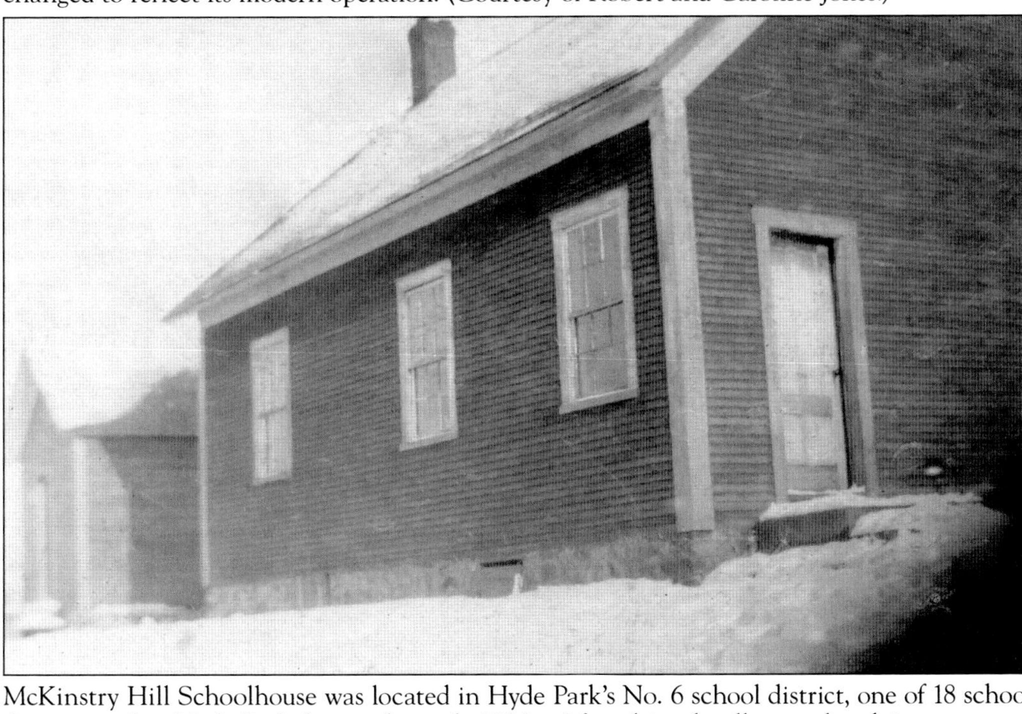

McKinstry Hill Schoolhouse was located in Hyde Park's No. 6 school district, one of 18 school districts within Hyde Park during the early 1900s. After this schoolhouse closed, it was turned into the home of Newton Brown. (Courtesy of the Stewart family.)

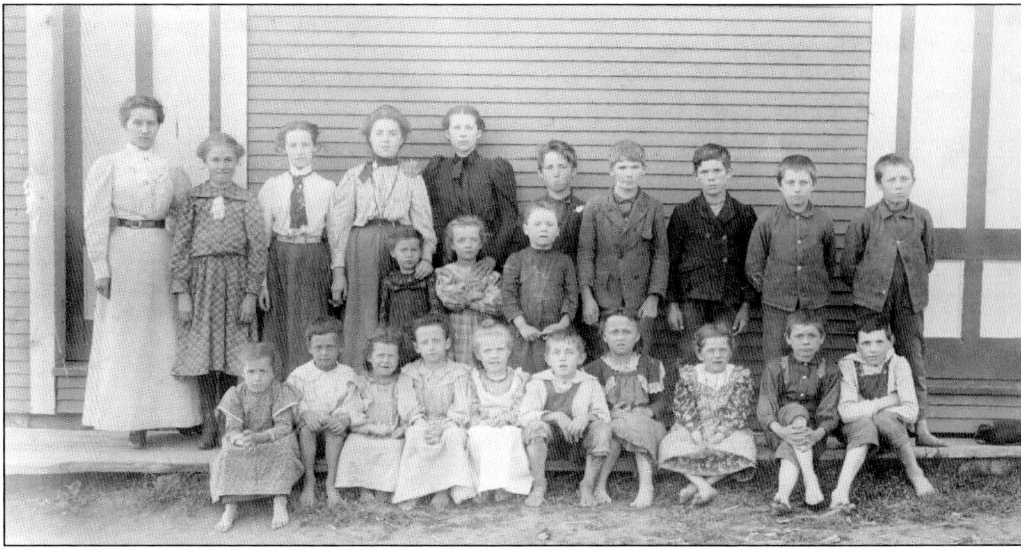

Students at the McKinstry Hill Schoolhouse are pictured with their teacher around 1900. From left to right are (first row) Augusta Jones, Tom McNally, Franty McNally, Ethel McNally, Annie Jones, Alton Jones, Nora Emery, Myrtle Bowen, Gordon Bowen, and Walter Jones; (second row) Winnie Hurlburt, Grace Jones, and Ola Stewart; (third row) Emma Lareabbe (teacher), Ethel Thompson, Goldie Hurlburt, Bertha Page, Gertrude Jones, Harry Page, Harry Bowen, Bert Bowen, Laurence Jones, and Ernest Jones. (Courtesy of the Heath/Savage family.)

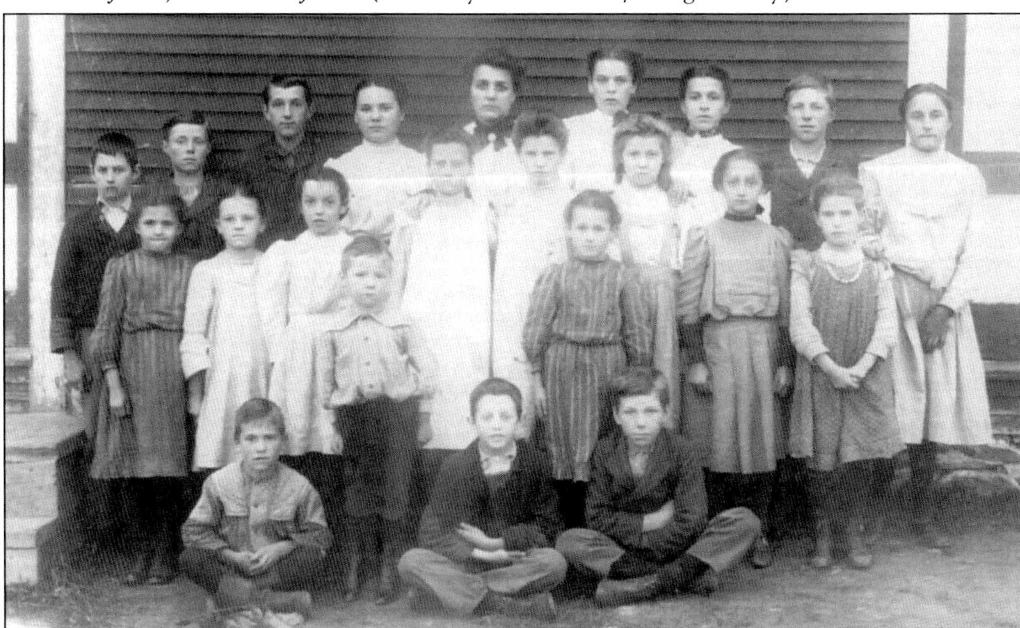

This school photograph was taken around 1904 at the McKinstry Hill Schoolhouse. Pictured, from left to right, are (first row) Merl Stewart, Rex Stewart (standing), Delbert Jones, Marion Jones (standing), and Glenn Thompson; (second row) Gladys Jones, Weldie Stewart, Ethel Chapman, Isadore Hurlburt, Winnie Hurlburt, Laura Hogaboom, Myrtle Jones, and Freda Hurlburt; (third row) Herbert Jones, Clyde Thompson, Alton Jones, Ola Stewart, Ella Davis, Myrtle Bowen, Augusta Jones, Ralph Thompson, and Etta Shepard. (Courtesy of the Heath/Savage family.)

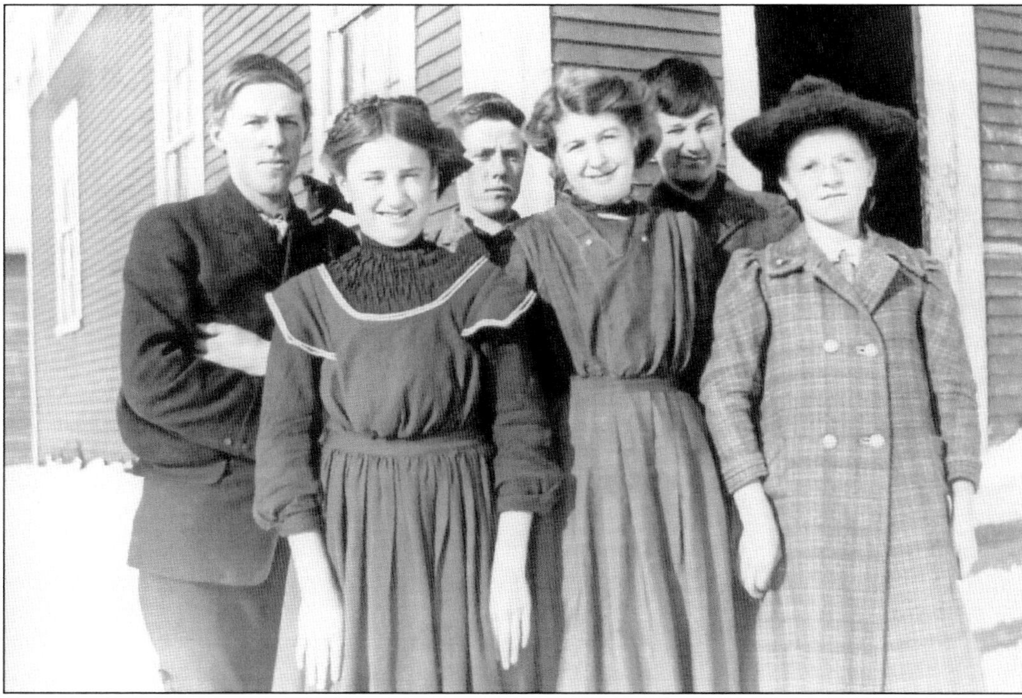

Children pose for a photograph at the McKinstry Hill Schoolhouse around 1908. They are, from left to right, (first row) Vera Davis, Laura Hogaboom, and Weldie Stewart; (second row) Ralph Thompson, Clyde Thompson, and Herbert Jones. (Courtesy of the Heath/Savage family.)

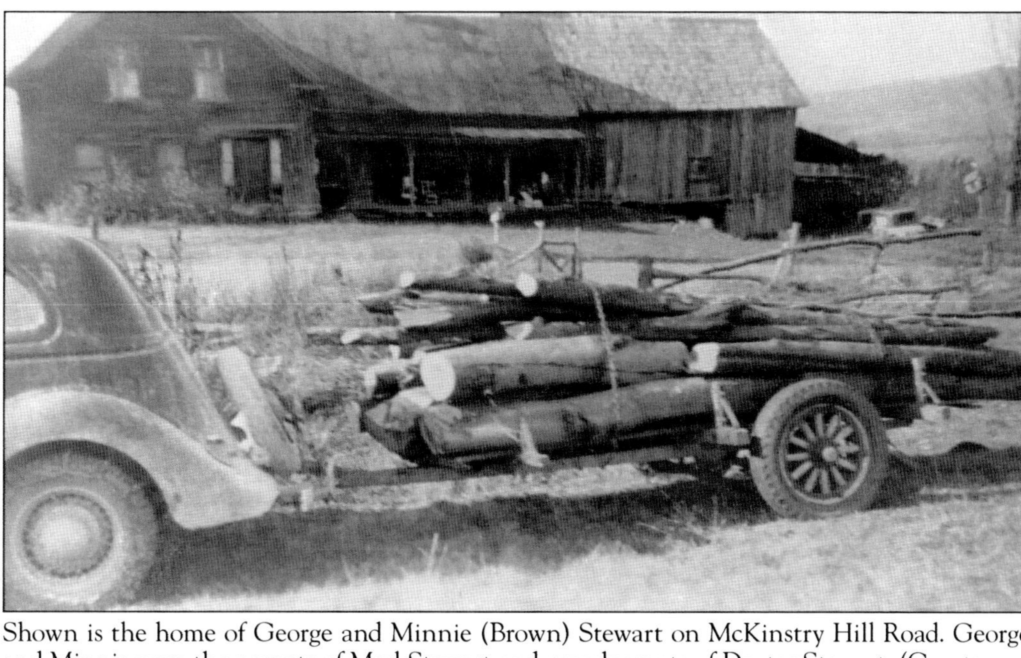

Shown is the home of George and Minnie (Brown) Stewart on McKinstry Hill Road. George and Minnie were the parents of Merl Stewart and grandparents of Dexter Stewart. (Courtesy of the Stewart family.)

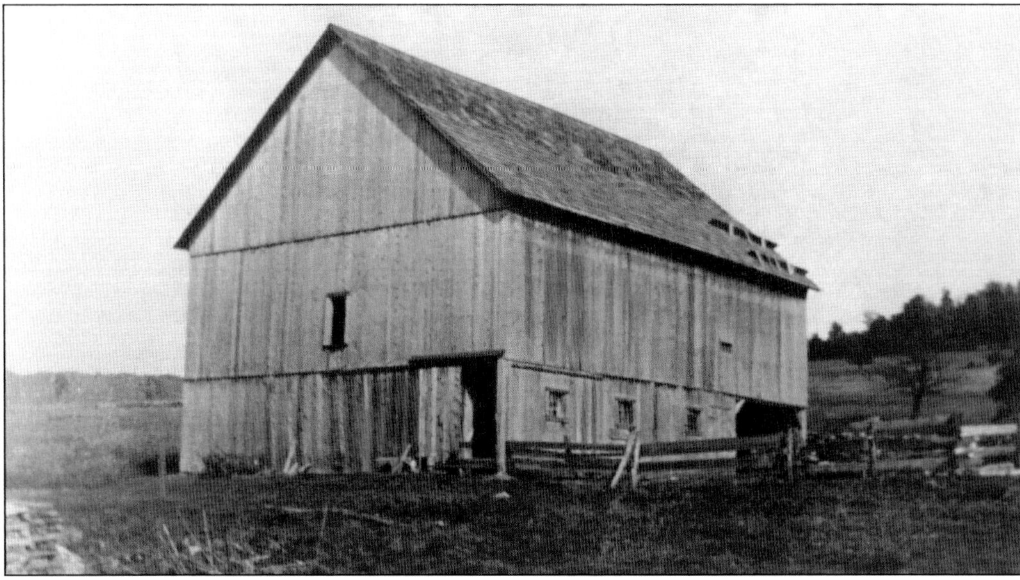

Shown here is a great view of the Stewart barn located on McKinstry Hill. This barn and the Stewart home are no longer standing due to a fire. The location of these two buildings was near the property of Morris Putvain. (Courtesy of the Larose/Manning family.)

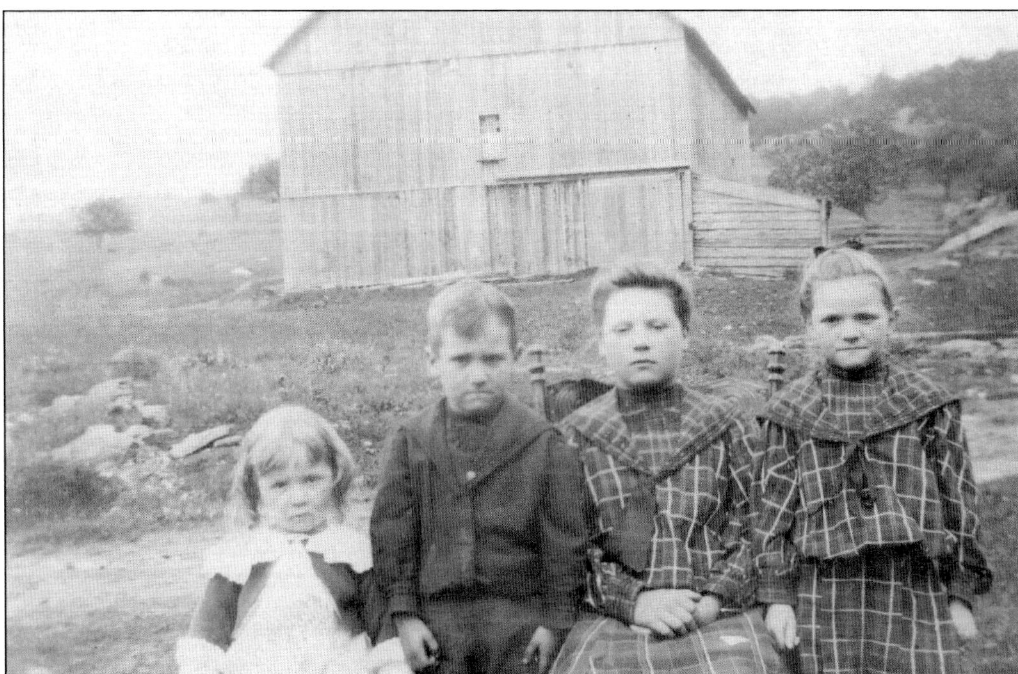

Children pose for a photograph at the Stewart farm on McKinstry Hill in Hyde Park in 1904. From left to right are Rex, Merl, Ola, and Weldie Stewart. (Courtesy of the Larose/Manning family.)

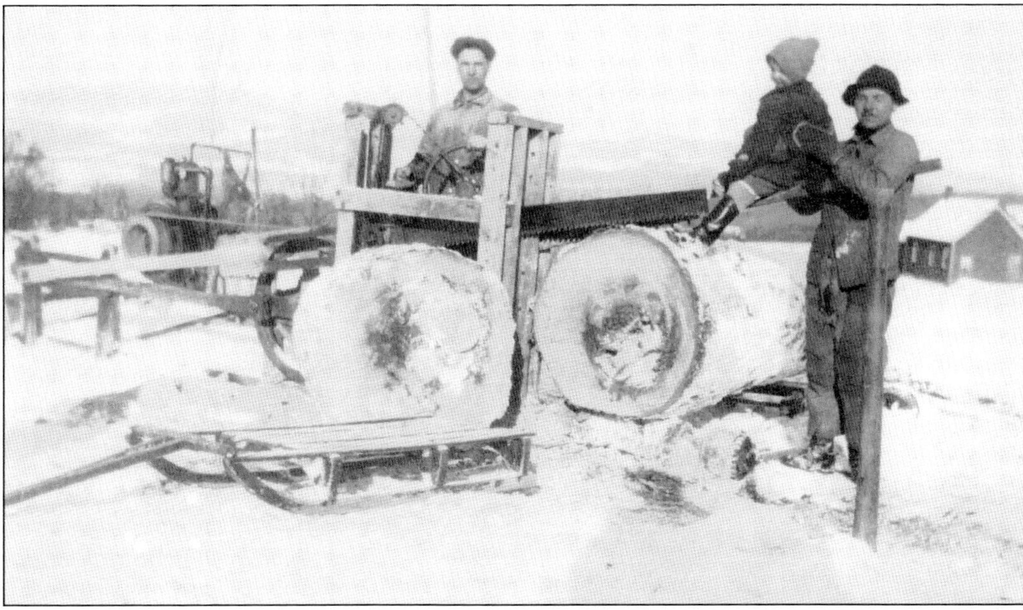

Pictured from left to right, Newt Brown and Merl and Rex Stewart cut firewood with a drag saw rig on the Stewart farm on McKinstry Hill. Notice the open view across the valley. (Courtesy of the Stewart family.)

Charles and Eva Burbank, the grandparents of Carolyn (Hanscom) Jones, are pictured at the former residence of the Wheeler family. (Courtesy of Robert and Caroline Jones.)

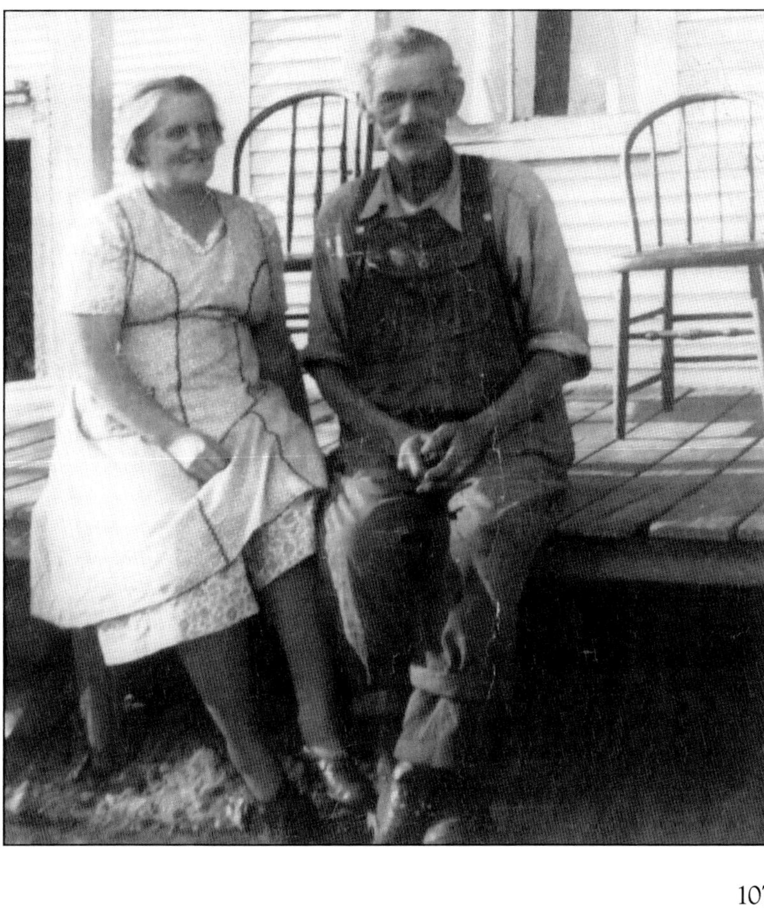

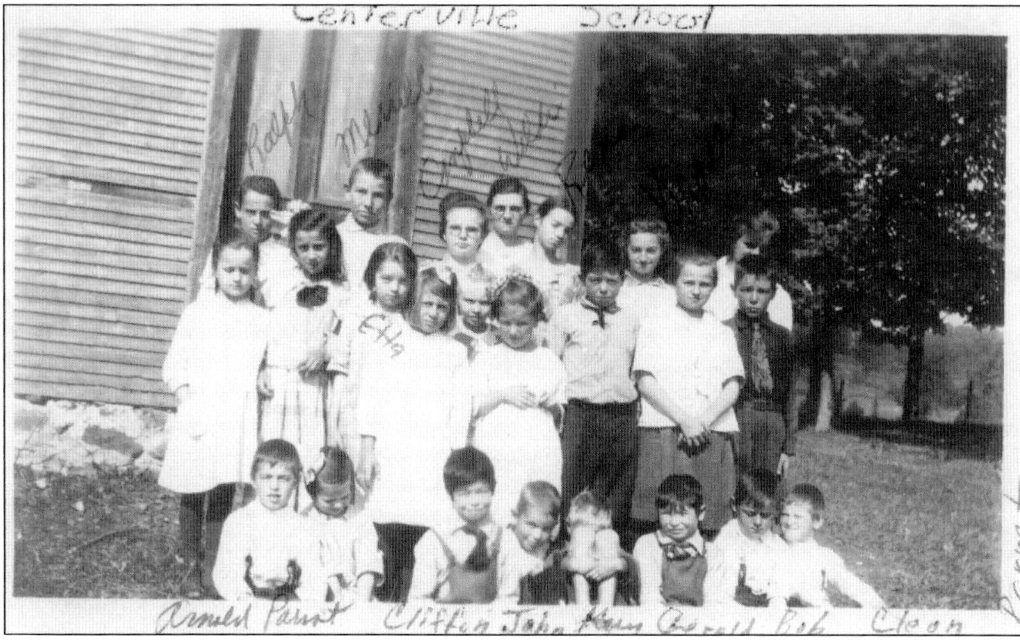

Children pose for their class photograph at Centerville School. Although many of the first names of children are written on the image, few last names are included. Merrill Jewett is pictured second from the left in the back row. The teacher is Weldie Stewart, who later married Hobart Manning. (Courtesy of the Larose/Manning family.)

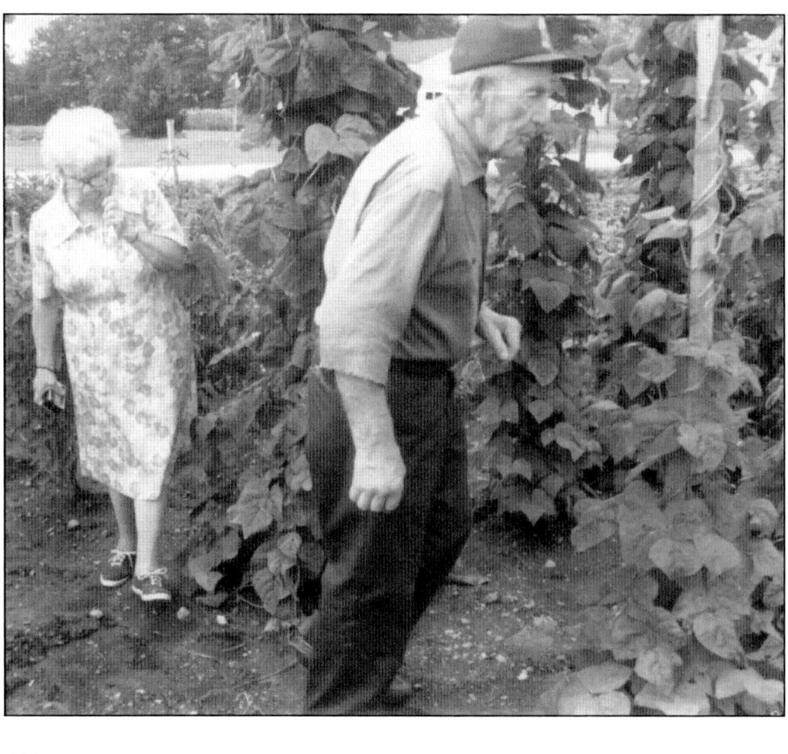

Merrill and Maude (Tenny) Jewett would conduct a daily check of their garden at their home in Centerville. They did a lot of gardening, as have many Vermonters. Merrill, a blacksmith by trade, raised and sold strawberries, strawberry plants, and raspberry plants. (Courtesy of Robert and Caroline Jones.)

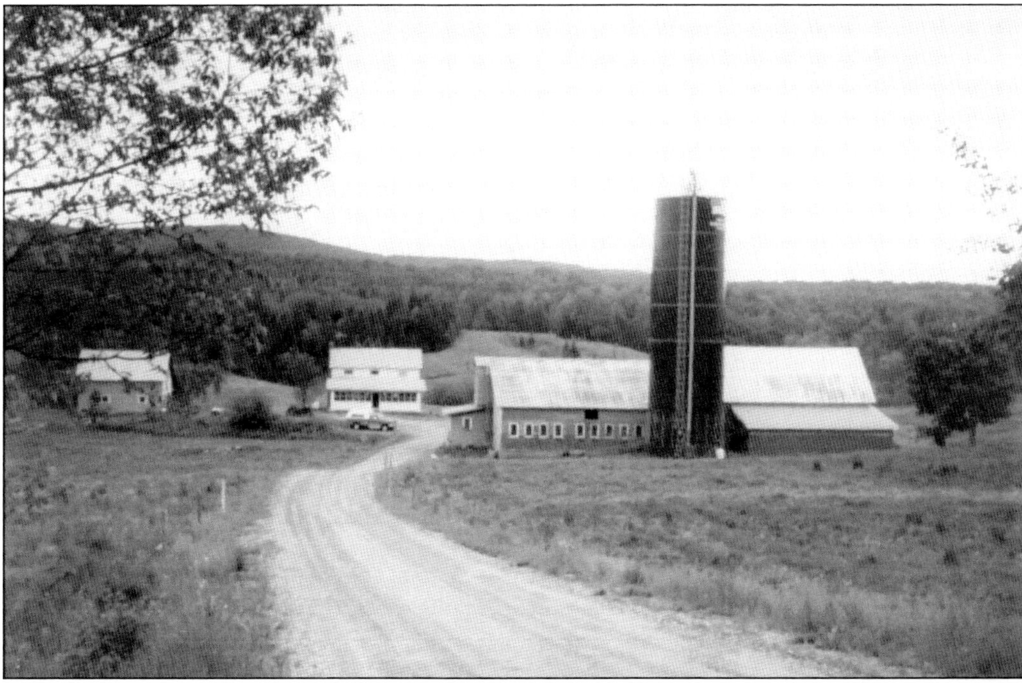

Shown here is one of the two Godin farms located in Hyde Park. Donald and Diane (Daigle) Godin's farm, pictured here, was located next to the farm that was owned by Andy Bourdeau. The other Godin farm, owned by Richard and Barbara (Petersen) Godin, was located on the Archie Longmore Road and sold many years ago. (Courtesy of Robert and Caroline Jones.)

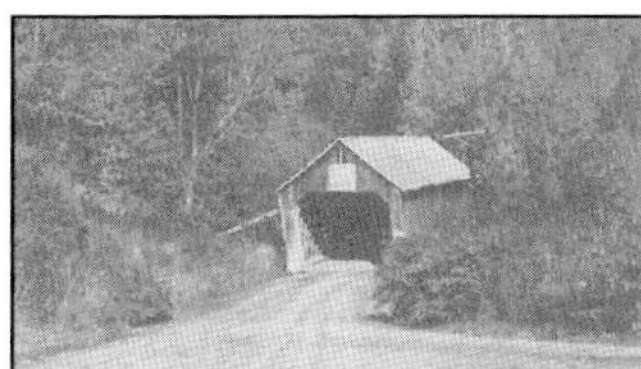

Garfield Covered Bridge

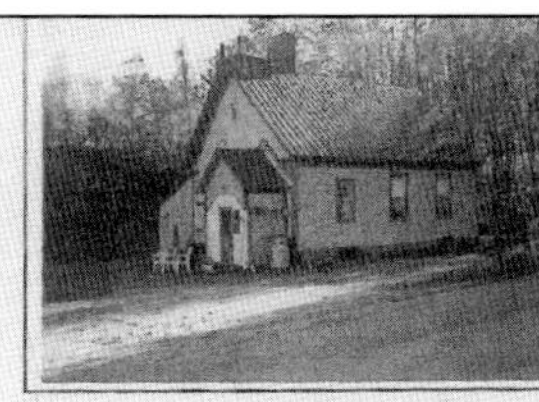

Garfield School No. 9

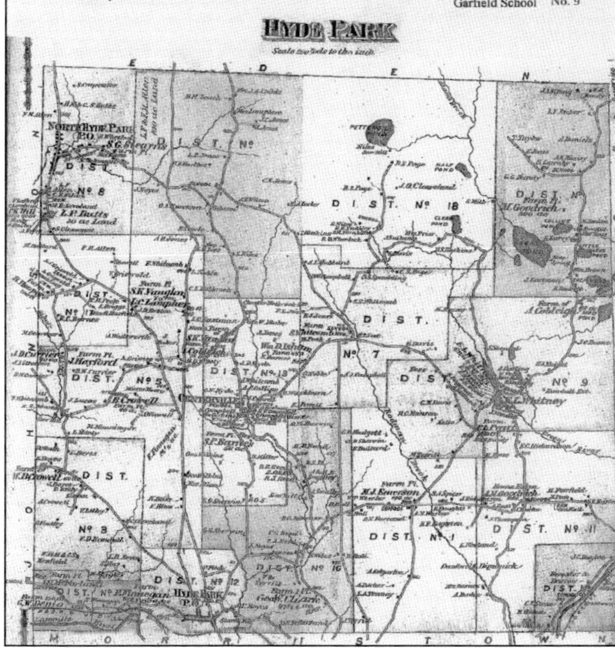

These images show the Garfield Covered Bridge, the Garfield School, and the many school districts that existed within Hyde Park, as seen on this Beers Atlas map. (Courtesy of the Davis family.)

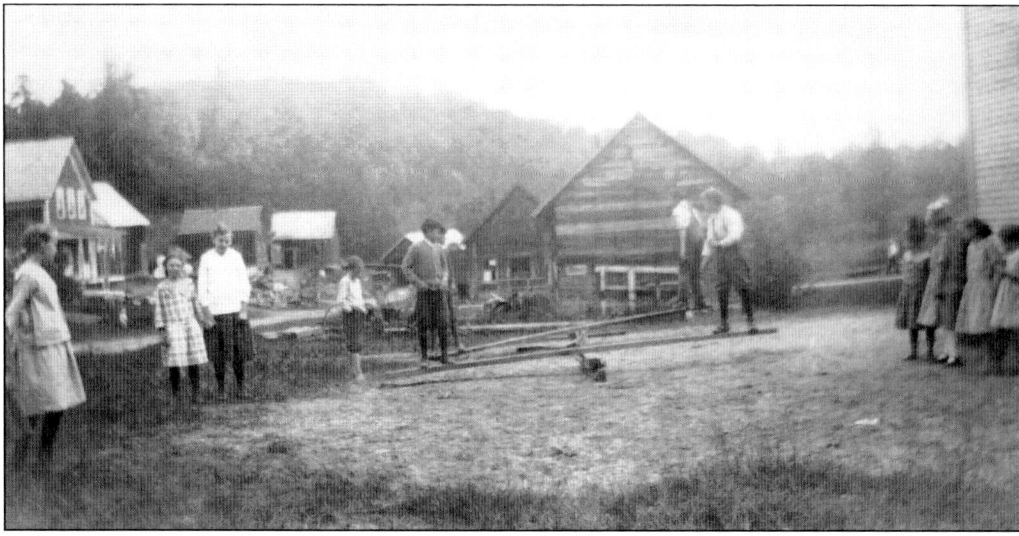

Children enjoy recess in the yard of the Garfield School in this rare 1924 photograph. Garfield, like so many hamlets within the town of Hyde Park, was well established, with many families for its time. The Garfield School, which was in school district No. 9, was later sold to Edward Jones in 1954 or 1955. (Courtesy of the Davis family.)

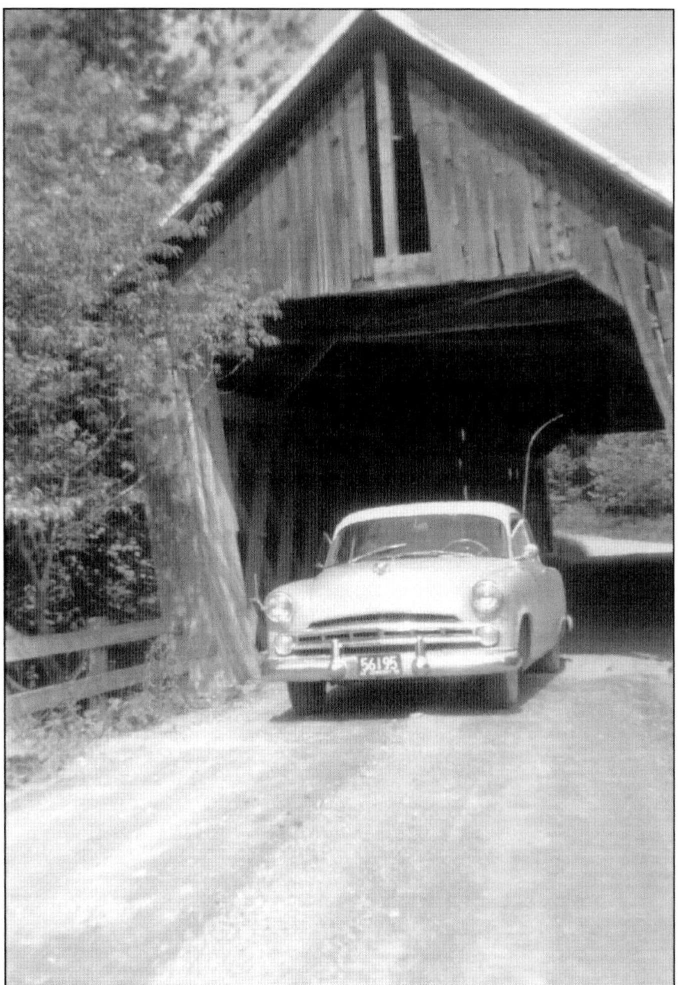

This iconic image shows one of the many covered bridges that were once so common around the state of Vermont. Located in Garfield, this bridge was typical and, considering its wood structure, held up for quite some time. (Courtesy of the Davis family.)

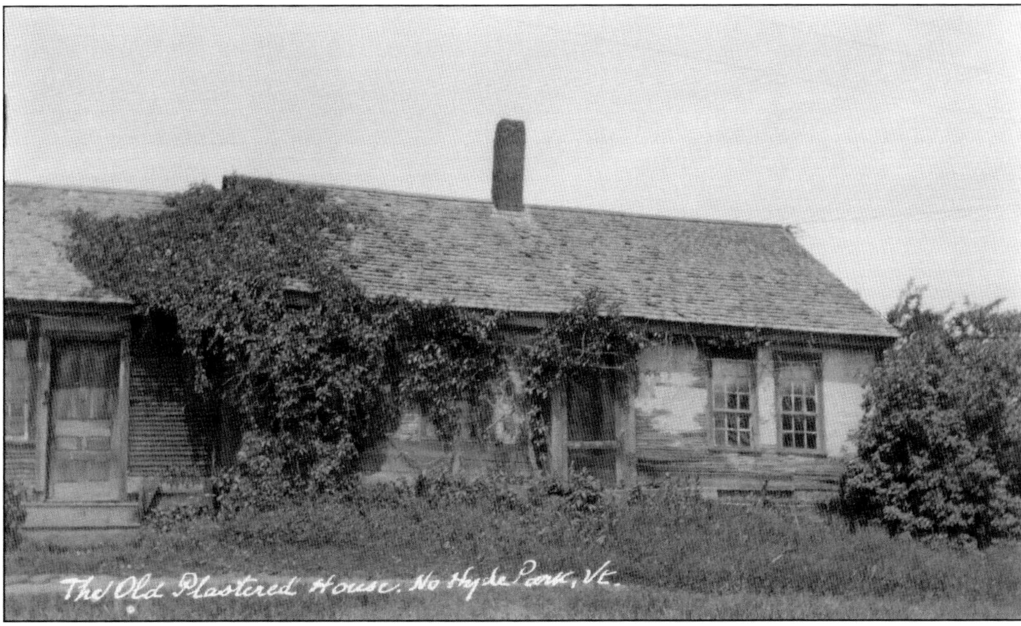

The Plastered House was home for many years to Libbey Felcher, who welcomed people from many walks of life into her home. Libby writes in the June 29, 1921, *News & Citizen* that "the Thompson boys . . . remembered the old folks in the Plastered House with a donation of as good flavored ones (strawberries) as I ever tasted." (Courtesy of Robert and Caroline Jones.)

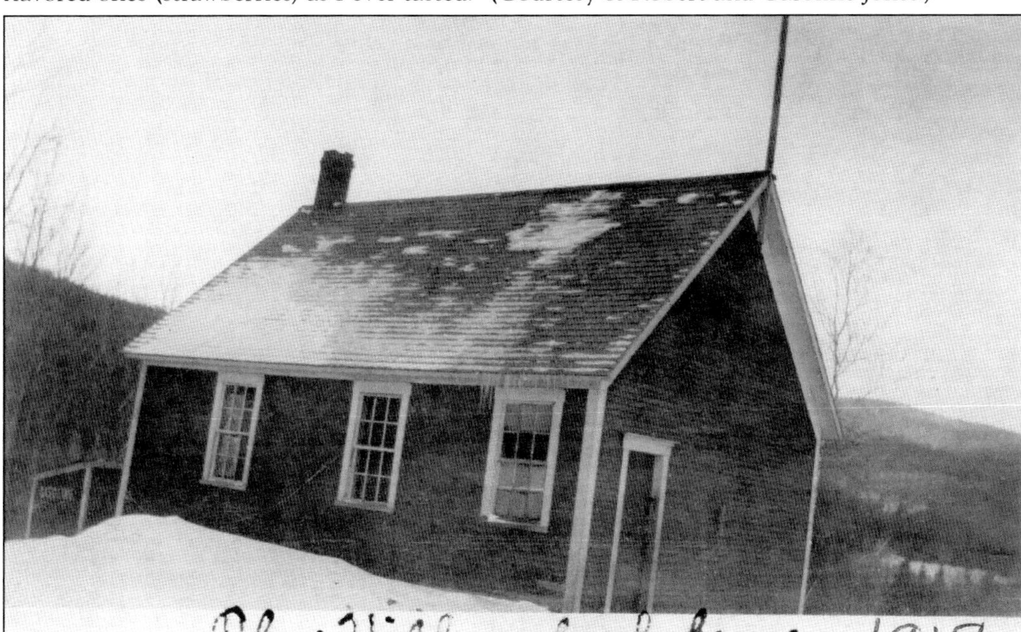

The Ober Hill Schoolhouse lies in the town of Johnson but is located just outside the perimeter of North Hyde Park. The school and community of Ober Hill were well known in North Hyde Park because many families living in town had relatives or friends living in the Ober Hill community. A few family names in this community were Manning, Dudley, and Ingalls. (Courtesy of the Larose/Manning family.)

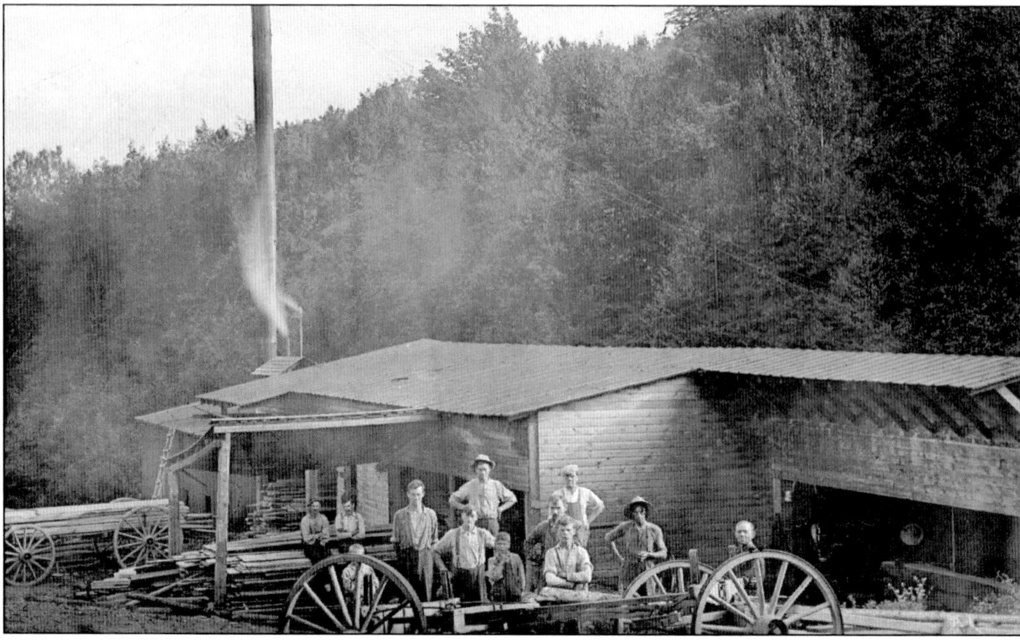

The Ober Hill sawmill was one of many sawmills that existed around the county. Pictured, from left to right, are (first row) Harry Manning (face hidden behind wagon wheel), Homer Manning, Hobart Manning, and Tom Richardson; (second row) Harry Brown, Wilt Driscall, and Bernie Lapan; (third row) Charles McAllister, Alonzo Bidwell, and Hezekiaha Baker; (fourth row) Carrol Newton and Ed Parker. (Courtesy of the Heath/Savage family.)

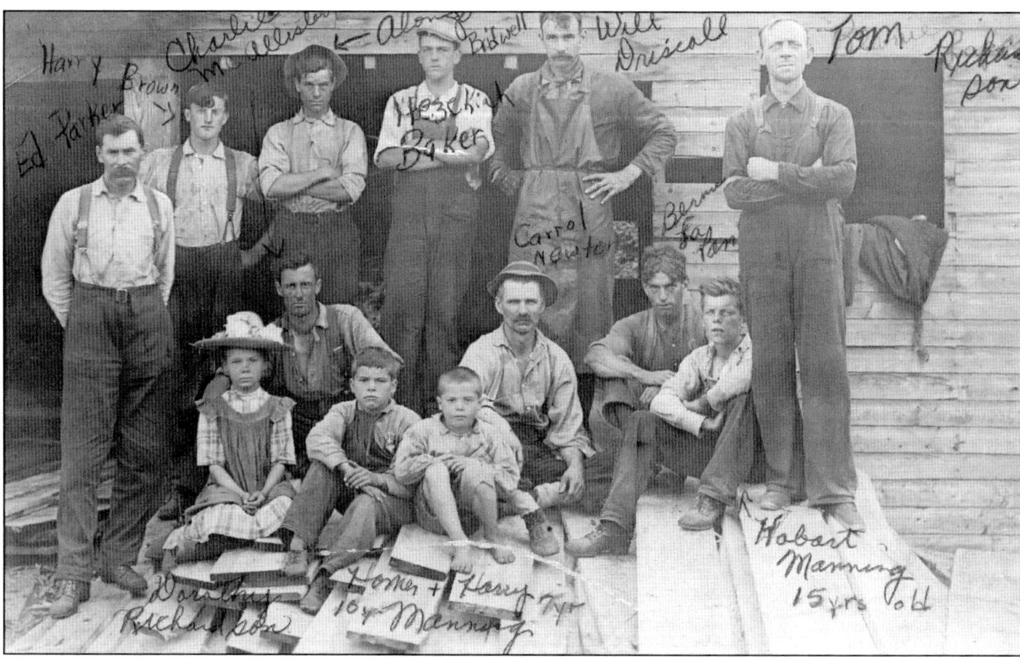

The Ober Hill mill crew poses atop recently sawn lumber that is ready to be stacked for drying. The names of the individuals pictured are written on the photograph, as are the ages of three of the children. (Courtesy of the Larose/Manning family.)

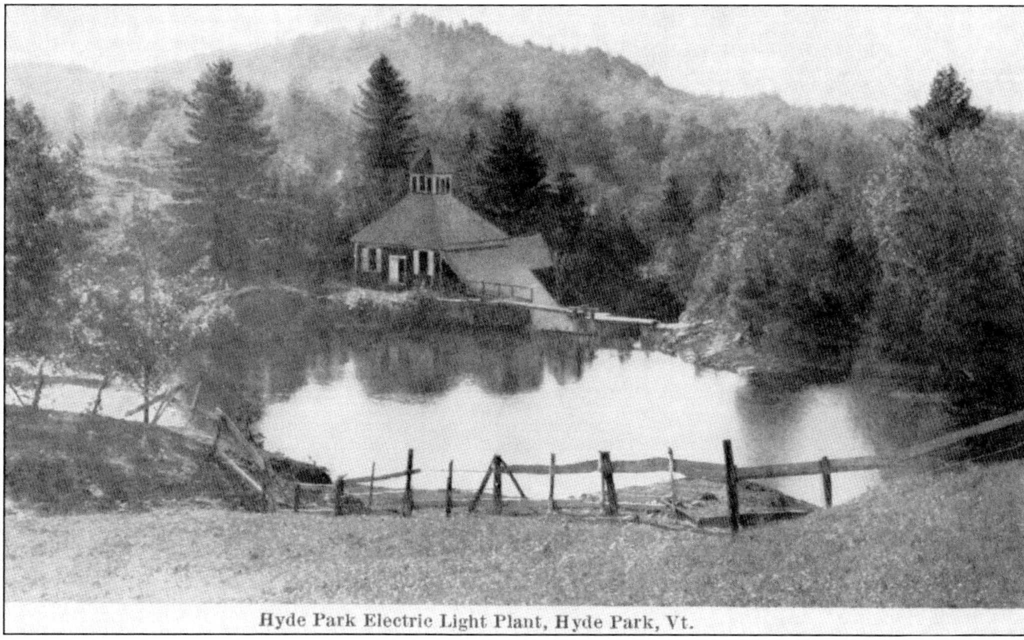

The Hyde Park power plant shown here was built in 1895, when Henry McFarland was chairman of the village board of trustees. Erected at a cost of approximately $15,000–$20,000, it represented a mark of progress as the town moved forward into the modern era. (Courtesy of the Page/McFarland family.)

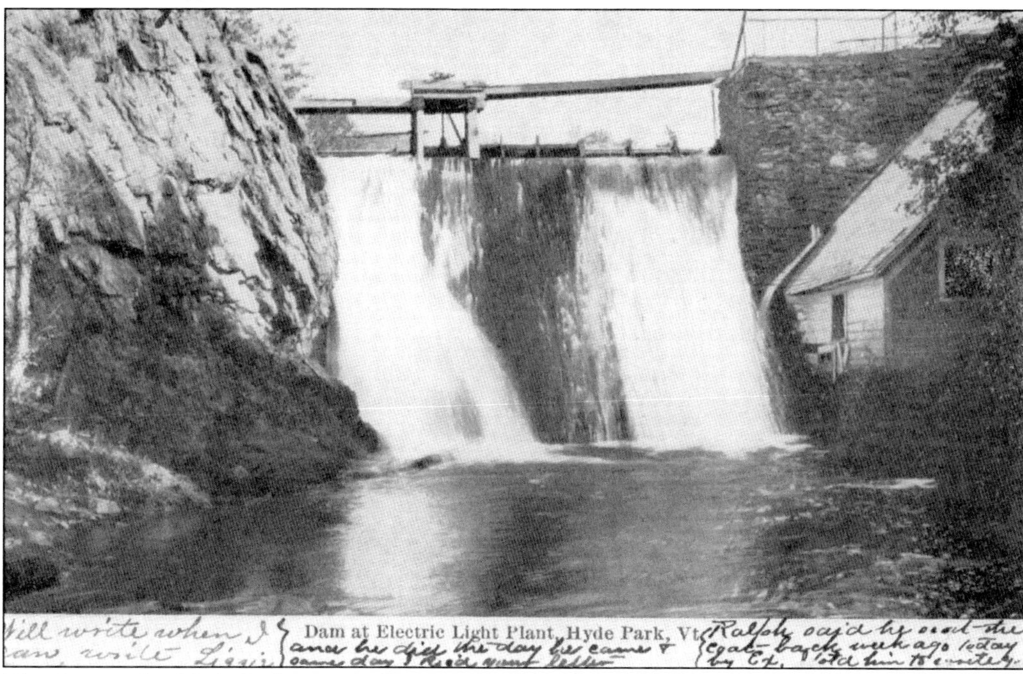

The dam at the Hyde Park power plant was built on the Gihon River to provide a head of water to run the plant. The land for the plant and dam was purchased from Edgar Pratt. Although the plant building still exists today, it has been converted into a private residence. (Courtesy of the Page/McFarland family.)

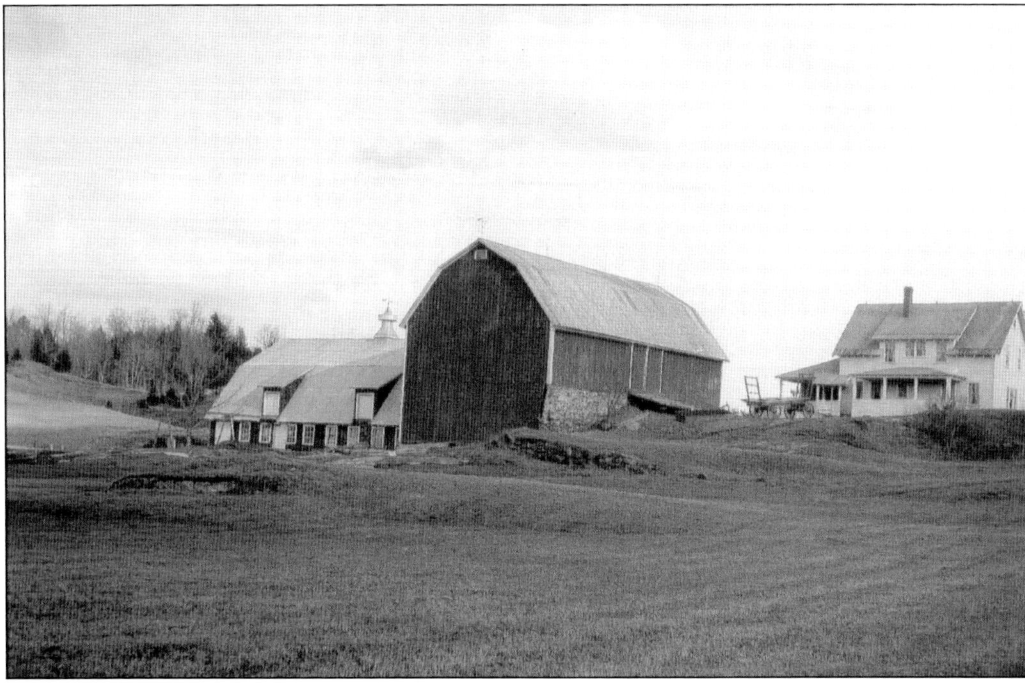

Cleveland Farm is located just off the east exit out of Hyde Park Village on Route 15. One of many farms in the community, it is still in operation today as a horse farm owned and operated by the Chauvin family. (Courtesy of Francis Favreau.)

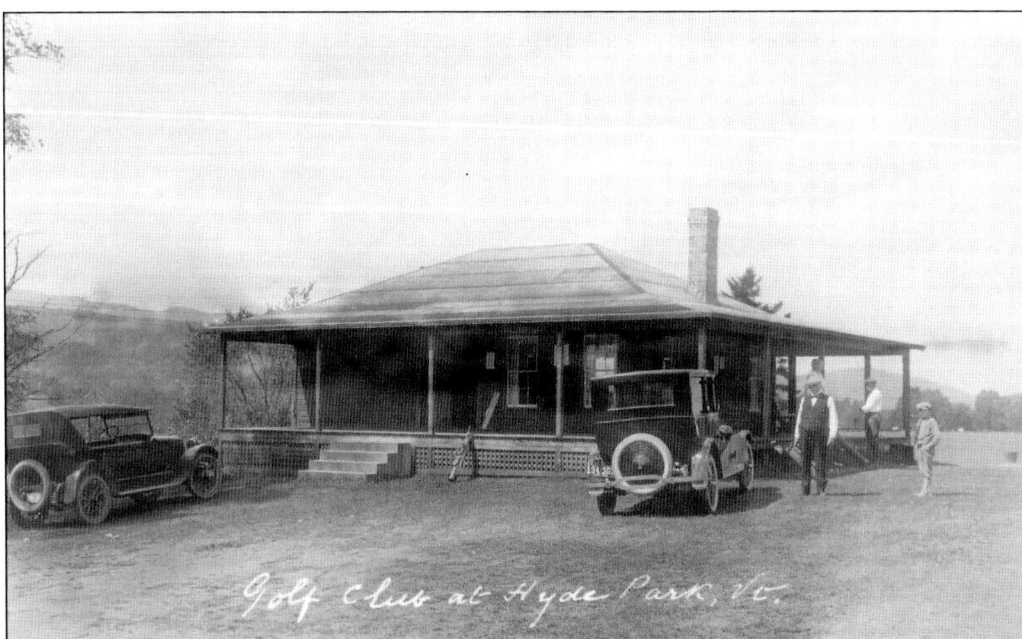

Gentlemen enjoy the newly erected Lamoille Country Club golf clubhouse, which was built in 1921. The clubhouse provided a place for avid golfers to gather before venturing out onto the course. (Courtesy of the Page/McFarland family.)

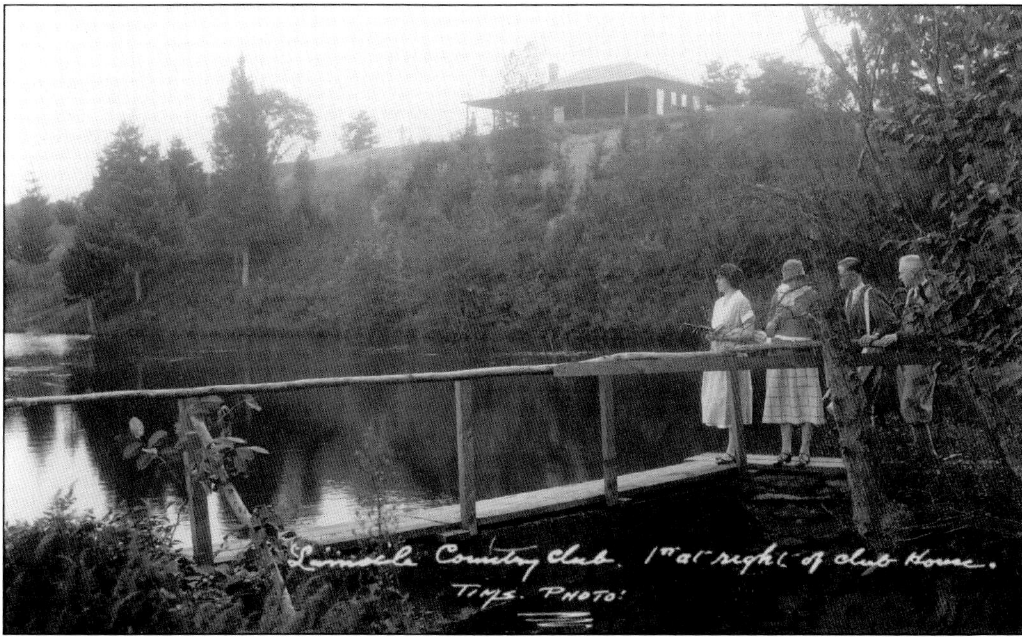

A path from the clubhouse, to the bridge, and on to the golf course became the normal route to the fairway. Here, two couples stop to look at the water before beginning their game. (Courtesy of the Page/McFarland family.)

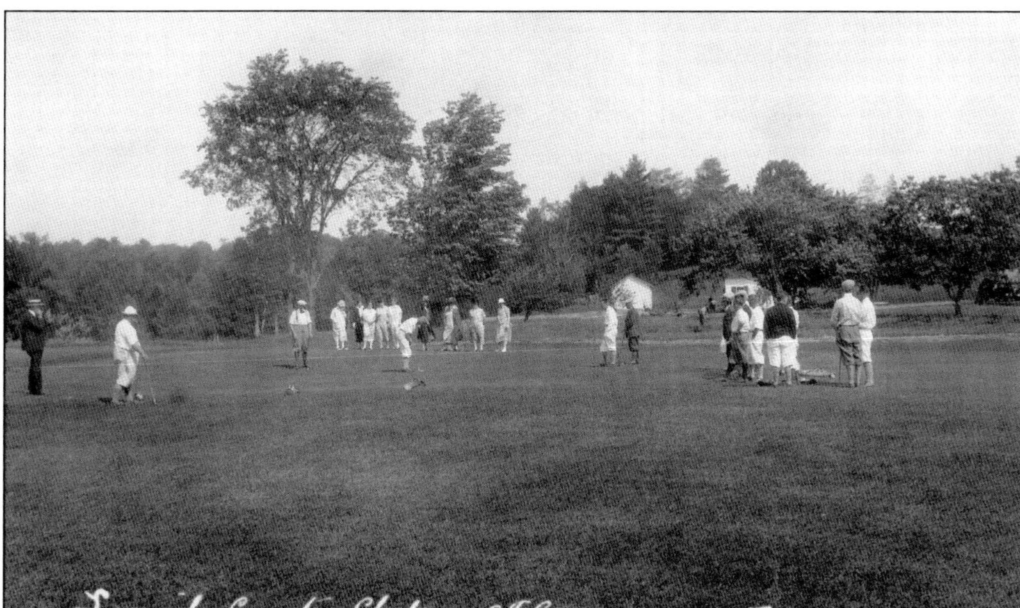

Golfers gather at the ninth green at the Lamoille Country Club fairway to wait their turns to complete the game. The site where the golf course was located used to be a softball/baseball field and is now occupied by Lamoille Union High School. (Courtesy of the Page/McFarland family.)

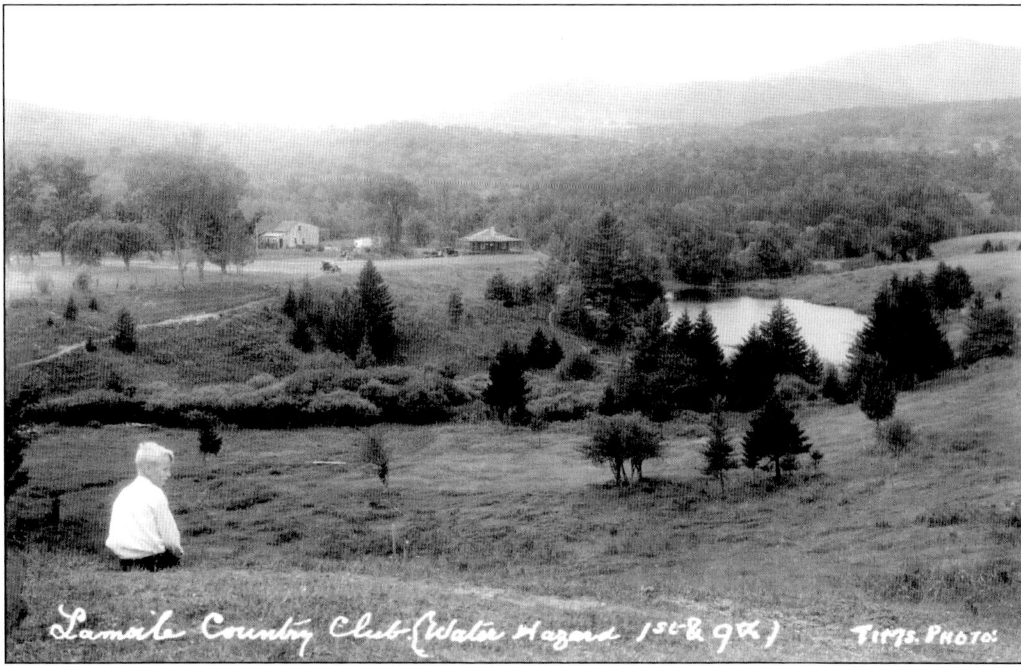

The clubhouse and the water hazard golfers faced are visible in this hillside view. Looking closely, one can see the path leading from the last hole back to the clubhouse. (Courtesy of the Page/McFarland family.)

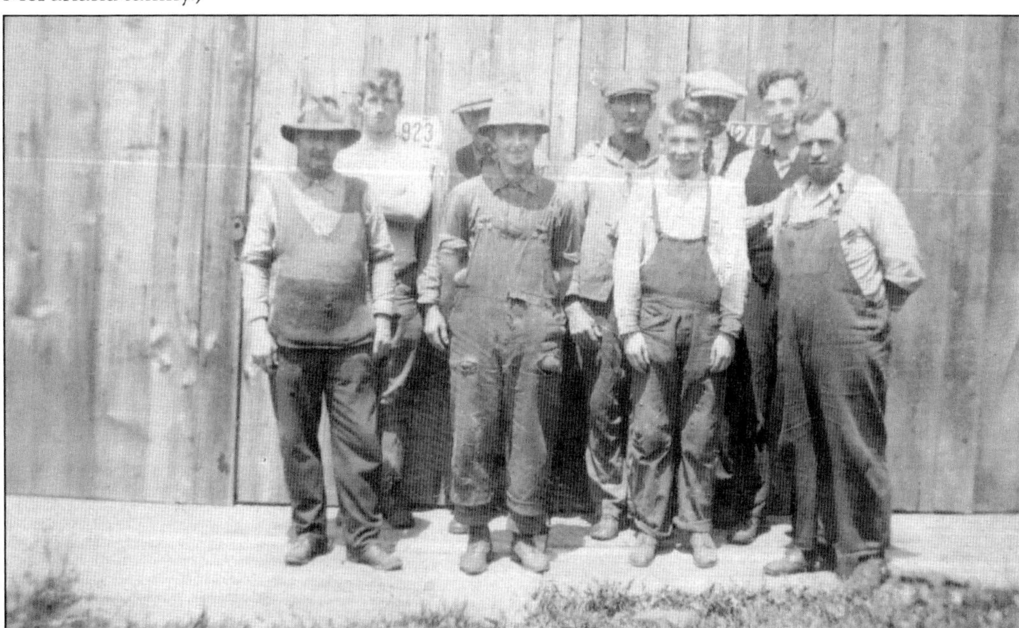

Pictured in 1915 is the crew of the Scofield Lumber Mill, located in the eastern part of town, known as the "diggins." This mill was an extensive business owned and operated by John Scofield, who came to Hyde Park from Elmore. Pictured, from left to right, are (first row) Lawrence Foss, Harold Foss, Ron Woodbury, and Walter Loomis; (second row) Burton Eastman, Charles Gates (partial view), Ed Parker, unidentified, and Curtis Farmer. (Courtesy of the Heath/Savage family.)

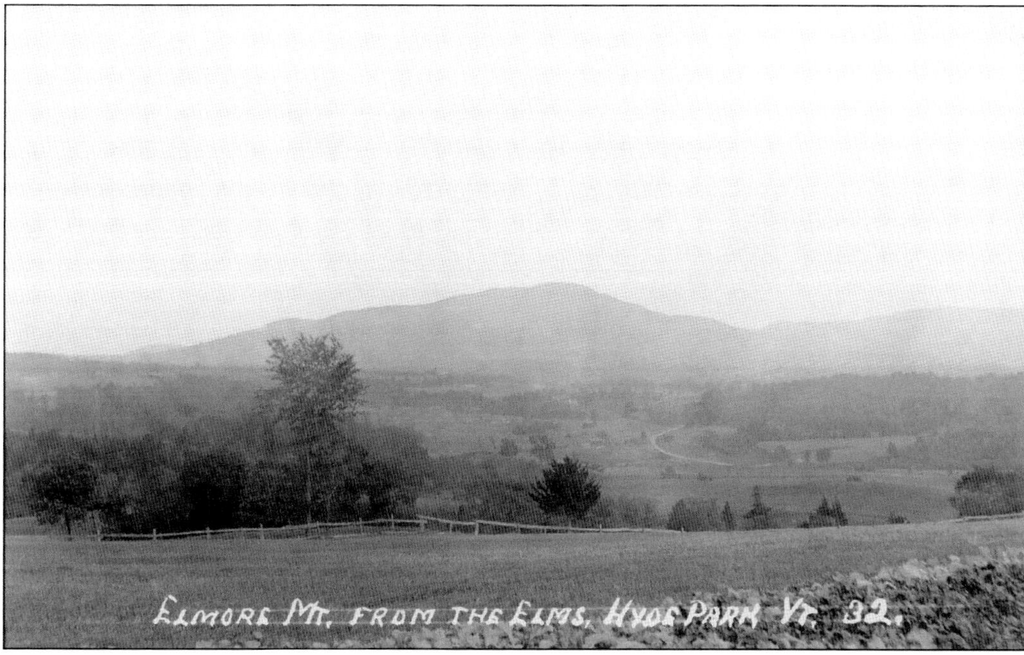

Pictured is a view of Elmore Mountain as seen from the boardinghouse known as the Elms, which was also the residence of Vernon D. Fitch. Looking closely, one can see the direction of the road and how it used to pass right through Hyde Park Village. The Route 15 bypass did not exist above the village at this time. (Courtesy of the Page/McFarland family.)

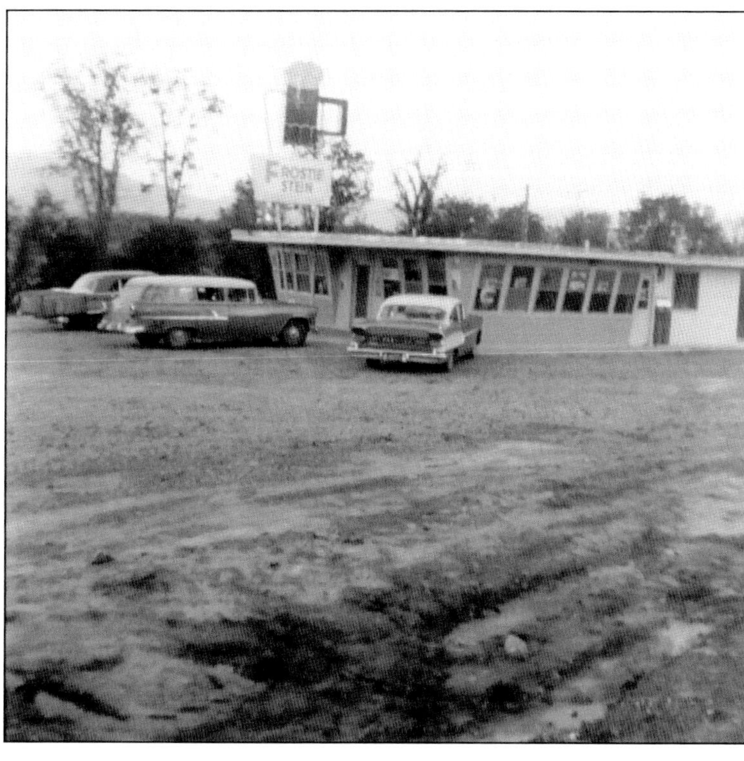

Adrian and Fern Larose built the Frostie Stein Snack Bar on Route 15. Adrian used to make homemade root beer, which was a treat for everyone. Later, it became Martin's Snack Bar and is currently the home of Lamoille Valley Veterinary Services. (Courtesy of the Larose/Manning family.)

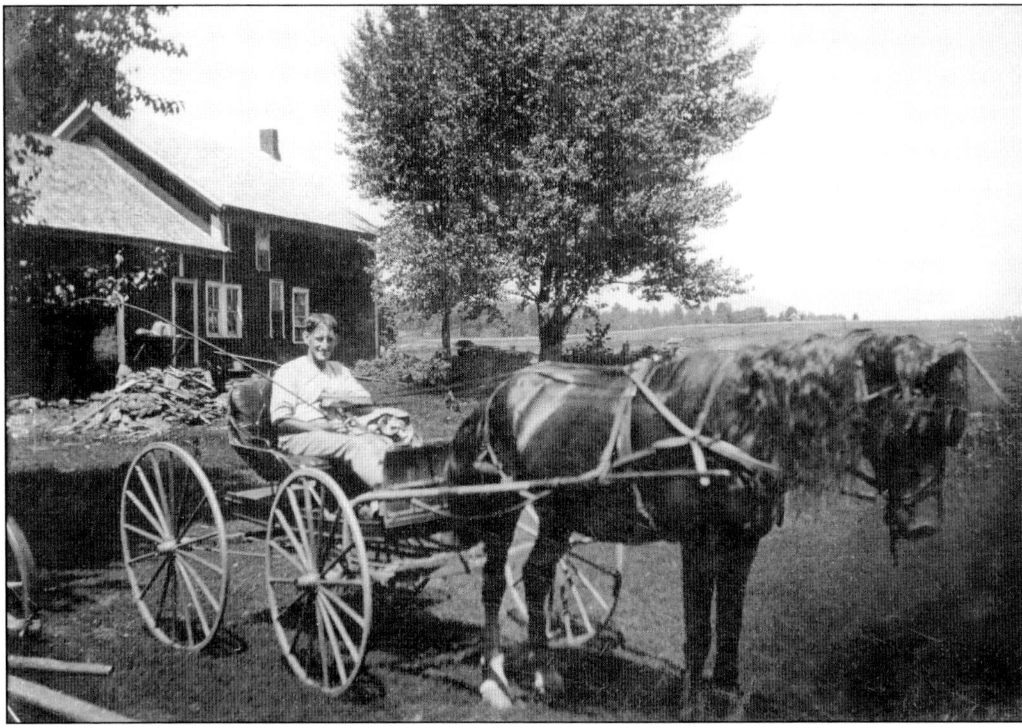

Robert Barnes is pictured in his buggy behind his farmhouse on Barnes Road (known as the Riverview area in the early 1900s). He owned this large farm his entire life. (Courtesy of Robert Barnes.)

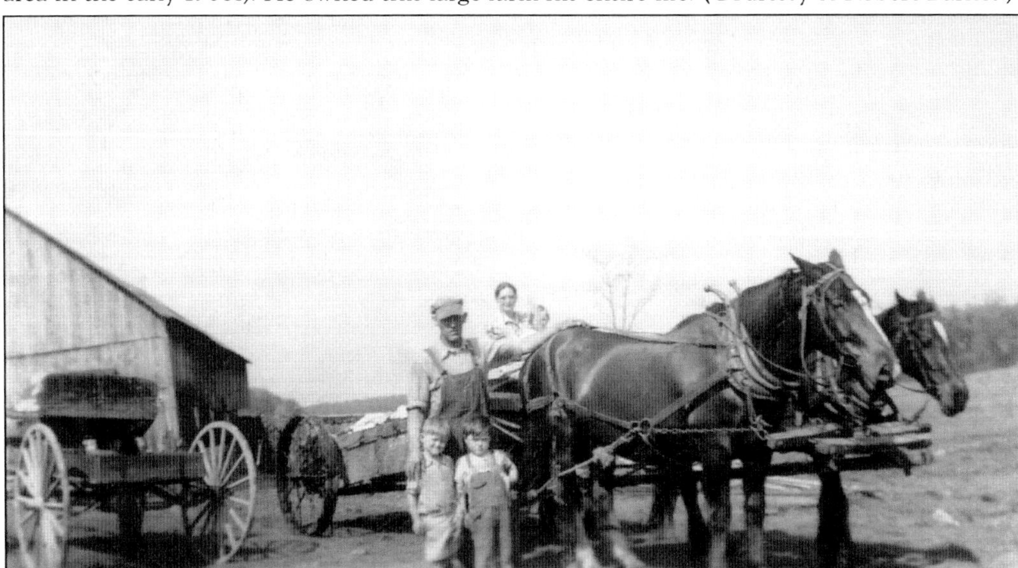

The Harry Demeritt family poses on their farm in June 1941. Pictured are Harry Demeritt (age 38), Gladys (age 34), and, from left to right, Cedric (age 3), Everett (age 4.5) and Doreen (age 1.5). This farm was located in the far northeastern corner of Hyde Park, with the eastern line of the farm property being the Craftsbury town line and the northern line of the property being the Eden town line. This farm was located within the larger area known as the Bundy District, named after the Bundy family, who used to live there. (Courtesy of Everett Demeritt.)

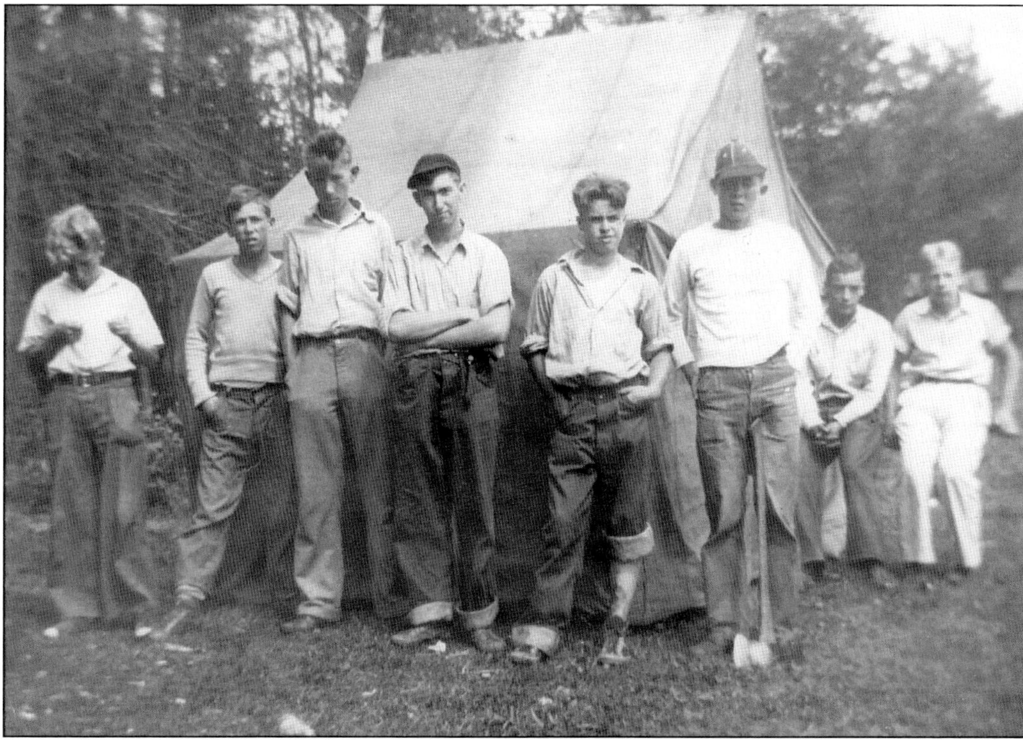

Members of the North Hyde Park Boy Scout troop are pictured during a camping trip on Lake Willoughby in Westmore, Vermont, from August 29 to September 1, 1935. Pictured, from left to right, are Haven "Bud" Bullard Jr., Harland O'Hear, Perry Jacobs, Norris Decell, Norbert Decell, Luther Parkhurst, Olen Marshey, and Vernon "Buster" Bullard. (Courtesy of Vernon Bullard.)

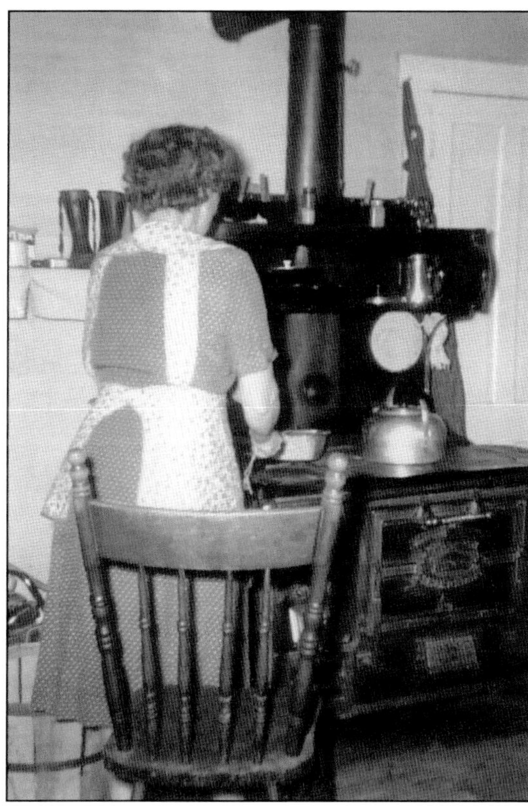

Iva Thompson, the wife of Guy Thompson, is busy popping Thompson Bear Paw popcorn on the wood cookstove. Stoves like these were also a key heat source for the home during the winter. (Courtesy of the Heath/Savage family.)

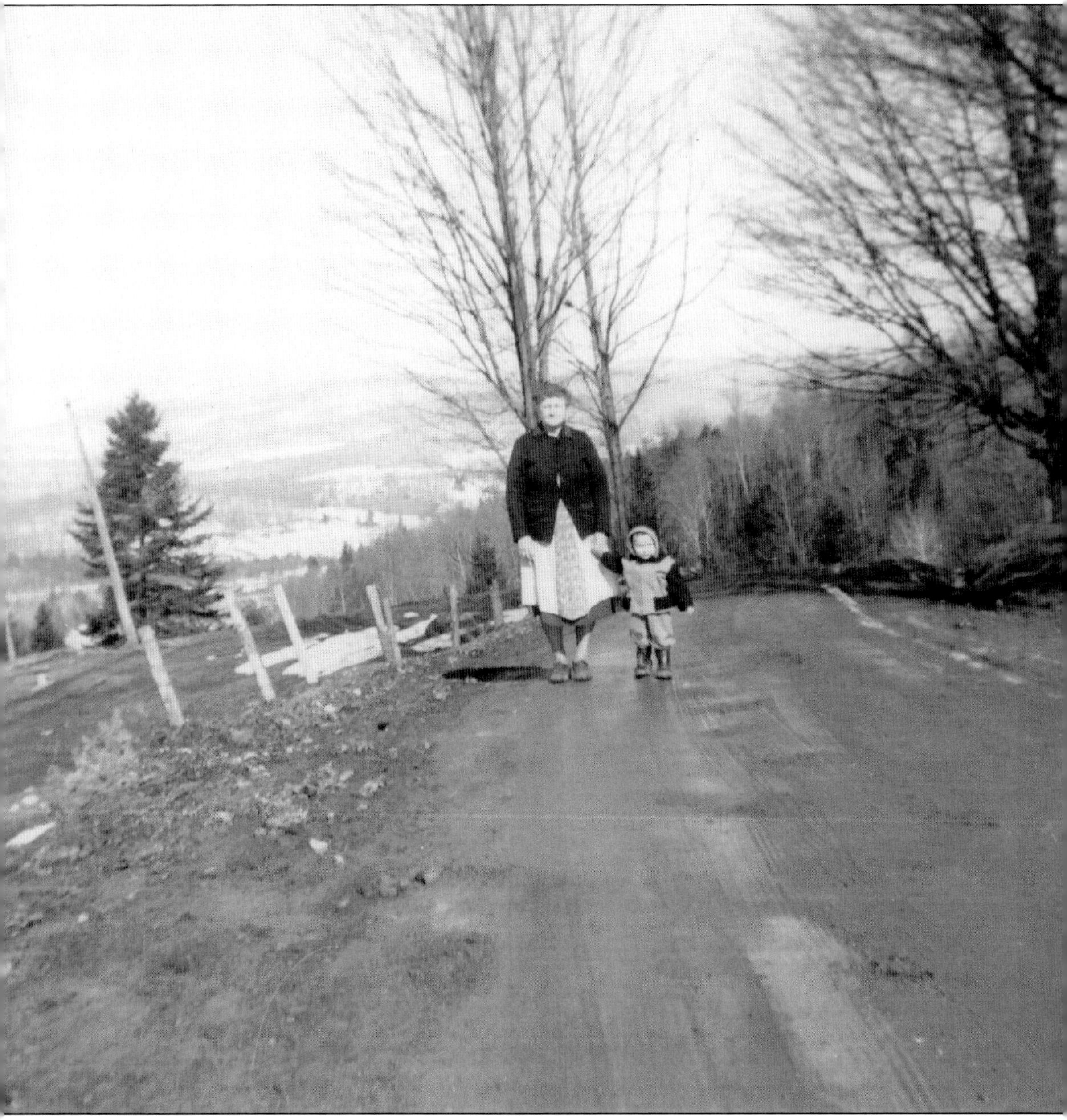

Florence (Ingalls) Whitcomb Smith and her great-grandson Arland "Bud" Ploof stand on Thompson Hill in front of Guy Thompson's house around 1953 before the road was paved. (Courtesy of the Heath/Savage family.)

Four

ODDS AND ENDS

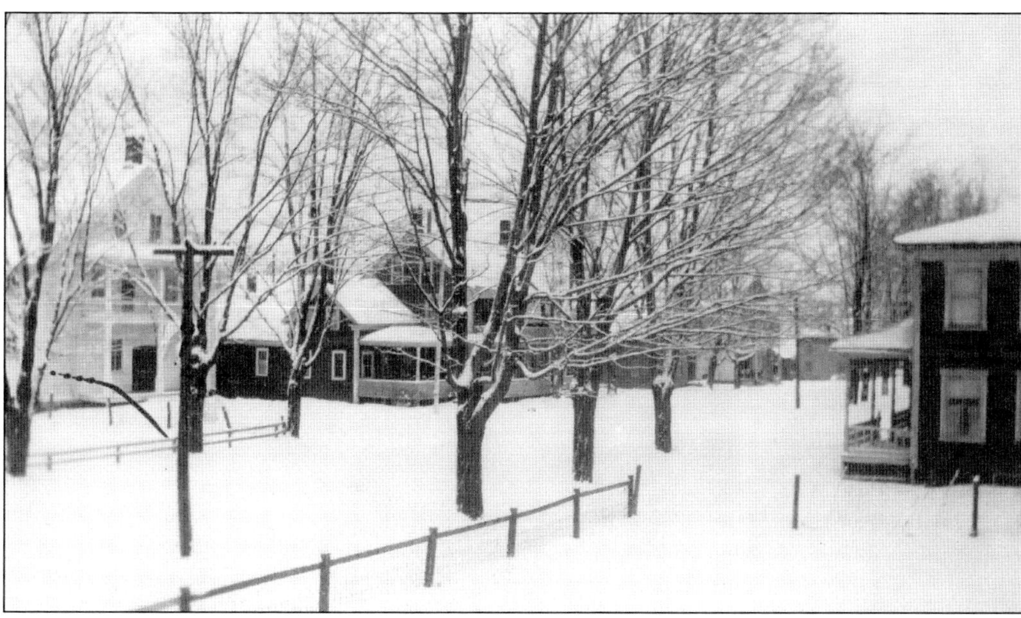

This is a winter scene of Main Street in North Hyde Park. It is a rather unique image as it shows the fronts of several key buildings in North Hyde Park, such as the Grange Hall (far left) and the Valley House (to the right of Grange Hall). (Courtesy of Jane and Eleanor [Grimes] Goodrich.)

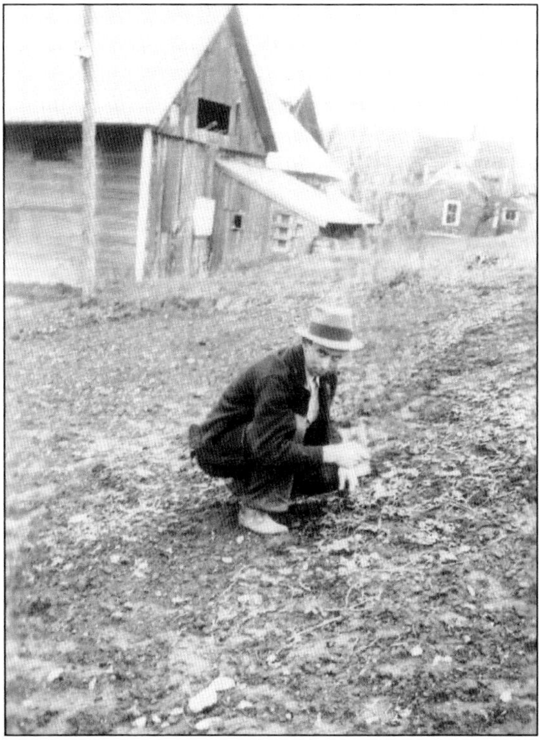

In this c. 1930 photograph, Feno Grimes works in his garden in either early spring or late fall. Feno, like so many other residents of Hyde Park, always worked in his garden to harvest fresh vegetables and fruit when ready. (Courtesy of Jane and Eleanor [Grimes] Goodrich.)

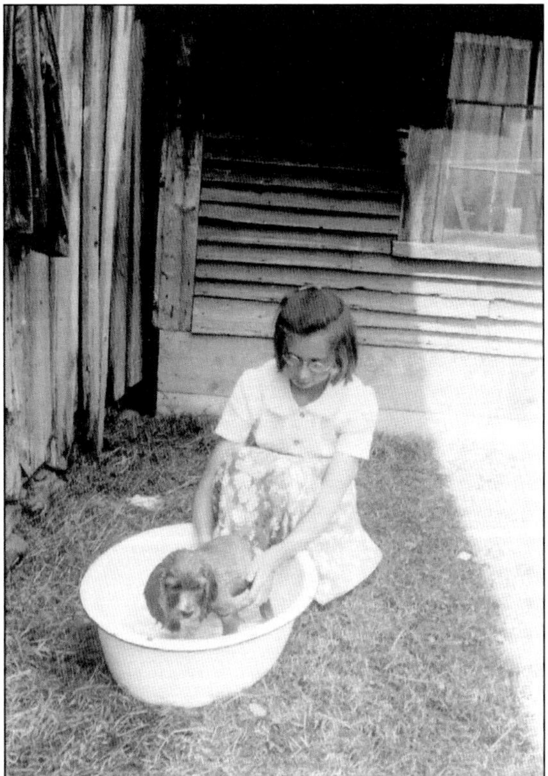

Eleanor Grimes gives her dog Teddy a bath in 1938. Eleanor was the daughter of Feno and Doris (Sherlaw) Grimes, who lived on Ferry Street in North Hyde Park. (Courtesy of Jane and Eleanor [Grimes] Goodrich.)

Russell Page plays with his dog Queenie next to the courthouse in Hyde Park Village. This photograph was taken around 1924. (Courtesy of Jane and Eleanor [Grimes] Goodrich.)

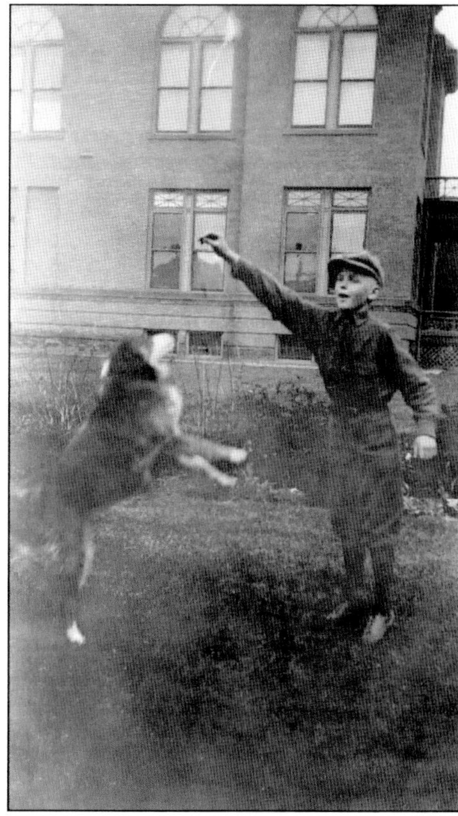

Young George McAllister is being watched over by a horse on the family farm owned by his father, Don McAllister. This photograph is thought to have been taken in the late 1800s. (Courtesy of the Graves/McAllister family.)

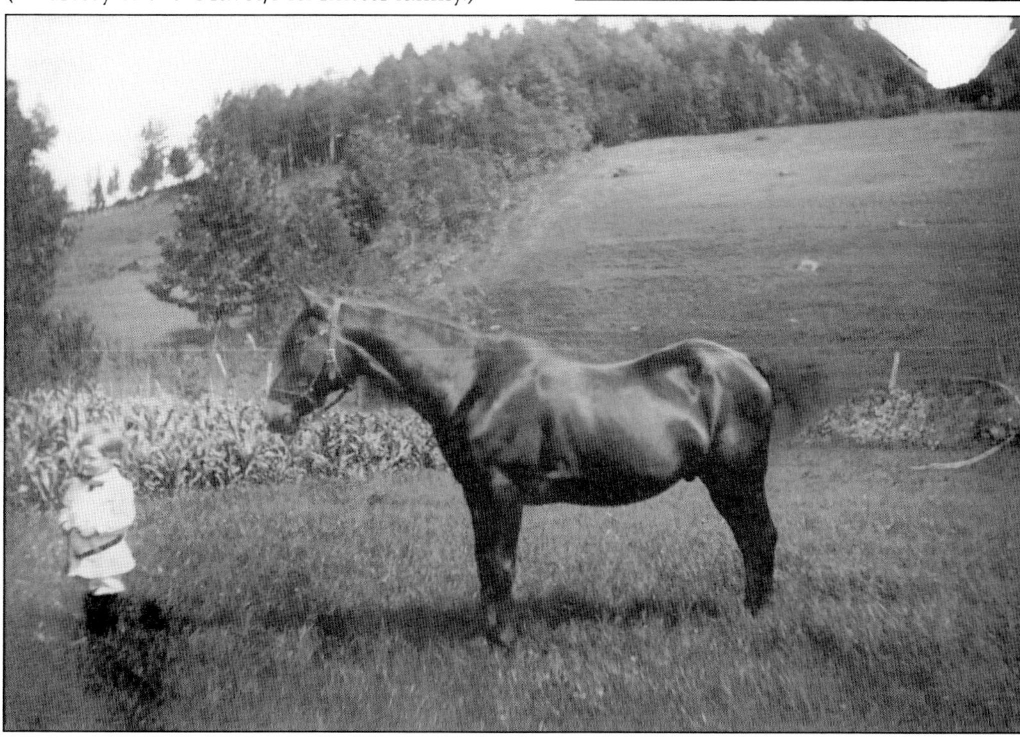

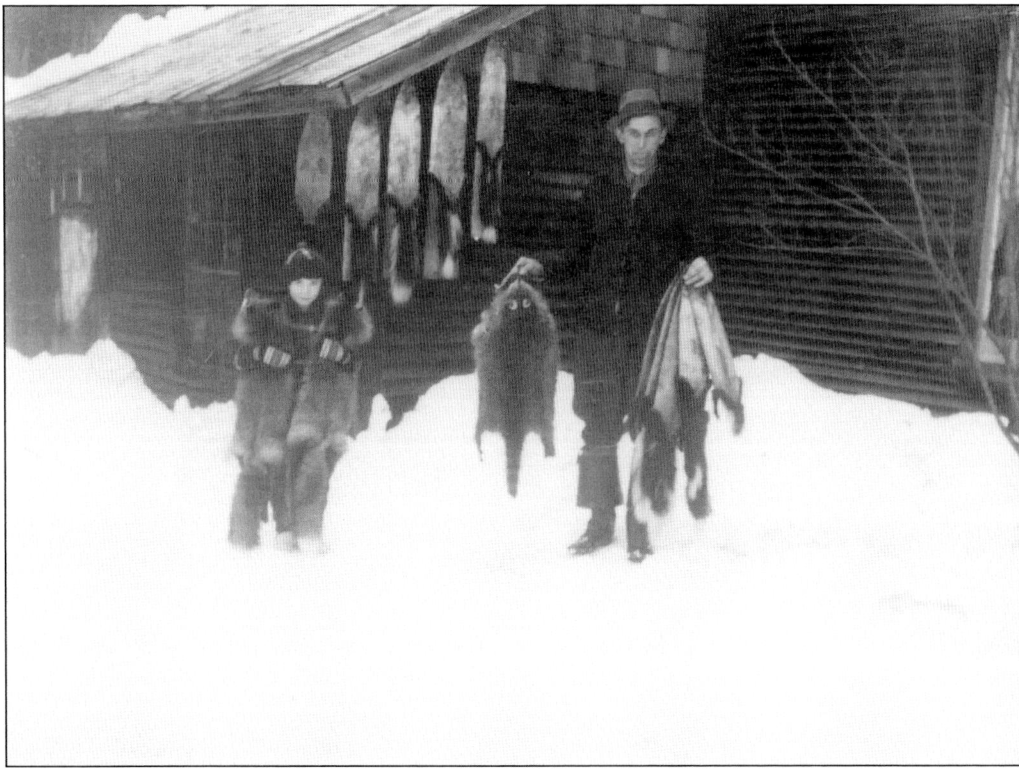

Feno Grimes was a fur trapper and is seen here demonstrating his success in 1938. He is pictured with his daughter Eleanor, who proudly helps her dad out in this photograph. (Courtesy of Jane and Eleanor [Grimes] Goodrich.)

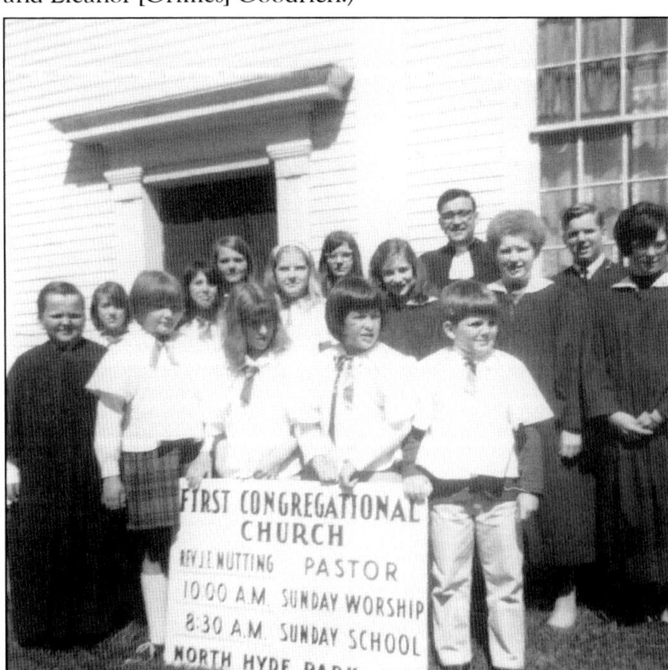

The First Congregational Church Choir in North Hyde Park is pictured in 1966. John Nutting, seen here in the back, was pastor of the church during this time period. (Courtesy of the Heath/Savage family.)

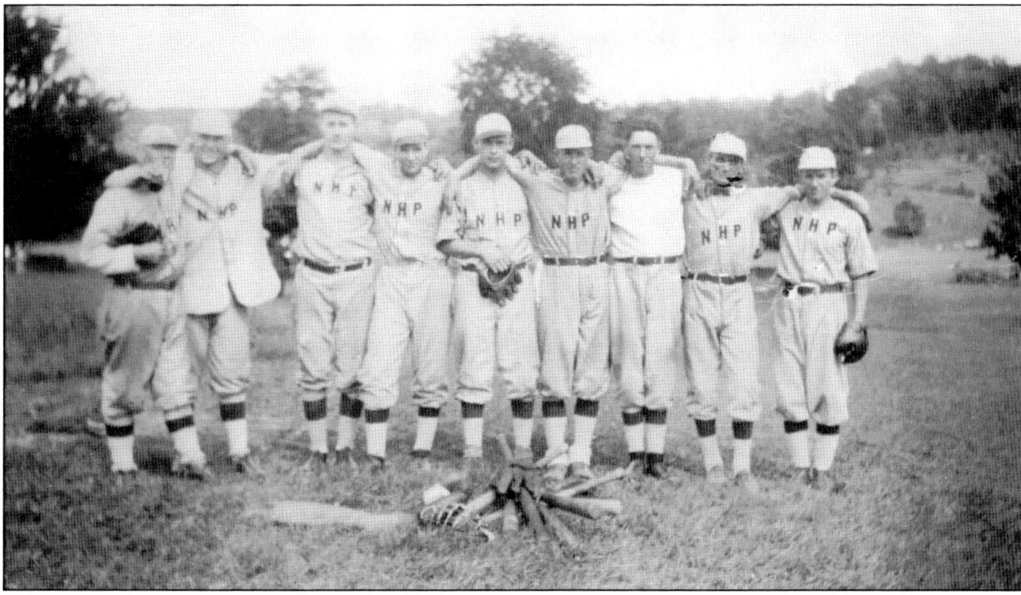

This is a rare 1925 image of the North Hyde Park baseball team. Pictured, from left to right, are Earl Gray, ? Foss, Clarence Wedge, Otto Foss, George McAllister, Perly Foss, Neal Sargent, Guy Newton, and Harold Foss. As stated on the photograph, there were more members on the team, but they were absent at the time this image was taken. (Courtesy of Jane and Eleanor [Grimes] Goodrich.)

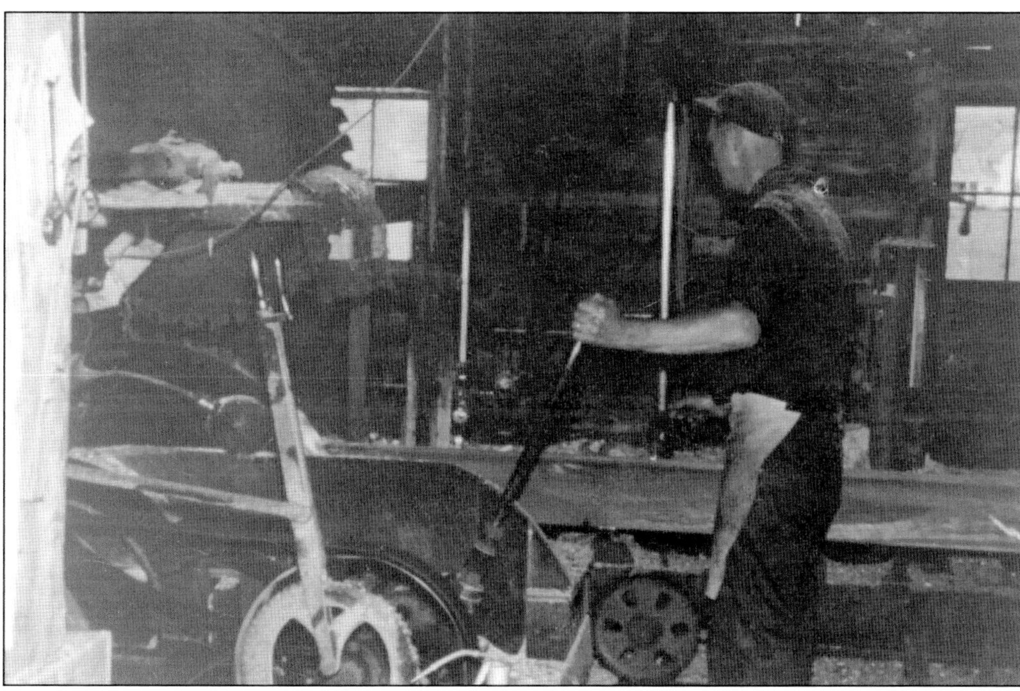

Merrill "Buck" Heath operates a circular board saw at his mill in North Hyde Park in the late 1950s, when the mill was powered by steam. The mill had a complex series of belts and pulleys that led back to the steam engine. (Courtesy of the Heath/Savage family.)

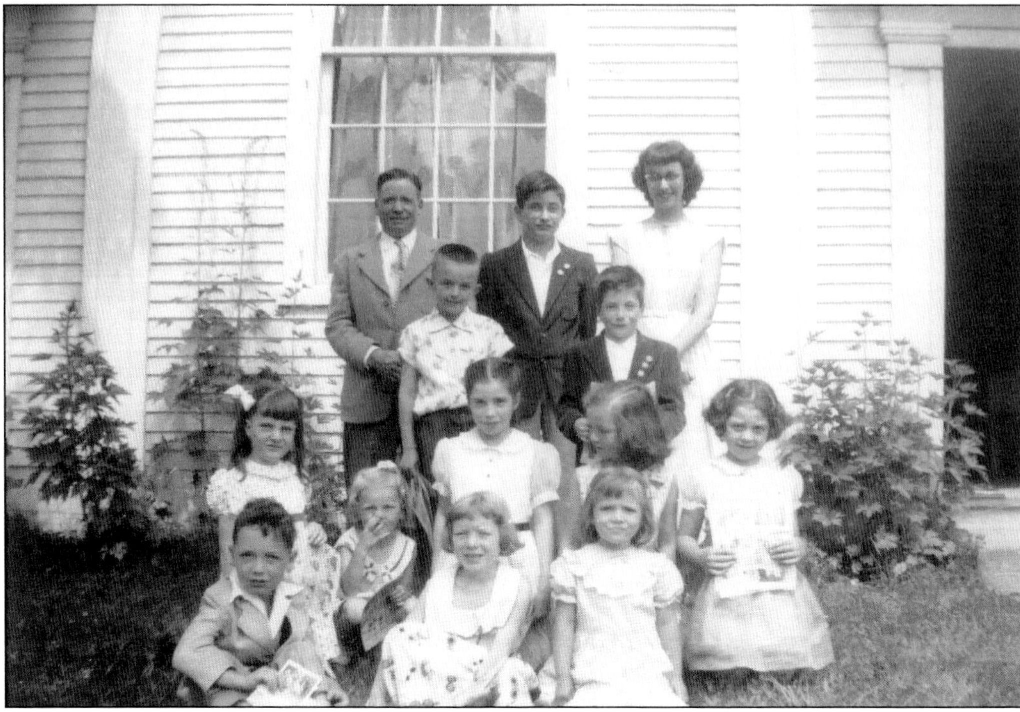

A Sunday school class at the First Congregational Church in North Hyde Park is pictured in 1959. The congregation was very strong during this time and required three Sunday school classes. (Courtesy of Madonna [Heath] Parker.)

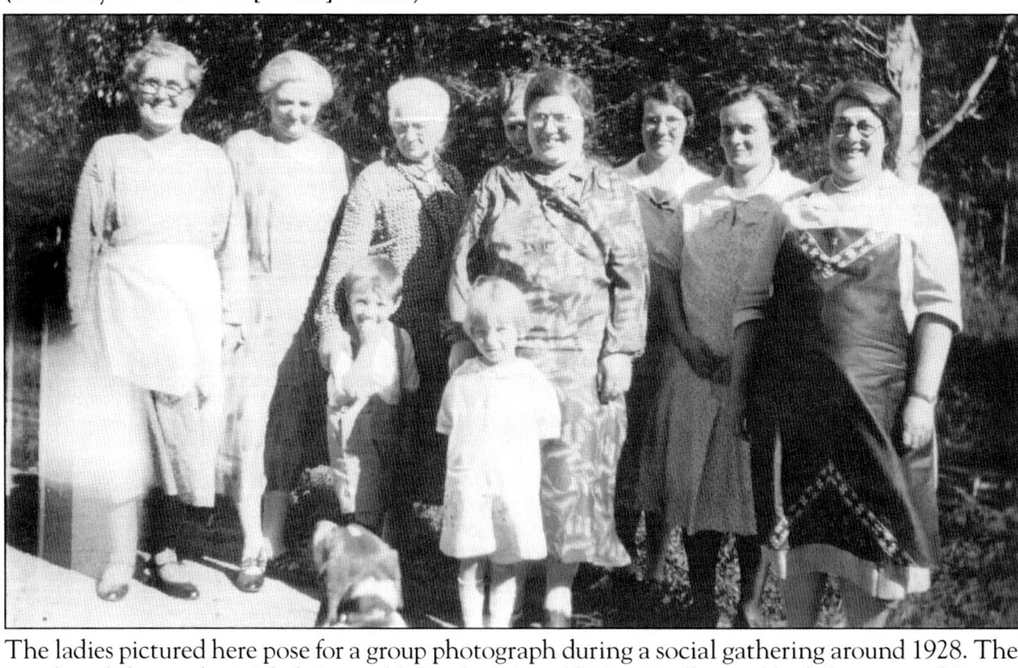

The ladies pictured here pose for a group photograph during a social gathering around 1928. They are, from left to right, Mabel Griswold, Bertha Metcalf, Mrs. Hadley and little boy named Proctor Gray, Daisy Foss (just visible in back), Doris Grimes, Vivian Sargent, Vivian McAllister, Ethel Hanscom, and Phylis Kidder. (Courtesy of Jane and Eleanor [Grimes] Goodrich.)

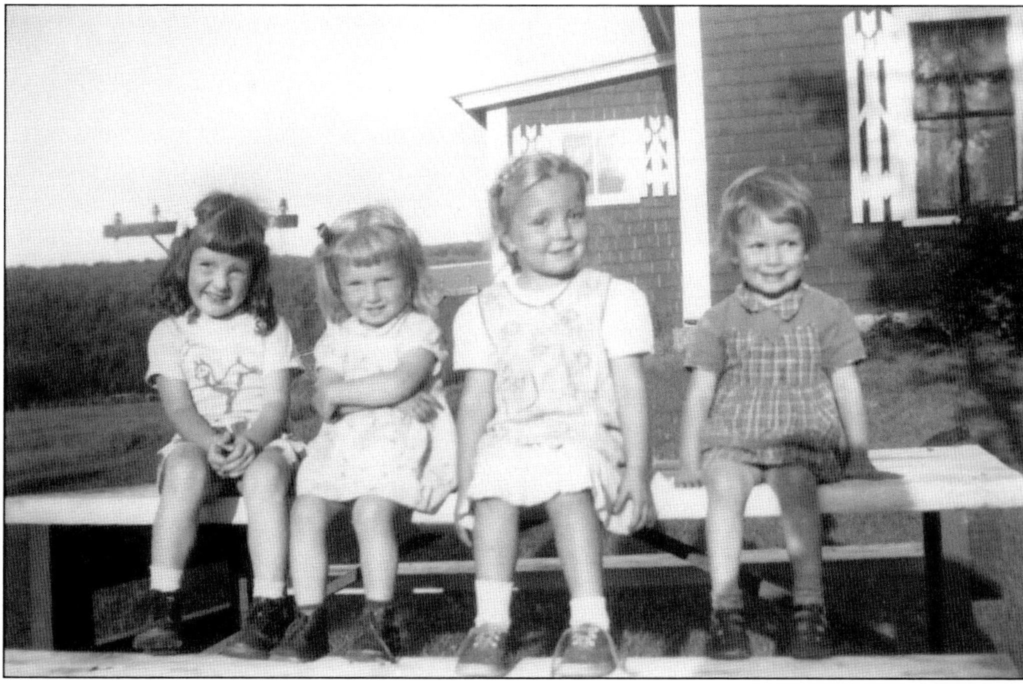

Four young girls sit on a picnic table at Margret "Peg" Mudgett's house on Ferry Street in North Hyde Park in 1953. From left to right are Shirley Dudley, Cheryl Dudley, Nioka Heath, and Madonna Heath. (Courtesy of Madonna [Heath] Parker.)

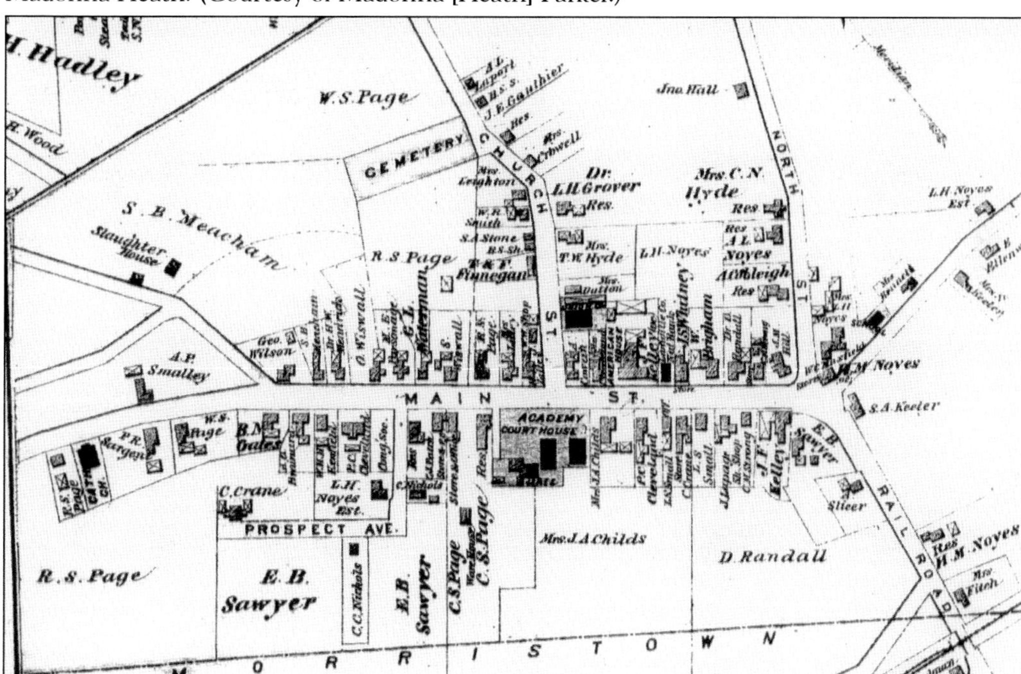

Pictured here is a Beer's Atlas map showing where the residents of Hyde Park Village lived in 1871. A county-by-county atlas filled with maps of many states across the country was published in New York by F.W. Beers, A.D. Ellis, and G.G. Soule. (Courtesy of Francis Favreau.)

Discover Thousands of Local History Books Featuring Millions of Vintage Images

Arcadia Publishing, the leading local history publisher in the United States, is committed to making history accessible and meaningful through publishing books that celebrate and preserve the heritage of America's people and places.

Find more books like this at
www.arcadiapublishing.com

Search for your hometown history, your old stomping grounds, and even your favorite sports team.

Consistent with our mission to preserve history on a local level, this book was printed in South Carolina on American-made paper and manufactured entirely in the United States. Products carrying the accredited Forest Stewardship Council (FSC) label are printed on 100 percent FSC-certified paper.

MADE IN THE USA